. . . and Changes

came on the land

North Dakota
Land of
Changing
Seasons

by Francie M. Berg

dedicated to this land and people

Third Printing

Library of Congress Catalog Card Number 76-45874
Copyright© 1977 By
Francie M. Berg
Flying Diamond Books
Box 1089
Hettinger, ND 58639

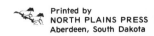
Printed by
NORTH PLAINS PRESS
Aberdeen, South Dakota

Contents

GO NORTH—it was a call to migrating game and birds of flight—to Indians, pushed up the Missouri from their homelands—to military men who followed—to the pioneer burdened with belongings and trudging beside a slow team—to Texas cattlemen, stringing out their trail herds.

North. Always north and west pounded the hoofbeats.

North—with the flights of wild geese in spring—north to watch the night sky shimmer with a million stars, roiling and flaming with the green fire of northern lights—north where red and golden sunsets billow across the heavens, silhouetting a horizon of butte and gully—north to open spaces, clear skies, rushing waters, broad plains, badlands, level croplands—north where the sun is always shining—NORTH TO DAKOTA.

A beautiful night. How amazingly clear the air is! Never have I seen so many stars, in Europe or America, and never have they seemed to shine with such brilliance, either at the zenith or at the edge of the horizon. The feeling of the spaciousness of sky and earth is more striking here than in any other place I have been.

The aurora borealis is so frequent and so beautiful in these latitudes that it would take too long to describe . . . splendid phenomenon . . . yesterday evening . . . the rays did not spring from the darkened vault at the edge of the horizon to the north. (Instead) the center . . . was at the zenith . . . where all the rays converge. So it was like a large luminous bell, and we were at the center. In all directions, the rounded sides went down to the edge of the horizon. It is an extraordinary thing, but the . . . illumination was as strong in the south as the north with this difference that . . . it moved in huge waves, perfectly distinct from one another, which swept toward the zenith in waves similar to those of the sea, although they moved much more rapidly. When one of these waves reached the point of convergence, the brightness redoubled, just as a transparent wave breaks into foam against an obstruction.

Regis de Trobriand
Commander at Ft. Stevenson

Stalking the bighorns: "The country is growing on me more and more," said Roosevelt.

Land of Changing Seasons

'tonight I heard the wild goose cry—wingin' north in the lonely sky—'

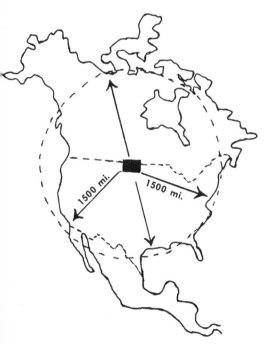

North Dakota's location at the center of North America insures striking changes of season and variability of climate

Spring, summer, fall, winter.

Every season heralds a striking change on the North Dakota landscape. The change, however, is never entirely certain nor irrevokable. Winter may announce her coming again and again, only to retreat each time before the persistent warmth of golden Indian summer. In the same way, spring can touch a frost-bitten January with joyful promise, then disappear and hide stubbornly behind mountainous April drifts.

Each season paints a new kaleidescope of weather patterns unlike any other. Old-timers may try in vain to recall two years alike, only to invite argument and qualification.

North Dakota's seasons deal a casual and unpredictable hand. It is this very unpredictability that strikes fear in the hearts of strangers. But the memory of the refreshing seasonal changes continues to stir with nostalgia former Dakotans who have moved away to gentler climes.

Spring, summer, fall, and winter—each has its magic moments, and through them all the Dakota sun is nearly always shining. Skies are pure and clear, with glorious clouds scudding into sunrise and sunset. Night skies sparkle with a million stars and glow green in the awesome spectacle of shifting northern lights.

Family of young prairie dogs stop in mid-chew to listen for springtime intruders

Ice melts, and rivers and creeks run high

Indian dances reflect nature; the sharp-tailed grouse struts his March courtship dance.

"It's time to get your WHEAT to grow!" sings the meadowlark.

Mares are brought in from the range, heavy with foal.

Suddenly

Spring comes swiftly sometime i March or early April, with perhaps a fals start or two in February.

Overnight, creeks and rivers are run ning bank full with melting snow and ice Hills, tinged with green one morning deepen and brighten day by day int emerald. Crocuses peep through pastur grasses and bloom in purple softnes Mayflowers, blue loco and yellow swee peas burst forth to wave their heads at th fresh breezes.

The honk of geese passing hig overhead fills the evening air and lifts th soul.

Calves and lambs run across th hillsides bucking and flipping their tail glistening clean in their newness. In th

A time to run: Spring fever hits the youthful.

t's spring—

deep brush a dappled fawn is born and, instinctively, it lies close in the sheltering leaves.

As fields dry, men are out on their tractors from early morning til late turning up black loam, preparing the land and seeding—trying to stay ahead of, or close between, the spring rains. These rains may begin in early April and are heaviest in the southeastern part of the state, lightest in the northwest. But spring is a time of swift, unpredictable changes and no one would rule out the possibility of a sudden March blizzard or even a light fleecy blanket of snow on the first day of May.

Spring fever hits the young people; their thoughts turn to vacation ("Will it never come?"), proms, graduation, track-meets—and down every country road come the joggers in their "sweats", running mile after mile.

And the song of the meadowlark greets the morning with joy. It's time, he says: "Time to get your WHEAT to grow!"

The crocus brings news of spring.

The honk of geese overhead fills the air, lifts the soul.

New calves, new grass, and all's well in cattle country

Spring in the air

... put in its appearance today in wonderful weather, a rejuvenated sun, and temperature which went up to 56 degrees . . . the water began to run in streams in all directions. The flocks of wild geese and ducks are becoming more and more numerous, and the prairie chicken are leaving the woods to mate and nest in the grass. The doors are open and there is no fire in the stoves.

de Trobriand March 21, 1868

Turtle River floodwaters break over banks to strand farmstead at left.

Rare whooping cranes, including these three above and below, stop each year in April and October. They fly with necks and legs outstretched, most often in small groups

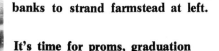

It's time for proms, graduation

Springs work: Tractors go non-stop to get in the crop

Concert choirs take a spring tour, right, amid rush of year's end school activities

Summer is packed with vacation-time events. Conventions and camps (left) bring young people together from everywhere. Fireworks highlight celebrations and fairs (center), and for those who follow the rodeo circuit . . . there aren't enough weekends

Summertime—
and the livin's fast-paced

Summer is vacation time. Camping . . . cabin on the lake . . . state fair . . . rodeo. It's swimming lessons and packing kids off to camps and exotic places around the world on tours and exchanges. It's company coming . . . and traveling far to visit and sightsee. Summertime, and there's work to be done. Cultivating corn . . . branding calves . . . hoeing garden . . . mowing lawn . . . 4-H projects. And there's the immense satisfaction of work well done: the stacks of hay, rows of plum jelly, full blooming petunia beds. Sunny summer weather is perfect for outdoor activity. Days can be hot, but nights are cool and air light and dry. Storms are sudden, pass quickly. A chilling of the air on a hot afternoon bodes hail, which can mulch a wheat field in minutes. But a summer thunderstorm is a joy, for all its crashing and flashing, and in its wake is fresh and exhilarating air, hills glistening green, and—like as not—double rainbows arching high.

Having fun at the old swimming hole, above. Summer is for camping, at its most luxurious—or this way, scrambling eggs over a wood fire

4-H'er shows her clean and shining steer at the county fair, left. Below, Carrington pool: It's filled with kids on a hot summer day

Days are long, nights

and sunny are cool—

Enjoy a water show at Lake Metigoshe—or try the real thing!

Left: Outdoor theaters flourish and NDSU's Prairie Stage brings tent drama to people across the state. Upper left: Summer vacation is more fun with a horse. Summer is for sailboats, below far left, on Lake Tschida. Calves grow fast on grass like this, left, once the range for thousands of buffalo; windmills and waterholes make pastures efficient.

Grain matures rapidly and combine crews move in to harvest.

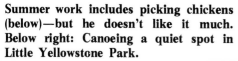

Summer work includes picking chickens (below)—but he doesn't like it much. Below right: Canoeing a quiet spot in Little Yellowstone Park.

School begins: NDSU class meets under a fall-brilliant tree; in center photo, high school students load down with books. Exuberant from the hunt, sharpshooter displays her buck antelope.

Fall—'this golden Indian summer'

Halloween: A break in routine for first graders.

Like spring, fall has well-defined beginnings: Labor Day, and the first frost which strikes toward the middle or end of September and swiftly changes the complexion of the land. Garden leaves curl; vegetables left uncovered turn squishy and soft; corn stalks droop; flower beds and tomatoes are still night-shrouded each morning with frosty blankets. Trees and shrubs glow with the brilliant red and golden colors of autumn.

Labor Day weekend plainly spells the end. Summer is over. And the mood of fall is on the land and people. Kindergarten begins . . . college . . . teaching jobs. It's a new beginning, and everyone is eager to settle down to responsibility and routine after the hectic pace of summer. Harvests are soon over, calves sold or put into feedlots. The farmer-rancher's production is over for this year and he's working toward the new one.

In many ways fall begins a new year more definitely than does New Year's Day, so it seems to everyone a lucky omen that the weather is just great. There might be a week of frost-bitten nights, or of drizzle. There may be whisks of snow. But soon the melting warmth of Indian summer breaks through with many weeks of crisp sunny mornings and golden afternoons of rich and mellow sunshine. The man who hailed out or sold his calves on a losing market, views his glorious land and can't help being swept by the familiar western optimism. He grins and tells himself . . . "next year" . .

The full red-orange harvest moon hangs low in the sky, sitting fat and bouncy on the horizon for a moment before it lifts off. High above, southbound geese cleave the evening air, calling to each other, unhurried, but never wavering from their dangerous journey.

Swans stop in North Dakota spring and fall; here they swim in serene dignity near Edmore.

Dakota at autumn

JoAnn Winistorfer

Dakota at autumn, a portrait in gold,
Repeating the cycle of ages untold,
Sends dying reflections in day's ebbing light
As the evening of seasons prepares for the night.

The blazing horizon at setting of sun
Signals to nighttime that daytime is done.
The harvest moon rises, and framed in her light,
The V-silhouette of wild geese in their flight
Is caught in that moment, suspended in space,
Ageless and timeless in beauty and grace.
Mournful the song of the wild honkers' cry,
Sounded in minor key, flung to the sky,

Faltering, fading, till infinity
Swallows all trace of its sad symphony.
An echo of silence still hangs on the air,
Pervading the mist that is gathering there.
The moon mounts the sky and the dusk becomes night.
The prairie is bathed in ethereal light
As Dakota at autumn lies waiting and still
For the frost's icy touch
and the winter wind's chill.

'the harvest moon rises . . . a portrait in gold'

The melting warmth of Indian summer makes fall a glorious season

Right: Geese by the thousands halt their southbound flight to feed, to swim and gabble in North Dakota lake country.

Buffalo berries (left) are best picked after first frost.

The grass is golden and cattle are fat (center).

Lower right: The zest of hunting may be heightened and prolonged for the bow hunter.

Winter sports are widely enjoyed; they include wrestling, state tournament photo at left, and ice fishing on Des Lacs and other lakes around the state. Small photo shows interior of fish house.

The drama of Winter

Hoar frost transforms trees into a fairy woodland. A Christmas snowfall lays a soft fleecy blanket of big flakes in the night. Wind-driven snow sculpts delicate drifts against the merest stem of grass. The sun dazzles snow crystals and cuts an artist's clean shadow from every fencepost. Winter can be a time of grandeur in North Dakota, with winter beauty in every badlands draw, every spring bubbling through the ice. Most always the sun is shining and the air is crisp and bracing.

But it's the blizzard, not the beauty, for which North Dakota winters are famous. Many outsiders are naively certain that winter is one long blizzard—some kind of raging will-i-waw that consumes this land for six months of every year.

Such legends die hard. North Dakotans themselves cannot resist the fun of telling tales of devastating blizzards they've experienced; listeners assume it's the commonplace. The legends have been fueled, too, by the variability of winter weather here, which makes it easy to dramatize one particular year, quote statistics, and "prove" whatever one wishes.

Actually, North Dakota receives less snow than any other northern state to the east, or the mountainous areas to the west. Many northern states, such as Michigan and the New England states, average over 100 inches of snow annually; North Dakota's heaviest average is 38 inches, in a belt across the state diagonally from the northeast corner.

North Dakota's record low of -60 degrees (at Parshall in 1936) is equalled or surpassed by Idaho, Colorado, and Montana (-70 degrees); Minnesota's record is -59, New York's -52. January average temperatures range from 2 degrees in the northeastern corner to 17 in the southwest—which is about the same as northern Iowa. Dry air, too, makes the cold less penetrating than in more humid climates. And there are the sudden changes: A cold snap—with 20 below five nights in a row—can end abruptly in a January thaw and water running in the streets.

North Dakota averages slightly more than two blizzards each winter. Seldom do they last more than a day or two, sometimes only hours, according to the state climatologist, Ray Jensen.

Yet blizzards can be spectacular. A proper blizzard needs three elements—wind, snow, and cold. To be classified severe, winds must blow 45 miles per hour, visibility be 100 feet or less, and the mercury drop to 10 degrees F. The falling snow is swept through the air by strong winds, forming in big drifts against trees and buildings. In open country the wind gets a long sweep, and the snow keeps moving. Blizzards are dangerous, and occasional tragedies still occur—here, as in every northern state. Most often it is not because people fear a blizzard's violence, but rather that they have no fear—they strike out confidently from a stalled auto toward some known or unknown point that is quickly lost in whipping, swirling snow.

A sudden blizzard calls a halt to everything. But for most people it's a mere inconvenience if loved ones are home and livestock fed and sheltered. Schools close for a day or two; meetings are cancelled. Dad joins the kids in a card game, or reads aloud to the younger ones—a rare treat—while Mom fries donuts and a teenager pops corn. Evening is cozy over a jigsaw puzzle or watching TV, with the blizzard dying outside. The holiday is especially pleasant because it was so unexpected. But next day, roads are scraped off and everyone is busy going about their usual activity.

North Dakotans prepare well for winter. Vehicles are winterized; snow removal equipment is ready; emergency shelter and feed supplies are available for livestock. Everyone takes for granted warm houses, insulation, and central heating—until they visit other states where these are not common.

Winter weather is generally pleasant, with bright sunshine and clear air. Winter sports are widely enjoyed. Much time, of course, is spent indoors. Sports like wrestling, basketball, bowling, and whist tournaments flourish in wintertime.

the winter sun is shining and the c

Sledding, left, can take a modern twist with a snowmobile pull up the hill.

Below left, hoar frost hangs on every twig in Christmas Eve stillness.

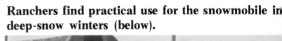

Ranchers find practical use for the snowmobile in deep-snow winters (below).

light—

Indoor pools are increasingly common in schools, motels and apartment buildings.

Deep snow is not usual in North Dakota but here in the Turtle Mountains there's plenty for skiing.

Antelope gather into big herds in winter; seemingly they become quite fearless . . . can run 60 miles per hour.

In fresh snow kids make their own fun.

Windmill against a dying sunset portends a winter evening's solitude.

Routes for the traveler

It's roughrider country; it's peace garden country. It's the sophistication of city streets, the simplicity of tenting out where coyotes howl. The history lover can find his dusty treasures; the light-hearted tourist, his bright shiny playgrounds.

Travelers—both instate and out—represent a fascinating spectrum of humanity, with enthusiasms as individual as their thumbprints. But whatever his tastes may be, the traveler can pursue and enjoy them right here in North Dakota. Perhaps he'll find his unexpected treasures close to home, almost underfoot—or they may be diagonally across the state in what is, for him, virtually unknown country.

Wherever the traveler goes, he will find in North Dakota a rare freedom from the crowds that swarm tourist-oriented sites elsewhere. He will meet, almost invariably, with consideration and personal attention from officials and local people. He will find that here there is room for flexibility; rules and regulations are no sacred cows to Dakotans—they can usually be relaxed for the interested individual who'd cherish a closer look. And the traveler will drive on excellent highways. In few places in the United States will he find roads so wide, uncrowded, well-kept, and easy to drive, including an east-west interstate that has won awards for its pleasing contours and integrity with the land.

The most highly developed tourist attraction is undoubtedly the Medora-Teddy Roosevelt Park area, just off interstate. There's plenty of diversion here for everyone, from riding historic trails up over a scoria ridge to watch a lone buffalo silhouetted in the sunset, to strolling the old cowtown streets, fully lined with tourist shops.

Another favorite, the Peace Gardens, has a unique character perhaps found nowhere else. It is sculpted and tended with delicate care for the ultimate enjoyment of the visitor, yet is strangely lacking in the familiar tourist hustle that would probably encompass such a spot anywhere else in the world. It is indeed the quiet haven of peace and beauty envisioned by its creative spirit, Dr. Henry J. Moore, a Canadian. Fittingly, the Peace Gardens is no empty showcase, for all its formal elegance, but a living classroom where young people from all over the world come to study, perform, and gain inspiration.

In North Dakota, no spot is far from a vacationland. The state's surface is two percent water. To the action-loving tourist this means boating, water skiing, fishing, swimming; to the relaxation-seeker it can mean a quiet cabin on a lake, a weekend's cruise in a houseboat. For everyone it means camping—high style in a sleek motor home, or intentionally simple. It means the high-wave cliffs of Lake Sakakawea or the quiet lapping at the shoreline of a small forested Turtle Mountain lake; the bright rippling waters of the Sheyenne or the surging waters of the awesome muddy Missouri.

For history buffs the ideal starting point is Ft. Lincoln State Park—or Walhalla's old trading post. Closer to home, every community has history worth exploring: filled museums, local history books and documents, old buildings. No one interested in pioneer history can avoid the fascination of old cemeteries . . . and the chance to ponder epitaths carved there in stone.

The traveler with ethnic interests can visit many nationality pockets in the state which keep up old traditions and where the language may be heard on Main Street.

On the following pages are listed some of the attractions in each section of North Dakota.

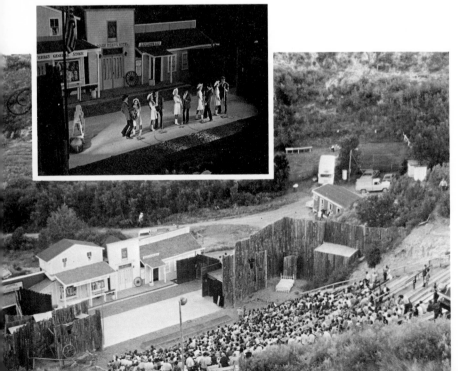

'no place in the state is far from a vacationland'

The Medora Musical entertains thousands of visitors every summer.

Badlands, range country: 'It grips the soul more than it pleases the eye,' said a 19th century visitor.

the Southwest

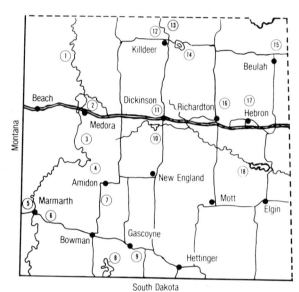

Buttes and badlands punctuate the horizon of southwestern North Dakota. This is range country, cattle country. In early days it was stocked largely with Texas longhorns, brought up the long trail. Then it was homesteaded, nearly quarter by quarter, with a shack, a dug well, a parched garden, thistles, and a tangle of barb wire on every claim. Most homesteaders left in drouth years, or sooner. Those who were able to stay on are today's ranchers. Beef is still the primary source of income for most of the area; small grains are important, strip farmed. Hay is raised on bottomlands.

Winter temperatures tend to be warmer here. Elevation is the state's highest. Lack of moisture is often a problem with an annual average of 14-16 inches.

Principal tourist attraction is Teddy Roosevelt park and the old cowtown, Medora. There's plenty here of interest for every visitor. Wildlife is abundant in the park and includes herds of wild horses and buffalo. South of Medora are Sully's Creek horse corrals for those who enjoy bringing horses — here bighorn sheep can be found on the higher ridges. Excellent horse corrals are also located farther north in Little Missouri State Primitive Park. Here the badlands trails are spectacular and overlook an expanse of rough country and the backup waters of Lake Sakakawea. Horses may be rented. Not far off the Killdeer Mountains still keep the secrets of the Medicine Hole through which, legend has it, spirits issue and Sioux Indians once made their escape.

Oil wells are a familiar sight in the southwest; coal development has begun.

Population is relatively light, with Dickinson the only large town.

1. **Roosevelt's Elkhorn ranch**
2. **Theodore Roosevelt National Park, south unit; Medora, historic cowtown, restored buildings; theater, hotel, saloon, western art gallery, museum; Roosevelt's Maltese Cross cabin; Chateau De Mores — original furnishings; zoo; Medora Musical; campgrounds; in park-trail rides, native wildlife, prairie dog towns, ranger talks and hikes.**
3. **Sully's Creek state primitive park**
4. **Burning coal vein and columnar juniper trees**
5. **Marmath, scenic Little Missouri town, restored theater plays vaudeville**
6. **Fort Dilts — sod fort built by beseiged immigrant train**
7. **White Butte, elevation 3,506 feet, highest point in North Dakota**
8. **Bowman Haley Dam**
9. **Knife River coal mine, strip mining**
10. **Rawhide City**
11. **Dickinson State College — summer outdoor theater Sosandowah**
12. **Killdeer battlefield in Killdeer Mountains**
13. **Little Missouri State primitive park, horse corrals**
14. **Lake Ilo National Wildlife Refuge**
15. **Beulah coal fields, strip mining**
16. **Richardton Assumption Abbey**
17. **Hebron brick factory**
18. **Heart Butte Dam, Lake Tschida**

Beef cattle, both registered and commercial, are a vital industry in the southwestern region.

Sharing a laugh in camp among the cottonwoods.

contrast, vigor

There is a strangely fascinating desolation to the badlands . . . I like this land because it gives me room to turn around without stepping on . . . others.

Marquis de Mores

Sharp-tailed grouse hunting near Amidon.

There's lots to see and do in historic cowtown Medora, entrance to Theodore Roosevelt National Park.

Little Missouri State Primitive Park has horse corrals and breathtaking trails; the Killdeer Mountains are behind, rough breaks of the Missouri below.

Rodeo—an old sport of range country—more popular than ever.

Pysanka—eggs hand-painted with wax, dyed with care and skill—symbolize Ukranian tradition.

Cheeky prairie dogs, once the scourge of rangeland, build their towns undisturbed in Teddy Roosevelt park.

Canoeing, below, near mouth of Little Missouri. Below right: Unique sod house stands in seed-planted pine grove north of Hettinger; was lived in from 1907-1960, has been built onto and improved many times.

the Northwest

Buffalo cross road in north unit Teddy Roosevelt park; longhorns also run wild here.

Lake Sakakawea dominates and divides this northwestern section. In historical times, the Missouri River dominated. Located along the river here were a great many fur posts, including the greatest of them all, Ft. Union, and a number of agricultural Indian villages. Later this became cattle country as southern herds trailed in to fill the grasslands vacated by buffalo. The more daring of the cattlemen pushed their herds across the Missouri and moved north. But the northern area was the one settled first by homesteaders, mostly Norwegian. Being level, it was more desirable farmland, and there was no river barrier to those coming from the east. Also it was Jim Hill's country: the Great Northern promoter was persuasive.

This is a country of big wheat fields, strip-cropped with ribbons of summer fallow; to the south is cattle country, with a small stretch of irrigation along the Yellowstone. Lack of moisture can be a problem with the state's lowest annual average, 13-15 inches.

Unlimited recreation possibilities are available in the Lake Sakakawea area with 27 designated public areas around the lake. The lake has 1,340 miles of shoreline, is 14 miles wide at its widest point, and 180 feet deep. Fishing is excellent year-around. Camping and boating are popular; resorts offer cabins, concessions, boat rentals and guide service — more are under development. Ft. Berthold Indian Reservation is cut into five sections by the lake with a crossing at the mile-long Four Bears Bridge near New Town. The bridge, named Four Bears after two chiefs — one Mandan, the other Hidatsa — actually honors 19 Indian leaders. Three Tribes owns a lodge, museum, and resort area and makes excellent pottery for sale.

This northwestern section of North Dakota is rich in oil and coal. Tioga's oil fields were the site of the state's first major oil strike, in 1951. Oil wells also pump the terrain south of the Missouri.

Again, a relatively light population, with Williston as the largest town.

1. **Writing Rock Historic Site**
2. **University of North Dakota Williston Center**
3. **Ft. Union, Ft. Buford historic sites — guided tours in summer**
4. **Theodore Roosevelt National Park, north unit; ranger talks, hiking trails**
5. **Ft. Berthold Indian reservation; celebrations, powwows of Three Tribes — Mandan, Hidatsa, Arikara**
6. **Four Bears Memorial Park, Four Bears Bridge; all-Indian museum, lodge owned by Three Tribes; agency office at New Town**
7. **Lake Sakakawea — campsites, fishing, resorts along 1,340 mile shoreline**
8. **Lewis and Clark State Park**
9. **Tioga oil fields**
10. **Lostwood National Wildlife Refuge**
11. **Des Lacs National Wildlife Refuge, Des Lacs lakes**
12. **Danish windmill — built 1902 for grinding flour**
13. **Broste Rock Museum**

Rugged buttes, wheatland, and lapping waters

Big houseboats explore coves of Lake Sakakawea. Right, Four Bears bridge; marker atop Crow Flies High Butte honors Hidatsa chief who founded village in valley below.

Ancient Indian carvings on Writing Rock near Alkabo.

This Danish Mill, one of six in nation, was moved to Kenmare town square from nearby homestead of Danish immigrant who used wind energy to grind flour.

Wheat country: 10-man plow at Makoti Threshing Show.

Land of lake and music

Northcentral

The only hope of preserving what is best lies in the practice of an immense charity, a wide tolerance, a sincere respect for opinions that are not ours.

P. G. Hamerton
engraved on Peace Chapel wall

The state fair in Minot presents a week-long program of entertainment, exhibits and contests.

International Music Camp students from all over the world entertain visitors with weekly summer concerts and a Festival of the Arts at the Peace Gardens.

Colorful Indian dances highlight pow-wows and tribal celebrations.

Sky-flying at the annual Lake Metigoshe water show.

Lake Metigoshe State Park in the Turtle Mountains offers beautiful vacation country.

That long Canadian frontier from the Atlantic to the Pacific Oceans, guarded only by neighborly respect and honorable obligations, is an example to every country and a pattern for the future of the world.

Winston Churchill

Our goal is not the victory of might, but the vindication of right; not peace at the expense of freedom, but both peace and freedom, here in this hemisphere and around the world. God willing that goal will be reached.

John F. Kennedy

The Peace Gardens: "We two nations dedicate this garden and pledge ourselves that as long as men shall live we will not take up arms against one another." (at the dedication, 1932)

Farmland, but plenty of pasture: Hereford cows and their Charolais-cross calves cool off by a spring-fed waterhole near Velva

1. Upper Souris National Wildlife Refuge
2. Minot State College; Roosevelt Park and Zoo; State Fair in mid-July; Minot Air Base
3. Ft. Stevenson State Park, campsites on Lake Sakakawea
4. Audubon National Wildlife Refuge
5. David Thompson monument honors explorer who came in 1797 and first mapped North Dakota area
6. Mouse River State Forest—canoeing, fishing, camping
7. J. Clark Salyer National Wildlife Refuge
8. State School of Forestry, NDSU, at Bottineau; Bottineau Winter Park—skiing, winter sports
9. Lake Metigoshe State Park
10. International Peace Garden, 2300 acres—colorful floral beauty and design, reflection pools, fountain, sunken garden, 18-foot electric floral clock, formal garden, All Faiths Peace Chapel; International Music Camp—weekly concerts
11. Turtle Mountain Indian Reservation, Indian Agency at Belcourt
12. Geographical Center of North America

THE NORTHCENTRAL region of North Dakota is sprinkled throughout with glacially-formed lakes of all sizes. Water runs north here; however, drainage tends to be poor and much rainfall remains in lakes, sloughs, and fields. This is excellent farmland for the most part and was settled early, predominantly by Norwegian settlers.

The Turtle Mountains—about 40 miles long by 20 miles wide—are a prime scenic and recreation area here. These rolling forested hills were a haven for forest tribes such as the Chippewa and Cree Indians. In the immediate area are Lake Metigoshe State Park, the International Peace Garden, State School of Forestry, and the Turtle Mountain Indian Reservation where decendents of forest dwelling Indians live today.

The Peace Garden symbolizes lasting Canadian-U.S. friendship and commemorates 150 years of peace on the longest unfortified border in the world. A walk through the formal gardens, and a concert in the outdoor amphitheater are musts for North Dakotans and visitors to the state. Young people have the unique opportunity to become familiar with the design and philosophy of the spacious gardens in week-long music and athletic camps held throughout the summer. Lake Metigoshe, not far away, offers a beautiful vacation spot. Besides water sports and canoeing, the park includes an extensive trail system for the hiker; 20 miles of snowmobile trail; six miles of cross-country ski trail; four miles of snowshoe trail; 10 miles for backpacking; and ranger talks.

North Dakota's 4th largest city, Minot, is in this section. Minot State College is a focus for cultural events of all kinds and in summer the North Dakota State Fair presents a week of excitement—big midway carnival, horse races, grandstand shows, country music, and barns full of the best livestock in the state. Pioneer village is located on the fairgrounds, with Roosevelt Zoo adjoining the grounds.

Cormorant and Great Blue Heron nesting in J. Clark Salyer wildlife refuge

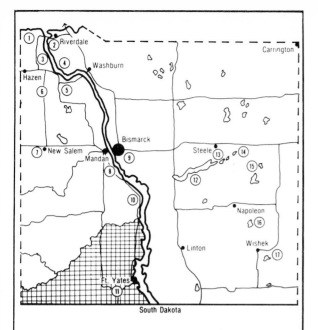

South Dakota

1. **Lake Sakakawea State Park**
2. **Garrison Dam and Power Station, guided tours; dam is 2 miles long, 202' high; Federal Fish Hatchery below; Riverdale, government town**
3. **Knife River Indian Villages, Sakakawea lived here at the River Hidatsa Village**
4. **Ft. Mandan, Lewis and Clark winter camp 1804-1805; Western 4-H Camp is close by**
5. **Ft. Clark, fur trading post built in 1829**
6. **Coal mining; World's largest lignite-burning electric generating plants**
7. **New Salem's giant Holstein cow, honors dairy industry and historical incident; pioneer village; Bachelor Days**
8. **Ft. Lincoln State Park, includes reconstructed Slant Indian Village, Ft. Abraham Lincoln, Ft. McKeen blockhouses, museum**
9. **State Capitol; Historical Museum and Library; Camp Hancock river warehouse and museum; Bismarck Junior College; Mary College; Dakota Zoo**
10. **Ft. Rice, blockhouses**
11. **Standing Rock Indian Reservation, Indian Agency at Ft. Yates**
12. **Long Lake National Wildlife Refuge**
13. **Camp Grassick**
14. **Slade National Wildlife Refuge**
15. **Streeter Memorial State Park**
16. **Beaver Lake State Park**
17. **Doyle Memorial State Park**

Southcentral

The southcentral region is rich in North Dakota history. Fur trade, steamboats, Lewis and Clark, military posts— Fort Abraham Lincoln, from which Custer and his 7th Calvary rode out on their fateful mission. Indian earthlodge villages, some current, some in ancient ruins, peppered the low plateaus above the Missouri.

A rare treat for the sightseer are the Mandan earthlodges in Ft. Lincoln State Park, reconstructed by the CCC's during the '30's. Farther north were five Hidatsa villages, where Lewis and Clark found Sakakawea. One of the exciting new projects in North Dakota is the excavation and reconstruction planned for these Knife River Hidatsa Villages. (See sketch, pg. 83) Visitors will watch a living laboratory: archeological diggings, processing of artifacts, rebuilding of ancient earthlodges.

In Bismarck are numerous interest stops for the traveler. Newest development on the state capitol grounds is the Heritage Center. When completed it will be a showcase for an enormous wealth of historical items and artifacts which have been unavailable to the public eye.

To the south is Standing Rock Indian Reservation, with Lake Oahe bordering the reservation to the east.

Farming is extensive throughout the southcentral region, with beef cattle on the rougher terrain. New Salem is a dairy center. Moisture is about average for the state with 15-17 inches; this area tends to have the warmest summer temperatures.

The state's major coal development is here—in the Beulah-Center area.

At right, the earthlodges of Slant Indian Village. Inset is aerial photo of the Knife River Village site slated for development. Circular depressions in foreground mark Sakakawea's village, to be restored. At top right are remains of the Lower Hidatsa Village

Indian girls wear traditional beaded dress for Ft. Yates celebration; at United Tribes training center in the second Ft. Lincoln, near Bismarck's airport, the emphasis is on action

A living

North Dakota's skyscraper Capitol: Inside, the will of the people is heard

New Salem's giant Holstein surveys grazing lands where the grass is 'right side up'

Sunrise and sunset on Lake Sakakawea is spectacular in any season

history

Coal mining in Mercer County: The machinery gets bigger

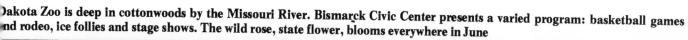

Dakota Zoo is deep in cottonwoods by the Missouri River. Bismarck Civic Center presents a varied program: basketball games and rodeo, ice follies and stage shows. The wild rose, state flower, blooms everywhere in June

Southeast—city suburb and bonanza farm

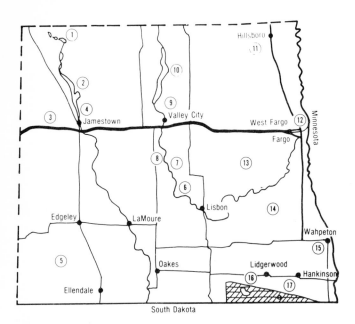

1. **Arrowwood National Wildlife Refuge**
2. **Jamestown Reservoir**
3. **Ft. Seward Military post**
4. **Jamestown College; Frontier village and fort, world's largest buffalo**
5. **Whitestone Battlefield, scene of state's bloodiest battle**
6. **Ft. Ransom military post; Bjarne Ness Gallery**
7. **Little Yellowstone Park; scenic drive and canoeing along Sheyenne River**
8. **Clausen Springs**
9. **Valley City State College; Valley City Winter Show**
10. **Lake Ashtabula; Federal fish hatchery is located below Baldhill Dam**
11. **World's tallest structures, KTHI-TV towers 2,063 feet high**
12. **North Dakota State University; Bonanzaville; Red River Valley Fair**
13. **Maple Creek Historic Site**
14. **Ft. Abercrombie, first North Dakota military post, beseiged for 60 days during Santee Sioux uprising, includes reconstructed blockhouses, stockade, museum**
15. **State School of Science; Chahinkapa Park and Zoo**
16. **Tewaukon National Wildlife Refuge**
17. **Sisseton Indian Reservation—considered a South Dakota reservation, since "no one lives on the North Dakota side."**

Cities, suburbs, and towns are more populous in the southeastern section. Fargo is the state's largest city and an urban distribution center for a wide area. Farms are smaller, closer, except in the rolling sandhills of the cattle country to the south. Soils are rich; land highly productive. Rainfall is highest in the state, averaging 20 inches annually near Wahpeton, and the growing season is longest.

Bonanza farms grew wheat in huge operations here during the late 1800's on grant lands speculators and real estate dealers bought from the Northern Pacific Railroad. In an earlier era, three military forts were built: Ft. Abercrombie, Ft. Seward, and Ft. Ransom. Ft. Abercrombie, North Dakota's first, was established in 1858 to guard traffic going north on the Red River, and west to Montana's gold fields.

Here are the level lands of the Red River Valley, brushed smooth and flat eons ago by water action on the bottom of glacial Lake Agassiz. But also there are beautiful valleys and scenic lakes; the Clausen Springs-Little Yellowstone Park area on the Sheyenne is especially delightful. The winding Sheyenne flows south, then cuts back northeast to the Red, ultimately dropping its waters into Hudson Bay—though for much of the distance its course is parallel and close to that of the James, which continues south.

Four colleges and universities in this region—North Dakota State University, Fargo; Valley City State College; State School of Science, Wahpeton; and Jamestown College—are centers for theater, art, and musical productions. Bonanzaville, near Fargo, is a favorite tourist stop. It includes the Northern Plains museum and a recreated pioneer town of 36 restored buildings covering 10 acres. Jamestown, too, has a frontier village on the bluffs above town near the landmark concrete buffalo which commemorates the enormous herds of buffalo once roaming here.

Fargo's downtown shopping mall.

Jamestown's 60-ton 26-foot-high buffalo is world's largest.

Bonanzaville, West Fargo, is a pioneer town of 36 restored buildings with authentic furnishings.

Jamestown Reservoir, below, on the James River and Lake Ashtabula on the Sheyenne are favorite vacation spots for camping, fishing and water sports.

The Battle of Whitestone Hill was fought here Sept. 3, 1863—North Dakota's bloodiest.

Four colleges draw students from all over state; are focal points for theater, art and music.

Valley City Winter Show reigns here for 10 days in March.

Beautiful forests, scenic rivers and lakes are here.

Northeast: Low valley and historic hills

This northeastern corner of North Dakota was first to be settled by whites, in 1797, with the beginnings of fur trade. Historic buildings survive: a trading post, mission, warehouse.

This section has the state's coolest average temperature and the lowest elevation. Pembina is only 750 feet elevation—and it's downhill all the way to Hudson Bay.

Here are beautiful forests, scenic rivers and lakes. Also the rich farmlands of the Red River Valley, level as the lake beds they once were. Potatoes and sugar beets are important, along with other crops raised through the state.

The Devils Lake region is particularly interesting. Here is the largest natural lake in North Dakota, plus a number of only slightly smaller lakes. Once Devils Lake was much larger; when Garrison Diversion is complete it will rival its former size as terminal point for waters diverted from Lake Sakakawea. Fort Totten Indian Reservation on the southern lake shore offers the sightseer rodeo, pow-wows, and the upper midwest's best preserved military post including 15 original buildings, built of bricks fired from local clay. Musicals run through summer in the Little Theater. Nearby, buffalo and other wildlife range Sully's Hill national game preserve.

Two state parks, Icelandic and Turtle River, offer year-around recreation and scenic trails.

Grand Forks is the metropolitan focal point here, second largest city in the state with both the University of North Dakota and Grand Forks Air Base.

1. **Lake Region Junior College.**
2. **Camp Grafton, national guard camp.**
3. **Sully's Hill national game preserve; buffalo herd.**
4. **Ft. Totten reservation; military post of Indian wars period established in 1867; summer musicals in Little Theater.**
5. **Devils Lake, largest natural lake in the state; goose hunter's paradise.**
6. **Carl Ben Eielson Memorial Arch, honors Arctic flier.**
7. **Mayville State College.**
8. **University of North Dakota; North Dakota Mill and Elevator, only state-owned mill in the U.S.**
9. **Grand Forks Air Base, SAC defense.**
10. **Turtle River State Park, forested, with trail riding, nature trails, skiing, snomobile trails.**
11. **Icelandic State Park, shoreline of Tongue River, lakes, camping, boating, swimming, hiking; Gunlogson Arboretum, an old homestead, preserves native prairie environment, animal and bird sanctuary.**
12. **Kittson trading post, built about 1851, oldest buildings in state; martyrs graves in Walhalla cemetery of missionaries killed by Indians during 1850's.**
13. **Pembina River Valley scenic drive, 30 miles of densely wooded valley.**
14. **Pembina museum and trading post, first in North Dakota, established 1797.**

Strategic Air Command jets take off from Grand Forks Air Base.

No fence, only sheared trees define Canadian border in Pembina Hills.

unflowers and beans, potatoes and sugar beets, grow well in fertile Red River Valley.

Devils Lake in the heart of the central flyway is paradise for goose hunters.

University of North Dakota campus.

Ft. Totten: l5 original buildings survive, most face into the cavalry square.

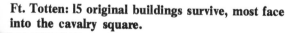

Skiing Pembina Mountain Skiway, above, and snomobiling the hills of Turtle River State Park, take advantage of the relatively deeper snows found here.

Bighorn ewes and young feed high on a ridge south of Medora

The wealth

North Dakota gained early fame from the wealth of wildlife that lived here. The first whites built a great system of fur trade; fortunes were made and lost; countless men died in the pursuit of riches from beaver and buffalo.

No less today is North Dakota famed for good hunting and for wildlife.

It was good hunting that brought Indian tribes out of the forests and onto the prairies and plains to form a new culture. Good hunting brought the adventurous and the wealthy: Teddy Roosevelt, A.C. Huidekoper, the Marquis de Mores. Big game of all kinds was abundant.

"The whole face of the country was covered with herds of buffalo, elk and antelope," wrote Meriwether Lewis, after climbing to the top of a ridge in western Dakota to get a good look. "Deer are also abundant."

But there came too many hunters, and settlers moved in from the east determined to subdue the land.

The terrible decline, that began when the first Indian discovered he could trade beaver pelts at the post for goods to make his life easier and more interesting, continued with a vengeance. Pioneers hunted down the predators and, with the big-time hunters, slaughtered the game.

Audubon bighorn sheep were annihilated for all time. Elk, buffalo, grizzly bear, black bear, wolves, and mountain lions were seen no more. The big birds continued their

spring and fall migratory flights, but many — such as the geese — learned to nest farther north in Canada.

Yet we are fortunate. Before it was too late, the people had enough foresight to say: Stop—and a reverse trend was effected. North Dakota is again rich in wildlife, both in variety and numbers.

A species of bighorn, the Rocky Mountain bighorn sheep, has been replanted in the badlands. They have reproduced successfully, now numbering several hundred, and the surplus offers permit holders a rare hunting opportunity. The Giant Canada geese are again nesting and raising their young along lakes throughout the state, migrating south and returning in spring, as a result of N.D. Game & Fish re-nesting programs. Wild turkeys, also, range wooded areas of western North Dakota.

Great numbers of out-of-state hunters come here for goose hunting, for ducks, for deer and antelope; many come for the superb fishing. But hunters, whether out of state or in, no longer have free license to kill indiscriminately as in the days of "that butcher, Sir Gore." Both hunting and fishing are carefully managed.

Even in the hottest front of goose hunting, shooting is permitted only until noon—geese are then free to feed in peace until morning. Wildlife refuges are sprinkled throughout the state and the geese know the boundaries as

Mule deer await their turn at the jump.

A successful bighorn hunter.

Corralling buffalo the modern way in Teddy Roosevelt park, south unit.

# of wildlife

The wily coyote adapts easily to changing environment.

well as anyone. Archery hunting is encouraged; bow hunters are given a month or more head start.

Hunting, however, is not as popular or as necessary as in days past. Wildlife is enjoyed for the pure pleasure of seeing it in native habitat, and perhaps taking a shot with the camera. Most people, including hunters, take greatest delight in discovering, but not disturbing, a mallard's nest in the grass, a wide-eyed fawn in the brush, or a den of foxes sunning themselves on a sidehill. A pair of fieldglasses or telephoto lens can add another dimension to exhilarating wildlife experiences.

Fleet of foot and keen of eye, antelope keep to the open country—in 1925 only 225 antelope remained in the state, now they number over 2500. In lower photo, Maddock hunters make camp near Rhame.

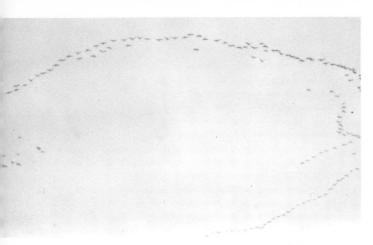

Sandhill cranes fly in great successive waves. Below, cranes coming in for a landing.

Geese are again nesting and rearing young in North Dakota.

Mallard ducks wintering over near Garrison; photo taken from a blind.

It's a record: 37 1/2 pounds of northern pike caught in Lake Sakakawea.

North Dakota records

Northern Pike—37 lbs. 8 oz.
Walleye—15 lbs. 12 oz.
Sauger—8 lbs. 12 oz.—World record
Rainbow Trout—9 lbs. 11 oz.
Brown Trout—5 lbs. 15 1/2 oz.
Largemouth Bass—7 lbs. 12 oz.
Smallmouth Bass—3 lbs. 10 oz.
White Bass—4 lbs. 4 oz.
Yellow Perch—2 lbs. 4 1/2 oz.
Bluegill—2 lbs. 12 oz.
Crappie—3 lbs.
Channel Catfish—26 lbs. 8 oz.
Paddlefish—60 lbs.
Ling—16 lbs. 8 oz.
Pallid Sturgeon—37 lbs.

From the edge of the smallest pond to the middle of Lake Sakakawea you can see the fishermen out most any day. Fishing season in North Dakota is year-around, except that game fish (such as trout, northern pike, bass, etc.) may not be taken in April. Consult N.D. Game & Fish for details on special seasons, limits, and where the fish are biting. List your whopper with them to qualify for the "Whopper Club"—and you could break a record!

Observe and enjoy wildlife more— by riding, walking, canoeing

North Dakota's famous flickertail gopher (Richardson ground squirrel).

The adaptable red fox is increasing in the state.

Watch your feet, but don't be scared—the prairie rattler is defensive, almost always he'll retreat if he can.

"just catchin' frogs"

the majestic eagle

Both golden and bald eagles nest in North Dakota. They are America's largest birds of prey, except for the rare California condor, and have wingspreads of 6-8 feet. Since 1782 the bald eagle has been America's official emblem. It differs from the golden eagle in having a white head when mature, and feet which are bare of feathers. The bald eagle usually nests in big cottonwood trees; the golden eagle on rocky ledges of cliffs. They mate for life and add onto their nests year by year until they are of enormous size.

Bald eagle, the American emblem; they nest in big cottonwood trees and mate for life.

The golden eagle prefers high cliffs for nesting. In the nest below, are two young golden eagles, an unhatched egg, and dead prairie dogs.

This eagle is using both beak and talons to carry a rabbit home to the nest.

the river

Oh Shenandoah, I long to hear you
Away, you rolling river.
Oh Shenandoah, I can't get near you.

> Away, away, I'm bound away
> Across the wide Missouri.

Oh Shenandoah, I love your daughter
Far away, you restless river.
She lives across the stormy water.

> Away, away, I'm bound away
> Across the wide Missouri.

Dakotans call it simply 'the river.'

The words evoke subtle shades of meaning: mystery, dread, and delight. Mighty Missouri—great surging river of history—powerful though shackled, a river to be reckoned with forever.

A river that for half a century was main highway for fur trade, living link between military forts, trading posts, Indian camps, gold fields, from St. Louis to the Rocky Mountains. Down the river went furs, buffalo hides and gold. Upstream went trading stock, military supplies, annuity goods for treaty Indians, and ornate furniture for gold field barons.

The Missouri sweeps turbulently under big cliffs and soft banks, gnawing hungrily until they topple with a roar and splash; meanders ceaselessly back and forth; rises at flood stage in wild raging violence. When the ice breaks up it cracks and pops through the night with shattering reckless sound. Rivermen called her, with affectionate respect, the Big Muddy.

Longest river on the North American continent, the Missouri constantly switched channels and snaked a changing circuitous route. Steamship captains plied every

River of history: Fort Yates troops at Bismarck.

sweeping curve and counted it 3,000 miles from St. Louis to Ft. Benton, highest point of navigation. Near Like-a-Fishhook-Village (just above Garrison Dam) the ships had to travel 75 miles—around the 'fishhook'—to make a distance of ten. But government surveyed across the loops to determine freight costs for hauling military supplies and Indian annuities. They called the distance 2,274 miles from Ft. Benton to St. Louis, and paid steamship companies on that basis.

But at least one writer questioned whether the Missouri did indeed end at St. Louis, and suggests that the Mississippi, instead, flows into the Missouri.

"There isn't any Mississippi left to view after it meets the Missouri," said George Fitch in 1907. "The Mississippi is a beautiful, majestic stream which minds its own business and flows placidly along the course laid out for it by nature ages ago. You can always count on finding the Mississippi just where you left it last year.

"But the Mississippi-Missouri is a tawny, restless, brawling flood. It cuts corners, runs around at nights, fills itself with snags and traveling sandbars, lunches on levees, and swallows islands and small villages for dessert. This description fits the Missouri to a 'T'."

There is Indian tradition with the same conclusion—that the Mississippi ran into another big river, opaque and turbulent.

For lands beyond the Missouri, Dakotans have coined a special term, west river, which means literally, 'west of the river.' Most Dakotans live east of the river and for them west river country is imbued with the traditions of a land that is different—wild, rugged, individualistic. West river people are thought to reflect these same characteristics.

Trains crossed on tracks laid on the ice.

Ice jams raised havoc with shipping. Both photos taken at Bismarck

'the ice is going out'

Water, swollen by thawing . . . lifted the vast layer of ice which held it prisoner, and gradually loosened it from the 2 banks . . . As soon as the vast shell of ice began to move, the debacle came. At first the ice floated adrift in enormous cakes. One of them was not less than half a mile long. Soon there appeared long fissures, with continuous rumblings; the cakes split, were shattered when they crashed together.

At the sharp bend in the river . . . the big cakes of ice, squeezed between the two banks and broke up into big blocks. These blocks pressed against the ones in their way, bumped together, went over each other, upset each other, and piled up so that soon this part of the choked-up river became a vast chaos of ice . . . The flood rose to ten or twelve feet in a few hours . . . swept impetuously across the flat bottoms . . . and disappeared in a few hours during the night . . . we have witnessed a grand and impressive spectacle.

De Trobriand

To be a boy when word flashed through town that the ice was going out was to know high adventure. Giant cakes, borne by a rushing, bank-full torrent, made bridges rattle as they smashed at piers. Often, in one of the river's many bends, the ice jammed, and the Missouri spilled into the surrounding low country.

George Moses

Part of this tradition stems from the extreme difficulty with which pioneers crossed the Missouri. They could swim it, perhaps, with their placid farm horses, their floating wagons, driving loose stock into the water ahead of them, but it was risky. At certain points ferries operated sporadically, or decrepit steamers were pressed into service. A pontoon bridge built in floating, detachable sections operated for a time near Mobridge. Pioneer stories are rich with lore of the crossing of the wide Missouri. Accidents, loss of goods and livestock were real risks of any crossing.

Ideally, they could have crossed on the ice if winter had been a time for travel in unfamiliar and unsettled western country. Building a bridge was so difficult and expensive that the North Pacific laid tracks on the ice at Bismarck and for ten years crossed their trains only in wintertime. When the railroad bridge was finally built, settlers often laid planks on the open ties to cross wagons and livestock.

Strong undercurrents and deep soft mud along the banks made Missouri River crossing additionally dangerous.

Libby Custer, wife of the general, expressed great fear at having to cross the river each time she went from Ft. Lincoln to Bismarck.

"I so dreaded that terrible river that we must cross going and coming . . . it represented a lifetime of terror to me. The current was so swift that it was almost impossible for the strongest swimmer to save himself if once he fell in: the mud settled on him instantly, clogged his movements, and bore him under. Some of the soldiers had been drowned in attempting to cross in frail, insecure skiffs to the drinking-huts opposite. As I looked into this roaring current, I rarely failed to picture to myself the upturned faces of these lost men."

I led (my pony) down the bank to the river where a couple of squaws with their bull boats were waiting to ferry us over. I got into one placed my saddle gun, & c. in & taking the lariats of 2 of the horses, towed them after snorting in the deep water, and plunging and splashing on the bars without any mishap we all crossed over. A bull boat is an original invention . . . a hide stretched over a round willow frame, & requires the utmost care to prevent **spilling.** The squaw propels it with one paddle, working very hard, and making slow progress.

Henry Boller, 1858

Libby's fear was increased by her distrust of the boat used as a ferry. "The western word 'ramshackly' described it," she said. "It was too large and unwieldly for the purpose, and it had been condemned as unsafe farther down the river, where citizens value life more highly. . .

"After we were once out in the channel the real trouble began. I never knew, when I started for Bismarck, whether we would not land at Yankton, 500 miles below. The wheel often refused to revolve more than halfway, the boat would turn about, and we would shoot down the river at a mad rate. I used to receive elaborate nautical explanations from the confused old captain why that happened. My intellect was slow to take in any other thought than the terrifying one—that he had lost control of the boat."

Indians favored the bullboat for Missouri crossings. Made like a tub, it was a single buffalo hide stretched over a willow frame, which the squaw could carry on her head when they reached the other side. Paddling bullboats upstream was nearly impossible, so they were only used for crossings unless they were to be disposed of at a downriver point.

Other craft used on the upper Missouri were keelboats, canoes, and mackinaws, which were little more than enclosed rafts. These 'floating shoeboxes' were used by miners returning from gold fields and by fur traders. Like the bullboats, they were not returned upstream.

The Missouri went on the rampage twice a year: in March or April when the ice broke up and snow melted, and again during the June raise when the river crested from rains and melting mountain snows. The ice break up was most dangerous and unpredictable. Towns and ranches flooded overnight as rushing ice-choked waters swept wide against an ice jam, giant blocks of ice smashing into each other, felling trees and fences.

And so: the dams. Now the Missouri lies shackled, chained by three huge dams. Garrison, Oahe, Ft. Peck, each among the world's largest. Garrison Dam, begun in 1947, six years in the building, is an engineering masterpiece, a tribute to man's penchant for progress. It backs the waters of Lake Sakakawea up to cover 609 square miles. Recreation opportunities abound—and are as yet barely tapped. Electric power is produced by great generators. Water is available for irrigation, industrial uses, municipal

water supplies. Flooding no longer holds its terrible threat over communities downriver and they now build far into the flood plain.

Yet, it is inevitable that other values have been sacrificed to these. Gone are the quiet bottoms with clear springs and brushy coulees that were havens for deer and other wildlife. Gone are the forests of big cottonwoods, thickly fringing the river's meandering course in a bright emerald green. Gone are thousands of acres of the best cropland and pasture. Gone are the homes of many, both white and Indian, and three towns: Sanish, Van Hook, and Elbowoods.

Ft. Berthold Indians bitterly opposed the dam, which ultimately took all their best land and split the reservation into five separate pieces. North Dakota's original farmers, they had tilled Missouri River bottom land since the 14th century. Now it was all gone and they were left with high and dry ridges and plateaus.

Just ahead of the rising waters archaelogical crews hurried to excavate remains of a 15th century village. Inevitably they lost the race. The remains of Indian towns and camps, trading posts and military forts richly abundant in the area were soon submerged.

In North Dakota the waters rose—not only westward from Garrison—but also up from the south, where Oahe was built close on the heels of Garrison. Waters backed up into every tributary to submerge land and drown out the thick stands of trees. Dead cottonwoods still stand as gaunt and silver skeletons raising their brittle arms to Indian people on the hills.

"You'll notice that all the big dams flood Indian land," comments a Sioux office worker, married to a Ft. Berthold Indian. "My father-in-law, for example, had a nice place down on the river with cattle, pastures and alfalfa hayland. He had to move out. The government paid him some, but he spent it all drilling a well, trying to get water up there on

Garrison Dam, below. Back-up into the Little Missouri, right, killed thousands of native cottonwoods and littered banks with debris.

North Dakota's original farmers tilled Missouri River bottomland for 700 years—lost it all

Garrison Dam site in 1946: across the river is a town which was flooded.

top. It was no use, he couldn't get his place built up again. He lost his cattle."

Only 90 miles remain in North Dakota of the natural Missouri River.

Now, new projects are underway, notably the "Big Ditch" diversion projects, long in the planning stages, designed to route water throughout the state for irrigation, industrial, and municipal uses. New dams are needed; broad deep ditches will be trenched out, requiring wide rights-of-way. More land and more homes will be taken.

These are important projects—North Dakota has a vital stake in using this water so impressively impounded within

Ft. Berthold Indians farmed Missouri River bottomlands since the 14th century, lost it all underwater.

Away, you rolling river—

her borders. But increasingly voices are raised in protest against the values of progress-at-any-cost. They question if the Army Engineers have not been somewhat overzealous in moving dirt and mapping out new projects for themselves—like a family of beavers who, with their own home and dam work complete, continue to fell trees compulsively. There may be other ways to accomplish economic goals which are not so disruptive to lifestyles, such as more use of existing river beds and pipeline for the big ditches.

Meanwhile, the old Missouri rolls on, ceaselessly, without stopping, pausing only to seek her way past man's obstructions.

Ninety miles of Missouri river bottoms remain in North Dakota; boats again tie up at Bismarck boat landing.

Lake Sakakawea: Two enormous lakes provide North Dakotans with unlimited recreation possibilities.

Layers of coal, clay and soils were formed as inland seas repeatedly swept the land and receded.

Once upon a time—
A vast sea flooded this land

80-million-year-old dinosaur skull from north of Marmath is packed for shipment to UND—horns were broken off as indicated.

Lower photo is of petrified wood, abundant in western Dakota.

A shallow inland sea once reached up from the Gulf of Mexico and flooded the interior lowlands of North America. Rivers flowing into this sea carried sands and clays, silting it in, washing away, building up.

Eons passed. The great sea receded, and as its waters drained away they left vast swamps and floodplains.

Tropical climate prevailed. Lush forests grew up where the sea had been; mighty redwoods, thick ferns and leafy brush. Year by year, century upon century, the luxuriant vegetation died and fell into the swamps, building up thick layers.

Then the rising waters of the inland sea returned. Silt and mud washed down onto the sea bottom again, covering the fallen vegetation, packing it nearly airtight under pressure.

Again the waters drained off and forests grew, only to be re-flooded and the process repeated through eons of time. Great trees, sequoias and redwoods, stood drowned and dying each time in white skeleton forests. Strange reptiles raised their heads to listen as the giant trees crashed and toppled into primeval swamp waters.

When vegetation rotted and decayed, the energy was liberated and the organic matter became just another layer of soil, darker perhaps than layers above and below. But when the thick layers of vegetation were trapped underwater, silted down, packed under pressure, hardened, the energy could not escape. Coal and oil, rich forms of energy, were formed by this process.

Lignite—North Dakota's coal—is only part way along in the forming process. It is less than 60% carbon and still contains, in addition, large quantities of oxygen, hydrogen and water. (By comparison, bituminous coal contains 60-80% carbon; anthracite 90%.) The lignite sometimes caught fire, baking clay layers into the colorful scoria seen today in buttes and badlands.

Fossils formed, too, when conditions were right. Reptile fossils have been found in this region in such numbers that it has been called a dinosaur cemetery. The best preserved fossils turned to stone, petrified. In this process dead plants and animals were preserved in a water-soaked condition until the minerals of the water eventually replaced the original living cells, leaving an accurate pattern of their design. Petrified trees, stumps and rock chunks of petrified wood are common in western Dakota. Original tree rings can plainly be seen.

Then came ice ages

A striking change then came upon this land. Tropical weather chilled into the ice age. Glaciers swept down from the north. Four times the ice sheets came and retreated.

The advancing glacier's action was that of a bulldozer: Leveling, grinding, crushing huge boulders, gouging, scraping up and pushing before it a ridge of soil and rocks to be dropped at the extremity of its reach. In retreat, a glacier's action was that of melting, rushing waters that cut waterways in the direction of least resistance, pooled into broad lakes when there was no easy outlet and when glacial ice blocked drainage to the north.

North Dakota's topography reveals clearly the action of the glaciers. It is almost as if some giant child played here with sticks and pails of water, leveling, pouring, scraping, leaving piles of debris.

The fourth and last glacier ground its way down from Canada pushing ahead of it vast quantities of glacial drift through the northern and eastern sections of the state. It extended nearly to the Missouri River before it stopped. This ice age lasted some 95,000 years. Then, a mere 25,000 years ago, the climate warmed and the last glacier began its retreat.

The glacier left its debris as a chain of hills cutting diagonally across the state, just east of the Missouri. Melting waters could not cross this barrier, but found some southern drainage through the James River.

The Red River Valley became one vast glacial lake. Lake Agassiz was unable to drain north because of the slow-melting glacier; its flood waters sought passage around the glacier's eastern edge and into Hudson Bay. Red River Valley soils are rich in ground limestone and organic matter which were leveled and silted in at the bottom of the lake.

Other glacial lakes formed a chain across the north from Stump Lake and Devils Lake to the Turtle Mountains. The valley in the Souris River filled with water. Some of this drained off into the Missouri River, and later changed to follow the course of the James along the edge of the glacier.

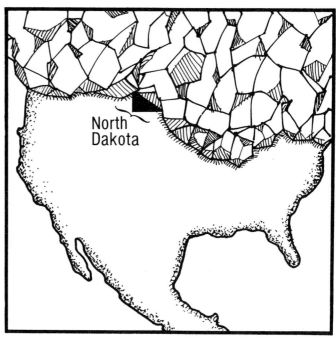

Extent of the last glacier; it receded 25,000 years ago.

Still later the Souris waters flowed through the Sheyenne, until they found at last their own tortured course north again into Canada.

This big mid-section of North Dakota, called the Drift Prairies, is diagonally sliced. It's a young region without a developed system of drainage and few rivers. Here are level productive farm lands; here also are many scoured-out low places and sloughs. Drift Prairie hills are rounded with sloping sides scarcely showing the effects of erosion except where rivers hasten the process. Soils are generally of richly ground drift, ideal for farming. But here and there the glacier played its tricks, dropping capricious loads of granite stones.

In the southwestern section erosion continued, unaffected by the final glacier. Torrential rains dug deeper gullies and washed away loose soil from the sides of rocky ridges and lone buttes. Walls dropped off cut-cliffs revealing the earlier story; the layering of silted ocean bottom, scoria clay baked red above burnt-out coal veins.

Glacial rock deposits are abundant, so there's plenty of 'rock picking'. Big glacial boulders, like the one at right, estimated at 2-2 1/2 tons, were pushed here from Hudson Bay regions.

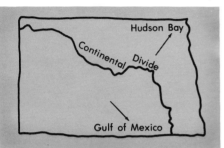

Like three broad steps

Like steps, North Dakota's terrain rises from the level Red River Valley of the east, once a glacial lake bed, up 300-400 feet at the Pembina Escarpment onto the central Drift Prairie. At the Missouri Escarpment there is another steep rise of 300-400 feet onto the Missouri Plateau. Low point of elevation is 750 feet in the northeast corner; high point is White Butte in the southwest at 3,506 feet. North Dakota's weather patterns tend to follow this diagonal lay of the land.

Drainage is poor in the young country north and east of the Missouri, terrain shaped by the last glacier. Potholes and lakes are common. There are few rivers and even lands close to the rivers often do not drain into them, but maintain their own systems of lakes and sloughs that swell and shrink with the rainfall.

By contrast, drainage is fast—often too fast—in the old eroded country west of the Missouri. No natural lakes survive in country like this; ancient basins have long since broken through into river channels. In Missouri River drainage, a rancher who wants to hold the run-off from spring rains, must build a dam to keep it. Flash floods are common. Small rivers and dry creek-beds can quickly become raging torrents as every draw and gully dumps in additional rainfall from a sudden summer storm.

Continental Divide cuts diagonally through North Dakota

Spring thaw looks like this in pothole country where drainage is poor

Badlands country drains fast and flash floods are common

Level Red River Valley farmlands

Drift Prairie combines farm and pasture lands

600,000 people—
a way of life

The character of a people, grown ever more cosmopolitan, but shaped by rural origins, ethnic heritage, great open spaces of prairie and plain.

North Dakota's most valuable resource is not wheat, nor livestock — nor coal — but people. The strength of a people who are, as a whole, honest, hard-working, neighborly, generous, optimistic and courageous.

It's a character shaped and hewed by rural origins, by foreign inheritance not very distant, and by broad open spaces of prairie and plain. In 1910, 71 percent of the population was foreign-born or the children of foreign-born — 21 percent was Norwegian, 20 percent German Russian and German. Eighty-six percent lived in the country or in small towns.

All this has changed as the population grows steadily more cosmopolitan. Today one-third live in cities over 10,000. But the three major influences are still steadily reflected in the character of the people.

Once Dakotans felt their remoteness, their isolation from population centers where things of excitement and importance seemed to be happening. Today the tables have turned.

TV has put everyone in instant touch with the pulse of the nation and the world. Fast cars and excellent roads have brought the opportunities of the entire nation within easy reach — whether it be for artistic events, sightseeing, shopping, attending distant Universities, or lying on palmy beaches. Dakotans now visit the cities for the advantages that cities can offer, and return home for the pleasures of easier, less congested living. Certainly, the best of both worlds.

No longer can Dakotans be called provincial. Their world knowledge and extent of travel exceeds that of the vast majority of metropolitan dwellers. Suddenly people in the cities know this, too, and it has given our youth a growing assurance, and a sense of the need to preserve the good life.

A high standard of living is generally enjoyed, even though statistically incomes tend to average low. Few people in the state have extremely high, or extremely low incomes. A higher quality of life costs less in North Dakota.

High moral character is reflected in the crime rate which — many years — is the lowest in the nation. According to the 1975 World Almanac, North Dakota was third lowest behind Mississippi and West Virginia, and that year exceeded those two states only in auto theft and property damage. North Dakota's murder rate was .8 per 100,000 population compared to all other states which varied between 2.1 and 17.4. In robbery, the N.D. rate was 7.3, Vermont's 8.8, and all other states between 13.3 and 439.6. For violent crime, North Dakota's rate was 60.8; Vermont 70.5; New Hampshire 82; the other states ranged between 102 and 731. Dakotans are able to live in a way no longer possible for many Americans — neither harming anyone nor fearful of harm.

In addition, most Dakotans enjoy good health. People live longer here and North Dakota has, in many years, the lowest infant mortality rate in the nation.

From an older generation youth can find its roots: strength, hard-work, faith, honesty, courage.

In North Dakota as elsewhere, there has been a great resurgence of ethnic pride. Norwegian influence has made this a state of blue-eyed blondes — and now the youngest of blondes are learning to turn the lefse stick. Young people are learning to make many traditional dishes, but not from the recipe book. They go instead to grandmothers who know from practiced touch when the dough is right for lefse, for fleischkuchele and kuchen. They listen to the voice rich in the sounds of the old country — though the grandmother was probably born close by. Girls in Ukrainian localities are again learning the delicate art of egg painting.

Volunteer work is a way of life in most North Dakota communities. It's the way things get done — instead of paying someone, as in bigger cities. The way to keep the hospital running, the ambulance service and the fire department ready-to-go; the way to obtain a new swimming pool, library, or senior citizens center; the way to bring many kinds of opportunities to the youth and adults of the community. Citizenship responsibilities are a part of growing up here — and are useful training for an active, rewarding life.

When population is light — as it is in North Dakota — it is clearly evident that it matters what one young person or adult does. Few faceless teeming crowds can be found in the entire state. Each person is important and needed. Fewer people mean more opportunities for leadership; young people learn to accept this challenge.

Civic groups of all kinds meet the needs. The accomplishments of North Dakota's extension service working with volunteer leaders for improving community living on many levels is well known throughout the state. Four-H has been a popular and rewarding program, challenging youth and adults to personal growth. It has consistently promoted an international scope, and since 1973 hundreds of North Dakota 4-H'ers have had the incomparable experience of living in Japanese homes, or of bringing Japanese exchangees into their own homes.

Young people grow up well-rounded, knowledgeable and in touch with reality. Out-of-state employers have long sought the young North Dakotan as a most desirable kind of worker and credit him with excellent trainability, positive motivation, superior productivity, mechanical ability as a result of general agricultural background, high degree of self-reliance, low turnover and absenteeism, high moral character, and a generally high educational level.

Such general traits may well be more common here. Yet, as everywhere, personality is unique and diverse. Every community, no matter how small, has its outstanding individuals who enrich the lives around them in a tremendous variety of ways.

Ethnic pride: The practiced touch on lefse.

Experiences in understanding: Young Dakotans live in Japan — Yumi unloads horse for a ride in Dakota hills.

In touch with reality: Teenage girls can sew their own; a farmer and his wife survey their acres, center; right, building a pole barn

a time to work—and time to dream

Daily chores can bring a proud moment, left. An intriguing problem, below, where to move next

School lunch cooks: Good food and a cheerful disposition

Small boy scales a sculptured rock atop a ridge and discovers the wonder of a hawk's nest; high above, the pair of hawks circle and watch

Presentation of flags at powwow.

Postcard-pretty princesses, costumes, dancing, beadwork and rodeo are all part — but only a part — of the North Dakota Indian story today.

Indians in transition

Fifteen thousand Native Americans live on or adjacent to four North Dakota Indian reservations. Standing Rock and Ft. Totten are Sioux (Dakota). Turtle Mountain is Chippewa; Ft. Berthold, the Three Affiliated Tribes — Mandan, Arickara, Hidatsa. A fifth, Sisseton in the southeast corner, is regarded as a South Dakota reservation, since few people live north of the border. Although Turtle Mt. is the smallest, comprising only two townships, 7,550 people live there, or about half the total number. The other reservations have about 2,500 Indian inhabitants each (including only the N.D. side of Standing Rock). Each tribe has a distinct heritage as plains Indians, forest dwellers, or river agriculturists.

During the '70's the movement to the cities has increased and many Indians also live in Fargo, Grand Forks, Minot, Williston, and Bismarck-Mandan, where jobs are more plentiful. Yet, the lure of the reservation is strong.

Populations tend to be young there — over half are under age 16.

Reservations today are places of change. There is much coming and going between reservations and from city communities. Children are sent off to Seattle, to Flandreau, or Wahpeton to live with relatives or attend boarding schools. Older youth go to and from vocational schools and colleges. United Tribes Training Center in Bismarck is unique in that entire families come there to live while taking vocational and basic education classes. Increasingly there are intertribal marriages.

Traditional Indians fear change — it causes instability, and a breaking down of cherished values. In the past it has brought mostly trouble. Some of the most disturbing changes are those set in motion by the bristling militancy of AIM — the American Indian Movement. AIM has shaken basic Indian tenants such as wisdom coming — not from

youth — but from age. AIM speaks out in arrogance, objects, pushes for reform; generations of reservation Indians have learned not to protest but to accept: "What is, is."

AIM rejects patriotism. Yet Indian patriotism and loyalty is well-known and has been tested in every American war with deeds of courage and the blood of young men. AIM has bred suspicion and distrust within tribes, set brother against brother, caused increased tensions and aggressive acts including beatings and murder.

But for all its violence and audacity, AIM has unexpectedly polished and brought into the light a long-hid jewel: the pride of being Indian.

A hundred years ago when they submitted to reservation living, Native Americans were stripped of their language, their dress, their customs, their traditional food sources, their religion. Children were taken to live in mission schools and taught to disavow their heritage and become like whites. "You can't do that . . . take everything away and build on nothing," insists a modern-day Sioux. The result was — and still is — an identity crisis for many Indians who tried hard, under the concerted efforts of others, to become "white." The identity crisis has manifested itself in self-defeating ways such as alcoholism, drugs, suicide, high accident rate, and aggression against family members.

The Indian is an alien in his own land, it has been said.

"We do not see peace of mind in this generation," says a young Sioux teacher at Standing Rock Community College. "There is not happiness for us in our time. We hope it for our children."

Many Native Americans today are seeking peace of mind by reaching back to old traditions to find out who they are, and re-establishing pride in old values of bravery, generosity, fortitude and wisdom.

They join other tribes in pan-Indian powwows and celebrations. The Native American Church has become a binding force as well, with its gentle precepts of friendship, meditation, family concern, self-reliance, avoidance of alcohol, and brotherly love.

A positive change evident on North Dakota reservations is improved housing. Each of the four reservations has 200 or more new homes, with additional ones planned, built under various aid and self-help programs.

Employment opportunities have improved somewhat. At Ft. Totten, a camouflage netting plant hires 300, 70 percent Indian. A cement block plant also hires a small number. At Rolla, the Wm. Langer Jewel Bearing Plant employs 95 Indians and two Belcourt companies hire another 90. The Four Bears Motel near New Town hires 30, and an electronics assemblies plant employs 33. Yet unemployment is chronic. For every job opening, many apply; there are no jobs at all for the youth. Principal work on the reservation continues to be government employment under BIA, public health, and other agencies.

Contrary to popular belief, North Dakota Indians do not receive any government checks just because they are Indian, and they pay income taxes on their wages. They may receive social security, welfare, or aid to dependent children checks the same as non-Indians. Education and medical service, granted by treaty, have been of such poor quality as to have done more harm than good, many contend. Individual Indians may receive lease money through BIA if they own land.

Land ownership is unbelievably complicated. About half the acreage on each North Dakota reservation is owned by non-Indians. Of the remainder some is owned by the tribe, some by the government, and some by individual Indians. Government policy has vacillated: at times it encouraged sale of Indian lands (most went to non-Indians), at others it sought to help bring lands back under tribal control. Of individual holdings, most are small and fragmented through a hundred years of inheritance. It is not unknown for a quarter, 160 acres, to be owned by 160 or more people. Selling or leasing such a piece of land requires agreement from everyone. BIA as administrator keeps track of the paperwork and portions out the money, which can be in exceedingly small portions.

Selling land is further complicated by requiring approval from tribal authorities and BIA personnel all the way up to Washington, D.C. Today, selling land to non-Indians does not win approval. Obtaining the money for land sales may require devious footwork, since it is channelled through BIA. One woman found buying beads to make jewelry for sale at powwows was not a convincing reason. A TV set, however, will probably get through. So an individual who

United Tribes Training Center at Bismarck: Mechanics class, left; below, students take a break in the cafeteria between classes.

Belcourt girl reviews her notes.

While parents study, at right, for UTETC classes, their children play at day care center, below.

Erasing the stereotypes —

Harriett Skye, an articulate and vivacious Sioux, seated at right, moderates her bi-weekly Bismarck TV show: Indian Country Today

has payments coming might requisition a $400 TV set, sell it to a friend for $150-$200 (on part-credit) and come up with the money he needs.

Government bureaucracy is at its worst on the reservation. With one hand it puts forth solutions and with the other, prevents their success, meanwhile protecting bureaucratic jobs and routes to personal power. Volumes of reports and studies fly back and forth to Washington, but incompetency and fraud cloud many reservation projects. A BIA official caught with his hand in the funds at Ft. Yates was merely promoted to another reservation. At best, government is the all-pervasive force — throwing out its many-tentacled cords which are both umbilical lifelines and siphons that drain off freedom and initiative, like an overpowering mother who cannot bear to part with her child. The government system has been to direct programs from the top down, heavy-handed upon every tribe alike, instead of encouraging grassroots programs to develop under local leadership to fit the specific need. By the time adjustments are made and the program becomes workable, it is dropped and replaced with another. One example of unresponsiveness to local needs: Ft. Yates keeps central time for the convenience of BIA officials east of the river, although the people who live there are surrounded by mountain time.

Educational opportunities are improving. Three N.D.

reservations have community colleges, branches of the University system. Parents have wide choice of schools to send their children. But often schools do not meet the needs of Indian children. Typically in adolescence, youth experience a time of serious crisis; school dropouts are common.

Crisis itself is common in the Indian home, and real tragedy touches the lives of nearly every family in a way that is hardly comprehensible to non-Indians. A small child dies; a teenager commits suicide; a father is killed in a car accident; an aunt dies of pneumonia; an uncle is murdered.

It is unfortunately true that most white Dakotans do not understand the Indian viewpoint, nor the everyday conditions with which Indians deal. Everyone looks for easy solutions. But the problems of Native Americans defy easy solution — perhaps they defy any solution under existing conditions.

Native Americans are sensitive to stereotyping that lumps them all together. But they see some hope in a real resistance at last from non-Indians toward civilization's obsession to "cut it down, dig it up, tear it out, dam it over — and move on." This nation may yet enrich itself by coming to a broader understanding of the great Indian traditions of brotherhood, cooperation, acceptance, wisdom, and living in harmony with nature.

A modern Indian mother: over half reservation population is under 16

Back to tradition: Veronica Baker, Gros Ventre (Hidatsa)-Mandan, prefers drying meat in the old style

City and town

Cities sparkle with the promise of excitement and opportunity and small towns glow with the warmth of an Indian summer morning when everyone you meet says, "hello."

But cities get big and the towns get small. The national dilemma of growing cities and shrinking towns has not escaped this rural state. One-third of the population now lives in cities over 10,000. Many more live in "commuter communities" close by.

The smallest of small towns are most vulnerable. There were, of course, far too many for modern day car-oriented society. Six or eight miles apart, the railroads decreed them in the old boom-town days, a reasonable journey by team and wagon. Weathered false front businesses now close one by one, suggesting haunting memories instead of an optimistic future.

But many small towns in the state are not only holding their own, but experiencing growth and vigor. They are trade centers for a comparatively large area, usually without close competition from towns of equal size. These towns have aggressive businessmen with the courage to build and remodel, to stock their shelves and to advertise. They build nursing homes and low-rent housing, a hospital, a library. School bond issues pass when they are needed and students ride the buses in from a wide area. Somehow these towns have turned the trick to attract and keep good doctors, dentists, veterinarians, teachers, ministers, and other professionals. Some have consolidated health services to fill the need from other towns. Hettinger's medical clinic, for example, is staffed with nine doctors offering day clinics in four other towns as far as 50 miles away.

Cities, meanwhile, continue to draw off both the talented and the desperate. North Dakota's cities are growing, spawning bright suburbs on every side.

Cities sparkle and spawn bright suburbs.

Fargo	53,365	Mandan	11,093
Grand Forks	39,008	Valley City	7,843
Bismarck	34,703	Devils Lake	7,078
Minot	32,290	Wahpeton	7,076
Jamestown	15,385	Grafton	5,946
Dickinson	12,405	West Fargo	5,161
Williston	11,280	(1970 census)	

Modern equipment in the science labs, left, and elsewhere; ample facilities for visual aids and flexible classrooms, center. Right, students pause briefly to pick up materials for next class

Focus on learning

Modern innovations in learning methods combine with solid teaching in the basics to give North Dakota students the opportunity for consistently excellent education from grade school through high school and college.

Education has progressed a long way from the sod-house school and the live-in teacher-tutor. Much consolidation has been brought about in the last 15 years. In 1961 there were still 1,146 rural one-room public schools in the state, but by 1975 this number was cut to 66. (In 1916, 4,722 rural one-room schools educated 51 percent of the students and employed over half the teachers.) During the same period many small high schools have been discontinued or consolidated with others Today there are 270 high schools in the state, a drop of 82 in 15 years. Forty-six of this number are non-accredited: 12 are private high schools.

The transition has not always been smooth. Losing a school in a rural area has meant losing a community center; for a small town it means a dwindling of population and business—both desperately needed for survival. For youth it has meant a ride on the school bus, greater distances to school, more time spent in daily travel. But the gains have undoubtedly been counted in better facilities, well-trained teachers, and broader course offerings. Teachers in North Dakota do an outstanding job of teaching, despite lower than average salaries, and their students rate with the top on national scholastic tests.

Fifteen colleges with an enrollment of 28,776, plus a number of private business and training schools, are distributed throughout the state. The two major universities, UND and NDSU, are located at the extreme edge of the state as a result of the early spoils system—a difficulty that has made them more easily accessible to Minnesota students than many North Dakotans. However, these and the other colleges offer excellent educational-opportunities to North Dakota's youth.

High school graduation: left, a speech from an honor student. Deciphering Spanish comic books. Library studies, lower left. A lesson on anatomy with a coyote skeleton. Lower right, a student learns to draw with precision. Right, down the stairs between classes.

Classes at N.D. colleges are often small enough for seminars and study groups—even for freshmen. Right, zeroing in on the subject at Dickinson State

The college student: a time alone to ponder

University of North Dakota, Grand Forks: a fast walk between classes

North Dakota State University, below: a moment of leisure and sunshine. Right, design students examine room plans

Dickinson's talented young gymnast, Robin Huebner, strikes a pose

For the sports enthusiast there's always another sport, another game, another tournament another match, another challenge — indoors, outdoors, no matter what season.

Sports of every kind

Two Indian boys take in a rodeo from atop the chutes.

Fans watch a college basketball game

the spectators are part of the fun

What's new is the tremendous upsurge in girls sports. In high school, college, and community, girls athletics strikes a chord of response that has been slumbering.

Girls take the 110 hurdles at 1976 state track meet

A hard game of neighborhood sweep ball, above. Below, a professional water ski team performs.

Melodrama comes to town, left. In photo above, Sosondowah theater presents "The Fantastics." At right, Hettinger high school calls on 6th grade boys to fill out the cast for a stunning performance of the musical "Oliver"

The arts—

Artistic events of all kinds are live and lively, centering on the college campuses and the state's urban centers. But the performing arts come to small towns, too, through the work of interested individuals and organizations. And when they do come — everyone turns out.

Increased leisure has meant a growing interest in the arts and today arts are much a part of everyday living all across North Dakota. Musical training begins early; high school students give near-professional performances on many occasions. Student groups go each year on state, national, and European tour. Artists—poets, potters, painters, writers, woodcarvers and others—find their inspiration where they live.

Five symphony orchestras are organized in the state, along with two civic opera companies, three dance groups, and more than a dozen art galleries and theater groups.

Piano students keep the beat in music lab. Below, Dickinson State's stage band goes formal.

New interest in an old art: 3-Tribes now produces high quality pottery for sale

Sidewalk art blocks view of Dickinson construction site

the churches

Modern architecture of Annunciation Priory, Bismarck, contrasts with traditional style of New Salem area country church

The churches exert a strong influence on life in North Dakota. Total membership, including children, is 484,342, or 71 percent of the state's population — considerably higher than the national average.

Conservative churches have predominated, especially Lutheran and Catholic, as these were the faiths brought by large numbers of immigrants. Both, however, experienced vigorous growth in the new world, unparalleled in the old. Together they make up 80 percent of North Dakota's church membership. In 1975 there were 216,579 members in the various branches of the Lutheran Church, and 171,185 Catholics. Others with fairly large membership are: Methodist — 28,880; Presbyterian — 18,636; United Church of Christ — 13,831; Baptist — 12,512. In all there are nearly 50 denominations in the state with a total of 1,678 churches.

Country churches once dotted the countryside. Almost anywhere the lone spires could be seen rising above the prairie.

With decreasing farm populations, many small churches have closed as congregations joined with those in nearby towns. In 1916 the state had 800 more churches than it does today. Yet a surprising number of country churches remain open, supported by a vigorous membership. Many town ministers still serve a rural parish — with 311 country churches still active in 1975. Of this number 240 are Lutheran. Many which have closed maintain a well-kept cemetery — and occasionally a grave is added for a local pioneer.

Foreign languages were common in the Lutheran and Catholic churches. By the first world war 63 percent of North Dakota's church membership was still hearing services in 13 foreign languages. The switch to English was long, and traumatic for older immigrants; even into the '60's some churches held occasional foreign language services.

Today religious leaders representing 14 churches and 425,000 members work together in the North Dakota Conference of Churches, an independent body pledged to support the spirit of ecumenism without infringing on denomination autonomy. The North Dakota conference promotes such statewide programs as world famine relief and the innovative Friendly Town program. Issues of concern are environmental, Indian affairs, legislative ethics, alcohol and drugs, prison rehabilitation, and mental health. Seminars and retreats are organized for religious leaders, and the conference has established summer ministries for Medora and the State Parks.

Contemporary worship has brought lively music, revitalized liturgy, and colorful banners to many churches

Today's modern farm may well support three families as does this McLean County father and two son operation. Photo at right shows "typical" cattle country in the pines west of Amidon — actually nearly all of North Dakota is cattle country.

Agriculture—North Dakota's lifeblood

Once when North Dakota was young, cowboy-poet Jim Foley set pen-in-hand and tongue-in-cheek and wrote about a seedy farmer named Jed Hicks. When Hicks came to town every merchant had the same anxious, avid query: "How's crops?"

Jed Hicks wasn't much to look at, but . . . "when he says the crop is hard to beat, you see the folks perk up all along the street." The banker . . . the grocer . . . the doc . . . all of them crossed the street to get that good news firsthand.

Old Doc Blake . . . he smiles, because he's got about
Five thousand on his books a-standin' out;
Si Gregg, he gives big orders for his store,
And says to Emmet Pew, the drummer: "Pew,
Make that one ton of sugar I said, two;"
Scrimp Short he rubs his hands and feels his oats,
And tells his customers he'll take them notes
At nine percent; and finds he's got about
Another fifty thousand to let out:
And thinks the notes can be renewed again
For mebbe eight percent instead of ten.
. . . and everywhere
You feel that easy-money-comin' air.

Intensive production: Knifing pinto beans in east Traill County.

Foley spoke the truth not just for his day, but for modern North Dakota as well. Agriculture is the most important business of the state. When crops are good and markets high there's that "easy-money-coming air" not just on small town main street but in every city in the state. When times are tough for agriculture, there are a lot of anxious people drawing salary, too.

In North Dakota agriculture is, as they say, everybody's bread and butter. The price of wheat and cattle has a profound effect on the number of new cars sold in Fargo. No matter what the business, one usually need not scratch deep to find the agriculture connection.

Commercial enterprises based on farming are the fastest growing industry in the state: processing of food, machinery manufacture and assembly, handling and shipping farm products. Retail businesses of all kinds are involved in supplying the producer. A great many federal and state employees are involved in agriculture.

North Dakta is known as the most agricultural state in the union. Forty-three million of the state's forty-four million acres are in farms and ranches. Thirty million acres are in cropland, making it third highest in total crop acreage after Texas and Kansas. (U.S. total crop acreage is 472.1 million acres.)

North Dakota leads all states in durum and spring wheat, producing 85 percent of the nation's durum and 44 percent of the spring wheat. It is second in production of all wheats, behind Kansas which raises mostly winter wheat. The state also ranks first in barley, rye, and flaxseed; ranks sixth or higher in production of potatoes, dry edible bean, sugar beets, oats, and honey, based on 1975 data. Other areas in which the state ranks high nationally are beef cows, sheep and lambs, also lambs on feed, wool production, and cheese. Of the nation's cows and calves, 12 percent are in North Dakota.

Better equipment, better methods: Above left, portable corrals, pickups for the rancher; center, taking the hand labor out of sugar beets; steel chutes for working cattle; Below left, welding know-how and good shop equipment is essential; air-conditioned cab and 4-wheel drive on a more powerful tractor; right, sunflowers — a new crop

Agriculture's success story—

Sixty years ago mechanization broke the "oat barrier" of feeding work horses . . . and since then agriculture has never looked back. Today a single operator not only farms more land, but gets vastly increased production per acre. Four kinds of change have accomplished this: machinery; chemical developments; genetic improvements; and the socioeconomic change which put the new technology into widespread use.

New machinery has taken the hand labor out of nearly every farming operation — although cost and size of operation do not always justify the expense. Wheat harvest, an enormous undertaking 60 years ago, is quickly dispensed with today. Haying is an example of a major job for which many kinds of machinery have been developed. A new popular baler rolls hay into giant bales 66" in diameter, weighing half a ton each, preserving the hay in good condition and resulting in a completely mechanized method of handling and feeding hay. The tractor has been improved every year since it replaced the horse to reach what surely seems to be the pinnacle: A 4-wheel drive 275 horsepower monster with air-conditioned cab and "fancy shift" costing $50,000.

Chemical warfare has virtually wiped out the threat of total destruction from hordes of creeping pests or clouds of flying insects. Weeds, too, are controlled in part by herbicides, often by aerial crop dusting. Use of chemicals has created much controversy because of possible harmful side effects to human health and environment. Some have been

banned and "ladybug" solutions espoused. But chemicals are obviously essential to modern production if farmers are to feed a hungry world and continue to produce cheap food. Latest chemical developments are aimed to be specific to the problem without harmful side effects.

The third change, genetic improvement, has tremendously increased yields of all crops and put pounds on every breed of livestock. Wheat yields have doubled nationally from 14 to 28 bushels per acre in 40 years. (Recent N.D. averages are: 1973-27.5; 1974-20.4; 1975-25.9;1976-23.) Improved varieties have resulted in heavier yield, better quality wheat, resistance to disease and unfavorable weather. Control of rusts through breeding in a resistant Scottish strain has, of itself, brought great stability to the wheat belt. Recent success with wheat hybrids now gives promise of perhaps 25 percent higher yields.

Hybrid corn has been a great success, increasing tremendously both size and number of cobs per stalk. Similar advancements in genetic breeding have improved every crop. In North Dakota a big expansion has taken place in sunflower production. Soybeans — the nation's No. 1 cash crop and leading export commodity — are another relatively new crop to the area.

Longhorn steers at one time took four to seven years to grow to maturity — today most steers are slaughtered at 1 1/2 years, a great savings in pasture use. In the last 30 years sire evaluation and performance testing improved the quality of every breed of cattle. Then cross-breeding began to prove again the value of hybrid vigor, unlocking ability for faster growth and better calf survival rate. Ten years ago there were few cross-breds on the market; today more than half the market is cross-bred.

Artificial insemination made its first impact on dairy cattle bringing swift improvement to commercial herds. But cattle ranchers laughed, ten years ago, at the suggestion they might try AI on a herd of 200 range cows. Now many have modified their management practices so they can do precisely that. At the same time the "exotics", all-purpose cattle breeds from continental Europe, made their sudden splashy entry into U.S. herds, causing considerable confusion and mixed reactions.

Sweeping changes have revolutionized the dairy industry — and squeezed many dairy farmers out of business. Cow numbers are cut in half from 1950, but milk yields per cow have doubled. North Dakota rates seventh in dairy food production and produces nearly a billion pounds of milk annually.

Hogs and sheep made similar advances. The hog silhouette has changed dramatically from the fat homesteader pig to the sleek lean one of today. Sheep not only produce more wool and meat, but are bred for multiple births.

U.S. and state experiment stations are constantly researching improvements and seeking solutions. North Dakota's experiment stations at Carrington, Cassleton, Dickinson, Hettinger, Langdon, Oakes, Minot and Williston sponsor field days and tours to report their respective specialties: Irrigation and cow-calf management on irrigated pastures; certified seed; beef cattle and grass management; sheep; farm management alternatives, small grains and row crops; small grains and tillage; land utilization and summer fallow. One practice now under question is the necessity of summer fallow when fall to spring moisture is sufficient. Cropping decreases the problems of saline seep which have developed with recent above-average rainfall, especially in western Dakota, and would increase the productivity of the land. Thousands of farmers and ranchers tour the experiment stations each year as well as the Northern Great Plains rangeland station at Mandan and the experiment station at NDSU where all experimental work is coordinated.

North Dakota's main experiment station at NDSU is credited with one of the five major successes in pre-1930 veterinary research — the development of the rumen fistula, removable window in the stomach of a rumenant animal. The simplicity and effectiveness of the fistula have enabled it to be used throughout the world for study of digestive processes. Veterinary medicine has also brought many changes to livestock operations.

Lastly, it was socioeconomic change which brought the other changes into focus. Farming became a business, with money invested and profits realized. Farmers wanted information of a scientific, practical nature — no longer did they look to their neighbors, or their fathers, for complete answers. Information came through private industry, farm papers, news media and, especially, through the county agent, whose job it was to get the latest experiment station and USDA information out to the producers. And because farming became a business, farmers were willing to spend their money on new machinery, pesticides, better seed and breeding stock, and their time in working out better management practices.

Experiment station tour, Minot: The latest in small grains under practical conditions. Below, dairy cows give twice the milk today

Setback for sheepmen: Chemical warfare against the adaptable coyote is banned; his kills are putting N.D. sheepmen out of business

Above, harvest goes fast with self-propelled combines — and custom combiners. Veterinary clinics, like Hettinger's in photo below, stress herd health, preventative medicine, good management practices as well as emergency treatment and surgery

North Dakota's
weather modification

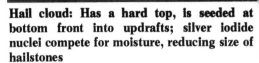

'most extensive in the world—'

Cloud seeding airplane: Tanks on wingtip are for rain; at rear under plane can be seen flares for hail — they ignite like 4th of July sparkler when releasing silver iodide

Hail cloud: Has a hard top, is seeded at bottom front into updrafts; silver iodide nuclei compete for moisture, reducing size of hailstones

Rain . . . hail . . . two sides to the same coin. The blessing, the curse. In southwestern North Dakota the keenness of both are intensified. It's a country subject to drouth, one of the heaviest hail districts in the nation. Hail insurance is outrageously high. Bowman County 1970 rates, for example, were up to $24 for each $100 of coverage, compared to $5-$8 for central N.D. counties. This meant that a grain farmer not only spent $240 for $1,000 worth of coverage, but that he had a 24 percent chance of getting hailed out.

This was ripe ground for fraud — and the rain-makers and hail-wizards had been there. But when former World War II pilot Wilbur Brewer and his aerial crop spraying partner Bill Fischer heard about silver iodide and seeding clouds, they decided to try. Both were farmers and "tired of getting hailed out every year." There was little precedent for their daring scheme in 1961 — the technique was newly discovered and barely used on a practical basis. They collected donations from a few neighbors to help pay for the expensive grams of silver iodide and began to fly hail clouds, perfecting their technique as they went. A telephone call from neighbors to the west: "It's hailing!" would put the two pilots in the air, bouncing around looking for the updrafts. Within a few years their hail-suppression program drew a solid mill levy from four convinced southwestern counties and an adjoining South Dakota area, and they bought radar.

Today North Dakota has the most extensive weather modification program in the world. In 1976 three radar stations manned by meteorologists were located in the state, each accurate for 100-125 miles and reaching 250 miles, connected by hot line and instant weather map transmitting equipment with the U.S. weather bureau in Bismarck. Planes are on 24 hour call and are in communication with radar at all times. Still they seem vulnerable to those on the ground, bouncing in the turbulence, shooting off "4th of July sparkler" flares as if they were on fire and ready to tumble to earth.

In essence, a hail cloud has too few nuclei. A large amount of moisture thus forms around each nuclei and the hailstones become bigger and bigger. When they get too big they fall, but a cloud with strong updrafts can hold up very large and destructive hailstones. Cloud seeding adds nuclei (one-hundred trillion per ounce of silver iodide) which compete for the moisture, making a greater number of the smaller ice crystals. They either do not fall, melt harmlessly as they fall, or fall as small or slushy hail.

Hail clouds usually result from moist warm air going north, passing under streams of dry cool air heading east. In this unstable condition the warm air tries to rise through the heavier cool air, causing strong updrafts when it does.

Seeding for hail is not yet perfected, as the still-high insurance rates indicate, but a success rate of 35 to 65 percent is estimated — an enormous saving in crop dollars.

Yet it was not hail, but rain-enhancement that sold east-central counties on cloud seeding. Cost of seeding in 17 counties was about 4 1/2 cents per acre in 1976.

What's an inch of rain worth in North Dakota? In an impressive study 33 NDSU specialists and consultants have come up with a very specific answer. They studied data from 1949-1970 on 15 crops, the weaning weights of calves, crop and livestock prices from 1960-1974, and weather information for those years.

An inch of rain over normal, they concluded, is worth precisely $1.89 an acre in western N.D.; $2.45 in west central; $3.13 in east central; and $3.33 in the Red River Valley. For two inches the figures are about double. Furthermore, farm income from one extra inch of rain generates business dollars worth $5.56 in the west; $7.61 in west central; $8.64 in east central; and $10.11 for the Red River Valley. With two inches, estimated added business volume in the east central section alone is worth $185 million.

Seeding for rain requires a very special cloud — and results are not easy to prove. The goal is to get half an inch of moisture from a cloud that would have given none.

Popular opinion has it that a rain-filled cloud travels until it releases its load — so one man's gain is another's loss. But meteorologists explain that cumulus clouds have a lifespan of only 20-30 minutes; the moisture begins to collect — then dissipates. It's a "rain machine" turned off too quickly. Seeding keeps the rain machine working longer, more efficiently, so more rain falls and over a wider area.

Silver iodide nuclei are added to trigger the precipitation process — but fewer than for hail supression. Too heavy concentrations of nuclei, as can be found in pollution laden air, create so much competition for moisture that no raindrops become large enough to fall.

Weathermen report that dams such as Garrison and Ft. Peck have probably increased moisture in the state, but only slightly; our real sources of rain are the Pacific Ocean and Gulf of Mexico.

Future research will make more clear the possibilities and limitations of tapping these "rivers in the sky." But there is little doubt hail suppression will continue, even more effectively, in hail prone country.

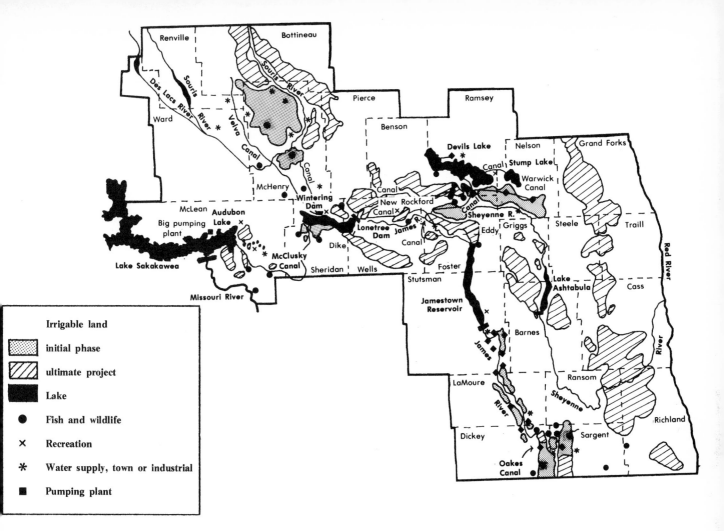

Legend:
- Irrigable land
  - initial phase
  - ultimate project
- Lake
- ● Fish and wildlife
- ✕ Recreation
- ✱ Water supply, town or industrial
- ■ Pumping plant

garrison diversion

The $500,000,000 Garrison Diversion project is now underway, with the initial phase to bring irrigation water to 250,000 carefully selected acres. (See dotted areas on the map.) Much underground pipe will be used and sprinkler systems constructed instead of the extensive open canals and drainage ditches that were originally planned for traditional gravity type irrigation. Use of the sprinkler system should provide efficient use of the water with lower operating costs, once installed. With sprinkling, farm labor is cut to a minimum, and fields can be farmed without leveling.

Essential features of this ambitious project include: **Snake Creek Pumping Plant** with three giant pumps lifting a million gallons of water a minute into Lake Audubon and maintaining that lake at 1,850 feet elevation (begun 1968). **McClusky Canal,** 73 miles long, connecting Lake Audubon with Lonetree Reservoir on the Continental Divide. Excavation depths of this canal reach 114'; water will be 17' deep, 94' across at the surface, 25' wide at the bottom (begun 1970). **Lonetree Reservoir,** a 20,000 acre lake on top of the divide, will be dammed at three points — Lonetree Dam on the Sheyenne, the James River Dike, and the Wintering Dam. **Velva Canal and New Rockford Canal,** both draining out of Lonetree Reservoir; the Velva Canal running 84 miles north. The 52 mile long New Rockford Canal will drop part of its water northeast into Devils Lake

and part into the James River headed south. The **Warwick Canal,** an offshoot of the New Rockford canal will move water 55 miles farther east. In addition are several smaller feeder canals and pumping plants. A number of towns will be able to get water supplies from this source.

Big earth and water-moving projects are always forged rough-shod over the backs of some individuals. Garrison Diversion is no exception. Some North Dakotans will suffer displacement of their homes and confiscation of lands. But the assumption is that many will benefit while those who make involuntary personal sacrifice are few. It's an old story.

Irrigation promises increased productivity of the land, stability in time of drouth, and diversity of crops. Water for 14 towns plus industrial sites will be provided and nine new water oriented recreation areas are planned.

Sprinkler irrigation cuts labor and need for leveling, provides efficient use of water

A high priced headache, the cost of new machinery: Combines can run $47,000, a drill $3,000, a new tractor $52,000

Caught in a cost-price squeeze

When a bushel of wheat costs $3.65 to produce and sells for $2.30, and calves cost $.75 a pound to produce and sell for $.43 — the cost-price squeeze is on, full pressure. That was the situation in 1976, with farmers and ranchers deeply discouraged by two years of low prices.

Prices rose swiftly in 1973 — calves peaked at $.75, wheat was $5. But the bottom fell out, almost more quickly. No doubt the cycle will swing again — up, down, up, down. But each time the squeeze of negative income becomes more painful with fixed costs rising. Crop failure or livestock losses can be devastating.

Capital investment is higher in farming than any other business. Assets of the typical North Dakota farmer or rancher reach a quarter of a million dollars; half a million for many. Yet the returns don't always seem to justify the investment. "You never have much to spend, but you die rich. And your kids have to go deep in debt to take over from you," says a ranch wife.

North Dakota's farmers are among the best in the world; but they often feel victimized by their own efficiency — the more they produce, the greater the surplus and the lower the price. They can come out ahead, some insist, only by benefitting from someone else's adversity in producing a good crop when others in the world have crop failure.

Production costs are at an all time high with inflation pushing them higher. New machinery is a major cost. Much is highly specialized, used only a few days each year. The producer must balance out the cost — $47,000 for a new combine, for instance — against going into debt for it, repairing the old one another year, or hiring custom combining. A tractor can cost over $50,000; fuel and repair costs have doubled.

The extension service has computed the 1975 cost of raising one bushel of North Dakota wheat at $3.65, including land investment costs, machinery, interest and $3 an hour labor.

Most farmers would like more land to spread costs over a larger volume, but land costs have risen steeply. Renting lands is expensive, too, and pasture leases run $9-$12 per cow-calf month. North Dakota's average size farm is about 1,000 acres; larger in the west — 2,700 acres, and smaller east — 660 acres. There are about 40,000 farms in the state,

Too much wheat?

Over a million bushels of 1976 crop is piled on the ground at Reeder elevator; center, unloading in the elevator; right, near Maddock, combined wheat pours from the hopper

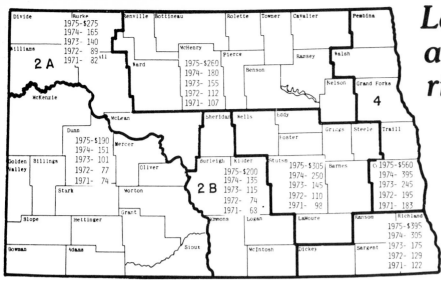

Land costs, leases and taxes keep rising

Estimated land costs: 1975 state average is $285. Average farm size in the west is 2,700 acres, in the east 660 acres.

most of them mixing owned and rented lands.

Producers have no more control over market than they do costs. World markets are complex, but in general the law of supply and demand works — the lower the supply of a desirable product, the higher the price. Yet all markets are subject to manipulation — by government, by monopolistic practices of powerful companies, by labor unions.

The grain embargo was a classic example of manipulation. A big Russian wheat buy was publicized while grocery prices were rising steeply, and consumers raised the cry that bread would go to a dollar a loaf — and furthermore, there may not be enough of it. It's a simple fact that Americans cannot consume more than a third of the wheat crop, so two-thirds of it must go on the world market. In addition the government had recently called on America's farmers for all out production to feed a starving world — and the farmers responded, all too well.

Seizing an opportune moment, longshoremen picked up the cry and said they were not loading one more pound of wheat while Americans starved. Not unless they got $9 to $16 per ton for grain carried on American ships — and an ironclad agreement that if one-third of the grain did not go on American ships they'd get their ransom anyway.

Prices dropped, with a glut of wheat on the market and no place to go. The longshoremen got their demands, but the embargo stayed for months. A political crisis over Middle East oil made the withholding of grain exports good leverage at the bargaining table. Wheat prices plummeted; foreign buyers went elsewhere.

Imports, rather than exports, are the cattleman's problem. By law only six to seven percent of meat can be imported, but preserved or processed meat such as hamburger does not count, so the figure sometimes reaches 10 percent. In addition the president lifted the restriction so the law did not apply, with meat prices way below the cost of production. In 1975 two and a quarter billion pounds of meat were imported with barely over a third of a billion pounds exported, much of it to U.S. territories.

what price lambs and wool? how much for calves?

Wintering costs are high: left, feeding lambs; keeping a cow costs $160-200 a year — with or without a calf

What's next?

It's an anxious question on the minds of North Dakota's farm and ranch families.

They do not doubt that varieties and breeds will improve; that they will increase their yields. They are convinced that new machinery will relieve them of even more hard work — if they can afford it. In a sense they will not have to work so hard in the years ahead. And their standards of living will be the highest.

Yet the scramble to keep income ahead of cost may be even more desperate. They accept the fact that costs will probably keep rising, but are saying that something has got to be done about the instability of the market.

Various solutions are espoused: Government support price and control of production; producer control by withholding actions; tighter import quotas; developing more extensive foreign markets with or without government inducement; promotion through consumer groups; contract marketing; and numerous others. All have certain disadvantages. But there are indications that farmers may be moving towards more control of markets. There is no doubt that agriculture could exert powerful pressure if farm groups worked together. But in the past, farm groups have tended to split, lining themselves up with opposing political parties — instead of keeping to an independent course to be wooed by both Democrats and Republicans.

USDA suggests that farmers may need a new way of financing in the coming years, perhaps selling shares to the public. Incorporation has a number of advantages in a family operation because of the stability of a shared ownership. But since the day of the bonanza, corporate farming has been a dirty word in this state. Hard-core corporations have invaded many sectors of American agriculture, and most farmers do not like what they see: bidding up of land prices; tax losses to offset capital gains elsewhere; control of market to the exclusion of the small producer. Few doubt that giant corporations, such as the meat packers and chain supermarkets, could make food a totally vertical operation from planting to setting it on the table, if allowed the opportunity.

But it's unlikely, given the strength of rural America in Congress, and the government's powerful influence on every phase of agriculture.

Farmers know good profits can come off their land; they know theirs is an important and needed product. Market prices are almost certain to average high on the world market with the increasing ability of developing nations to pay, and their increasing needs. All in all, forecasts for farming are optimistic; USDA predicts it will be increasingly profitable.

Wheat for the world's hungry and a constant reshaping of rural America

business and industry

Business and industry in North Dakota is inevitably linked to agriculture.

Manufacturing is in large part directly aimed at serving agriculture. Two important farm equipment companies have their headquarters here: Melroe and Steiger Tractor. Other farm machinery and equipment manufacturers make or assemble tractor parts, haying equipment, feed mills, and steel buildings. Fertilizer plants process and sell to the producer.

At the other end of the scale is the food processing industry. Potato chips, potato starch, and instant potato flakes are all processed in the heart of Red River Valley potato-growing areas. Milk takes a number of forms: powdered, processed in whey form, made into cheese. Flour mills produce flour, cake mixes and cereals. The meat packing industry is a big one and the state has new processing for sugar beets, malting barley and pinto beans.

Feed mills and elevators both supply the farmer and purchase from him, processing grain into specialized feeding ration for feeders.

Much of the wholesale trade such as storage and moving grain and livestock to market depends on agriculture. So does a great deal of finance, insurance, and real estate. In 1975, $654,446,000 in non-real estate loans were made to North Dakota farmers.

However, the non-agriculture sector of business and industry is also growing in volume. Construction, and making supplies for construction such as concrete and ready-mix, is thriving business with much building investment going on as well as home construction, and modular housing. Printing and publishing has a big share of business revenue with 101 newspapers active in the state. Business is generated by the U.S. defense system, and aircraft are assembled. Oil and gas refineries do a considerable volume of business.

In 1972, of $207 million from manufacturing, 36 percent was in processed food and related products; machinery 10 percent; printing and publishing 11 percent.

North Dakota's right to work law permits workers the right to join or refuse to join a labor union, and permits both union and closed shops.

The state has long been an exporter of raw materials, an importer of manufactured goods. Efforts of state planning groups to reduce this flow have met with a measure of success in bringing more industrial development to the state, and attracting light industry which in turn attracts other light industry. In the 14 years between 1960 and 1973 manufacturing grew nearly 300 percent. Industrial growth in 1975 created 1,100 new jobs in the state. North Dakota offers a number of tax incentives and exemptions to relocating or new companies. Among these, the company may negotiate for exemption from property and state income taxes for up to five years, or claim income tax credit up to one percent of wages paid for three years.

Construction: A new building goes up on DSC campus

Storage tanks at Mandan oil refinery line the Missouri River

Manufacturing is closely linked to agriculture; above, Dakota Maid feeds and a Steiger tractor

coal

"Queen O' Buttes" dragline removes overburden from Knife River's Gascoyne mine with 32 cubic yard bucket and 235' boom.

Coal . . . the subject can be emotional. Western Dakotans are apprehensive; they forsee destruction of a unique way of life, of historic landmarks. Environmental groups call it the "rape of the plains". Electric co-ops and companies say more electricity is urgently needed. Many are apathetic: "No one lives out there. What's the difference?" Chambers of commerce groups, especially statewide, look forward to new business, new paychecks. Everyone knows North Dakota needs new jobs for young people.

Decisions must be made . . . far-reaching decisions that will affect the future of the state, that will determine if North Dakota is to become the victim of another boom and bust operation. This is an opportunity to choose . . . instead of hope for . . . industry and growth; to develop a more balanced economy not totally dependent on weather and agricultural markets. The challenge is for the entire state, although it is true that eastern Dakota will probably enjoy more of the positive benefits from coal operations, and get less of the negative aspects. Since legislators are overwhelmingly eastern, they will ultimately decide the destiny of western Dakota.

Coal mining is not new in North Dakota. In 1936 there were 366 mines working in the state, most of them underground mines. What is new is the size of modern mining operations and the intense interest in conversion of lignite to other forms of energy such as electricity and gaseous forms.

Coal companies today take care to promote a positive, friendly image. They employ local people in public relations positions; they christen their big shovels with local-sounding names . . . Beulah Belle . . . Queen O' Buttes. Consolidation Coal Co. pays radio stations to keep airing their swinging tune: "Be proud you know a coal minin' man!" Legislators are reminded it is "our duty" to share the coal.

Dakotans must not take all this at face value. These mammoth subsidiaries of big international companies are not just more of us home folks, and it is irresponsible to trust their good intentions (whether one knows a coal mining man . . . or *is* a coal mining man). The intentions need to be spelled out in law.

There are many complex questions to consider.

How much coal is here?

North Dakota's share of the Ft. Union coal formation is about twenty-two percent of the nation's total, 16.1 billion tons of strippable reserves. It's been estimated that under original plans for western North Dakota's coal development, an amount of coal would each year be mined and consumed equal to half that consumed in the entire U.S. in 1973.

Is it our duty to share this coal?

Advertisements in national magazines encourage this attitude. One proclaimed, "The clean Western coal is the people's coal. And the people need it . . . now." Exxon bought seven consecutive pages in an issue of Newsweek to promote the need for stripping Northern Plains coal, and to wear down stiff western resistance. In-state, company advertising has been friendly but firm, "We North Dakotans must share with the nation in this grave crisis . . . We must be generous as we have in the past."

The question about duty is superficial and irrelevant, in particular when raised by mammoth profit-seeking corporations. North Dakota has and is sharing coal. And there are other areas of duty: to Dakotans who will be displaced; to the nation that depends on us for food supply, which could be decreased by destruction of cropland and by air pollution; to future generations; to stewardship of the land. All these must be put in balance against the insatiable appetite of our countrymen for more goods, produced by ever more energy.

Nevertheless, the coal will be shared in one amount or another. What may not be necessary is for western Dakota to bear the burden of heavy industrialization. The coal *can* be shipped out for conversion at the points where the energy is demanded.

Who owns the mineral rights?

Unfortunately not the people. A surface owner may own a percentage of rights on this or that quarter but, no matter how many generations the land has been in his family, his total share is about 15 percent. In North Dakota this means an individual's land can be mined against his wishes as long as he is paid compensation for use of surface land and removal of buildings, if necessary.

It was a fluke of settlement years. First, that the N.P. railroad, now Burlington Northern, was awarded alternate sections (one-quarter of the state of North Dakota) and then was not required to sell them with mineral rights intact . . . as was Congress' intent. Second, that the federal government decided to withhold mineral rights from homesteaders after 1909, when much of western Dakota was being settled. Now the federal government owns approximately 20 percent to 50 percent of the coal rights in 13 western counties, ranging from 90 percent in Grant to three percent in McLean. For four years a moratorium on federal coal leases halted progress. Under pressure from energy companies, Secretary of Interior Thomas Kleppe ended the moratorium in early 1976, whereupon it was announced that more than 100 coal developers expressed interest in bidding for the leases of 500 tracts in North Dakota, Montana and Wyoming. Four and a half million acres were opened for exploration in North Dakota alone. Because of potential disruption to land owned by North Dakotans, the state hopes to exercise some control in this area, according to the governor's office.

Burlington Northern's share of coal rights in these counties is about 10 percent, from one percent in McLean to 17 percent in Stark County. In addition, mineral rights are owned by the state (11 percent in Adams); the Bank of North Dakota (three percent in Grant and Mercer); and the Federal Land Bank (five percent in Hettinger).

Of remaining mineral rights, a share are owned by absentee owners through land sales, and also through an oil lease swindle in which, some 20 or 30 years ago, landowners were persuaded to sell mineral rights in the belief they were only leasing them to oil companies.

Other states have passed laws permitting landowners to veto strip mining on their property; North Dakota's 1975 legislature considered such a bill but voted it down in the face of lobby pressure.

Of those landowners who do own mineral rights, many leased years ago during coal depression under the $.10 a ton, 40-year lease. Says a Beulah farmer, locked into such a lease, "That's a whole lifetime. It's not fair. You can't lease farm land for 40 years."

This sort of situation is one reason western Dakotans put up such determined opposition to the proposed West River Diversion project which would bring Lake Sakakawea waters south nearly to the South Dakota border with needed water for heavy mining industry, and forming a broad network of dams and canals throughout the entire area. The possibility of irrigation was offered, but much more land . . . 150,000 to 1,000,000 acres, depending on size and number of dams . . . would be taken out of production. "They wanted us to pay for building this big open canal right across our lands," said one man. "So they can condemn our property for coal mines and power plants. And our taxes go on all the years they're mining."

Indians own rights to the coal under 350,000 acres of the nearly one million acres on Ft. Berthold, the only Indian reservation in the state with coal reserves. (The remainder is owned by the federal government.) Although they are in the heart of extensive coal development, the Three Affiliated Tribes have not yet leased.

Will there be more jobs for North Dakotans?

Yes, there certainly will be, and are more jobs . . . a long-time goal of North Dakota planners. Not all jobs will go to Dakotans, but a substantial number will . . . and at good pay. Probably the more slowly the industry develops the more jobs will go to in-staters; the faster, the more out-of-staters will be needed and hired. The additional people and the steady paychecks will surely help stabilize businesses in small towns. Again, if development is fairly slow, local businesses can keep pace. If population influx is sudden and large, this will invite nationwide chain and cut-rate stores to step in and take over retail business.

How much in taxes will the state gain . . . the impact area?

The 1975 legislature set a $.50 per ton severence tax on coal mined. Of this amount, impacted areas will get only five percent, with 35 percent to go into a fund for special needs of impacted areas. Thirty percent goes into the general fund, with an additional 30 percent held in temporary trust, the income to go into the general fund. Tax was also levied on production of conversion plants.

North Dakota's severence tax will rise with the wholesale index, a scale that is, however, unrelated to the price of lignite. Straight percentages are set in some states; Montana, for instance, requires 30 percent of value on subbituminous and 20 percent on lignite coal, with lignite prices spiralling.

How much land will be needed for mining?

The coal companies say less than two percent of the

Major lignite coal beds in North Dakota

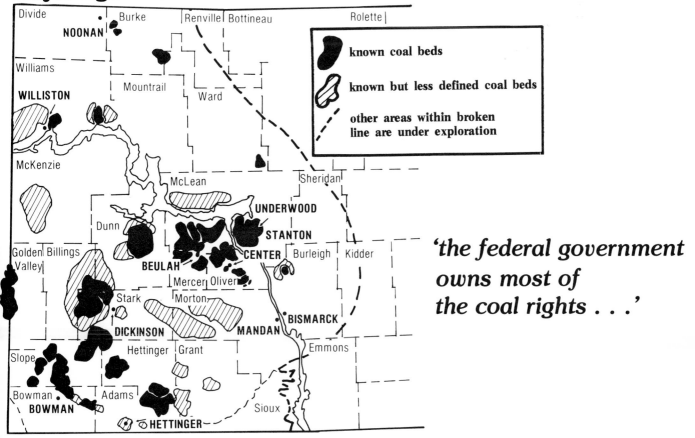

known coal beds

known but less defined coal beds

other areas within broken line are under exploration

'the federal government owns most of the coal rights . . .'

After overburden is removed, coal seam is drilled and dynamited; 100 ton trucks are loaded by an 18 cubic yard shovel for haul to the tipple (right) where coal is broken and loaded into unit trains

state's land surface. Realistically, there's little point in averaging in the entire state; it will be a sizeable percent of the western counties.

What about damage to underground water?

Each mine will differ in its effect on underground water depending on the nature of the water-bearing layers as well as size and depth of the mine. It is possible both for water supplies of wells in the area to be lowered, and for them to be contaminated by leaching of toxic materials.

Water is vital to western Dakotans, and the prospect of cutting trenches, long, deep and wide, through water-bearing layers of sand, gravel and coal, makes local people distinctly nervous.

NDSU researchers have suggested legislation, as in other states, to require companies to provide evidence through ground water studies that their planned development will not be harmful to ground water supplies.

What's the difference between mining . . . and mining plus industrial development?

Coal mining disrupts the land and ground water systems; it does not cause severe air pollution, nor does it require a big water supply. It does not involve the great population influx of heavy industrial development and thus does not have the same potential for social and physical disruption.

But lignite coal is to be converted to other forms of energy, and it is this conversion . . . to electricity or natural gas . . . that involves heavy industrialization because of the size of planned facilities. Conversion can be done either at the mining site or the place where the new form of energy will be used. Original industry plans placed gasification and generating plants at northern plains mining sites.

In 1971 these plans were revealed in the North Central Power Study. Twenty-two gasification plants were slated to be in operation in western North Dakota by the year 2000. In the public shock over the implications of such massive industrialization, the states involved . . . especially Montana and Wyoming . . . began to stiffen regulations. Industry plans were considerably dampened and, since 1973, no new applications for big coal conversion water permits have been approved in North Dakota.

Water applications have been filed for 12 gasification plants and 10 big generating plants. Three 450 megawatt generating plants (Minnkota Power Cooperative; United Power and Cooperative Power Associations) and one 250 million cubic foot per day gasification plant (Michigan Wisconsin Pipe Line Co.) have been approved. Michigan Wisconsin's gasification plant is scheduled to begin operations in 1981 and will be the first of its kind anywhere. Its rezoning application in the hands of Mercer County's

zoning commission was opposed by petition with a reported 1,500 signatures.

The approved generating plants are for cooperatives. Mike Jacobs, in his book ONE TIME HARVEST charges that big energy companies have been using co-ops, noticing how well they are regarded in North Dakota, and have sent them time after time to Bismarck to "lobby for lower taxes, for lesser environmental standards, for speedier action on granting water permits." He questions whether the rural electrics themselves are losing sight of their traditional grassroots concerns for the common man. Minnkota's Square Butte addition to the Center power plant, Jacobs says is actually financed by three New York banks and 13 insurance companies, one of which (Prudential) invested $50 million dollars. The plant will be leased and operated by a specially formed cooperative. Most of Square Butte Electric Cooperative's power delivery will go to Duluth and suburbs.

If the coal is not converted on site, it will need to be shipped out. Unit trains presently do go daily to supply out-of-state generating plants. Another method of shipping under consideration by coal companies is through slurry pipe lines, mixing ground coal with water . . . this method requires a considerable water supply. The Farmers Union favors opening the Missouri to barge traffic and shipping coal down the river.

On the other hand, if conversion is done at the mining site, the plant production must be shipped out. Natural gas can go by pipeline, but electricity will require more high voltage power lines. Several of these already leave the state, branching out from Garrison Dam's five 80,000 kilowatt generators. Utility companies have exercised the power of eminent domain in taking the land they need for these big power lines. Again, the landowner has no veto although many consider the lines a nuisance in farming, an eyesore, and even a hazard. In present legal action Square Butte Electric Cooperative is appealing with the N.D. Supreme Court a lower court ruling that they have not shown sufficient evidence of public benefit to warrant use of eminent domain for their high voltage power lines to Duluth.

Many Dakotans are increasingly convinced the problems of heavy industry should be borne by the localities which demand the energy. Although heavy industry generates growth, it has been shown that it discourages the coming of light industry. Light industry can offer as many job opportunities without the adverse effects.

What are the water needs of coal industrialization?

Approved generating plants have permits for 7,500 acre feet each; Michigan Wisconsin's gasification project has 17,000 acre feet allowed annually. The water is to come

Unit train with 100 covered cars leaves Gascoyne mine every day bound for Big Stone City, S.D. 440 MW power plant with 10,000 tons of coal

from the Missouri River and Lake Sakakawea.

The question of whether state or federal government should control Lake Sakakawea water is unclear, though the state has assumed its rights. To complicate matters, the Ft. Berthold tribes have stated their prior rights to waters impounded and passing through their reservation, based on the turn of century Winters Doctrine, which guaranteed Indians a prior and paramount right to use of waters within their reservations.

Water is used for cooling in the big plants; when it drains off it can add a degree or two of heat to river water all the way down the Mississippi, altering the plant and fish ecology.

Will industrialization cause air pollution?

Unfortunately, yes, with present day regulations and know-how. North Dakota's Health Department, which has the responsiblity of the state's air quality, has already set secondary standards for coal areas of the state. This means that additional development is permitted to pollute air to the level of EPA set standards.

The Interior Department reported in October, 1974, that probable effects of the planned massive western strip mining would be: long-term damage to plants, animals and humans from air pollutants; smoke and dust would increase by 12 percent despite pollution controls; hydrocarbons and nitrogen oxides would more than double; sulphur dioxide would more than triple.

"The air here is so clear . . . you can see for miles." Since early days, travelers have remarked on the purity of the northern plains atmosphere, the radiance of sunrise and sunset, the sky full of clear sparkling stars. Dakotans tend to take fresh air and blue sky for granted . . . until they come home from somewhere else that has smoke, haze, and smell, and they hasten to reassure themselves that the big

open sky has not changed.

Elsewhere skies have changed. People have learned to live with smog. East coast residents observe inversions of sulphurous smoke hanging overhead, sometimes for days; they and other industrialized areas of the world have experienced sulfuric acid rainfall. Industry is now prevented by 1970 EPA standards from adding to the pollution of such air — so they are looking for new areas not polluted up to legal limits.

It may be, as some have charged, that what industry wants in the northern plains is, not so much our coal, but our clean air. Mike Jacobs has written in his well-documented book a fervent appeal not to let the coal industry take over western Dakota. "The coal industry has come west," says Jacobs, "in search of four basic resources: cheap clean air, cheap coal, cheap water and cheap politicians." (In the sense of underrating what belongs to the people.) "They've found each of these in North Dakota."

Lignite, measured by ton, is low in sulphur — which is one of the most troublesome by-products of coal conversion. It has caused respiratory infections and increased the effects of asthma and lung ailments in polluted areas especially when the air does not move. But while lignite is low in sulphur, it is so low in heat value that two tons must be burned to equal one ton of higher heat coals . . . thus doubling the amount of sulphur, bringing it back into the range of other coals. Expensive pollution controls, such as scrubbers, will be needed. A coal company spokesman says one-third of the cost of a new plant goes toward required pollution control and that 20 percent of the energy output of the plant must be used to operate the scrubbers and other anti-pollution devices. These costs, he adds, will be passed on to the consumer.

A persistent problem with pollution control devices in North Dakota has been that they break down, or are deliberately shut down on occasion, and the black smoke rolls until local residents complain enough for the Health department to begin issuing and extending deadlines. (It is important, however, that individuals notify the Health department by letter every time they see black smoke from industrial stacks, since inspection manpower is limited.)

Dr. J. M. Ramirez of NDSU's experiment station, says coal development will need to use the air for disposal of some of its wastes regardless of pollution devices. One gasification plant of the size already approved will, he says, produce daily as waste products, 2,000 tons of char, 450 tons of elemental sulfur, 14,000 tons of carbon dioxide, plus phenols, thiocyanates, ammonia, and potential air contaminants such as COS, CS2, mercaptans, thiophenes, aromatics and NOx compounds. The usual air movement through this area is helpful in mixing the contaminants with clean air, but Dakota is also subject to inversions, especially on calm cold winter days, which can hold pollutants near the ground and prevent mixing.

Climatic changes are possible with the immense amount of heat, water vapor, and fine particles distributed into the atmosphere. This could decrease rainfall downwind, perhaps 10-15 percent with industry's original plans, according to atmospheric studies scientists at the South Dakota School of Mines where pioneer work on cloud seeding was done. The great amount of fine particles in the air could "over-seed" clouds, causing so many fine droplets of rain that they cannot fall — an increasing of the effect of hail-seeding in which additional nuclei are added

Mining near Beulah: Ahead the green valley, with natural cover for wildlife; behind, Beulah-Hazen mining area looks like this (right) from years of abandoned spoil banks. Present law requires leveling to "gently rolling"

to decrease the size of hail. The decrease in rainfall would be most pronounced in central and eastern Dakota . . . but the entire state is downwind from the planned extensive coal industrialization in Montana.

The particle load in the air would also decrease visibility.

Will extensive coal development cause "people problems"?

Estimates call for a doubling of western Dakota's population (some estimates for three times that number or nearly 300,000). The new population would settle in towns, tripling their size. Towns close to industrial sites would bear the heavy increases, being multiplied many times in size.

New people moving in can be a boon to small towns . . . an opportunity for development and enhancement of the quality of life. But few Dakotans believe the quality of life will be improved by such an influx. People on the move coming into highly industrialized areas generate problems. A Gillete, Wyoming counselor has listed job problems in the boom community as alcoholism, absenteeism, and accidents . . . and home problems as depression, divorce, and delinquency. These overlap into community problems such as overcrowding in schools; the need for more health facilities, police protection, water supply, garbage collection, better streets and highways. Increased taxes are the only answer and have been experienced inevitably by boom communities despite new tax revenues and impact funds. They also see a cost of living rise.

100 coal developers want to dig in . . .

The Soil Conservation Service, Game and Fish, and other groups have planted trenches of spoil banks with surplus trees. Some sites have grown well, as here near Garrison, and become a haven for wildlife

Can the land be reclaimed?

Strip mining has never been done on this big a scale before . . . removing such deep layers of overburden . . . so no one knows for sure. But even for shallower strip mining, there are no long-term studies of successful reclamation. Fortunately the question of reclamation is taken seriously today by coal companies, by legislators, by state regulatory agencies.

Reclamation begins when the mine is planned, says North Dakota's geological survey team. However, North Dakota requires no environmental impact statement of mining companies even though some sites could be unreclaimable because of highly toxic soils, or because ground water will be drastically affected.

By contrast, Montana requires a company to file application before mining with a detailed plan for mining, reclamation, revegetation, and rehabilitation of affected land and water. Included must be the past "track record" of the company's reclamation efforts; results of test holes; overburden and potential for toxic materials which would need to be buried; cross-section of all formations; maps of both surface and subsurface. Intentions must be advertised in daily newspapers to inform the public of mining plants. One-year permits are renewable with full compliance. Bond of $200-$2,500 per acre must be posted against the possibility that reclamation is not done — but no company can move their equipment from the mining area until restoration is complete.

NDSU researchers say there will be few major problems reclaiming land from shallow mines removing 30 to 50 feet of overburden. Deep mines present more serious problems because they are generally high in toxic materials, in adsorbed sodium and clay content. It is reclaimed areas from shallow mines which have become company showplaces; one such showcase, for example, is a green field from which, long ago, several feet of slack coal were scraped from under two or three feet of topsoil. This is quite different from reclaiming lands deeply mined.

Basically there are two methods of reclamation: burying toxic soils, and changing their physical and chemical properties. The first method is quite successful, but expensive. Toxic soils must be buried below root growth which is four feet for small grains, six feet for grasses, eight feet for alfalfa. Experiments suggest a minimum of five years to restore land to productivity under this method.

In the second method the aim is to prevent surface sealing, reduce adsorbed sodium content, and promote natural structure development. Most success has been achieved in soils with only 15 percent exchangeable sodium,

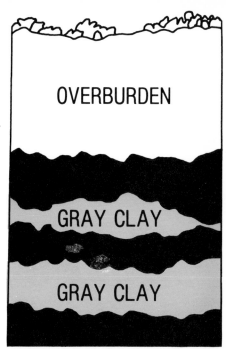

Cross-section of Gascoyne coal seam: Overburden is six to 73 feet thick averaging 45 feet; three coal seams are each eight to 10 feet; layers of gray clay are one and one-half to 16 feet; total depth to be removed is around 100 feet or more; cut is 150 feet wide and up to two miles long

using straw mulches and treatment with gypsum.

A basic question that must be settled is how the land should be returned: As level cropland? In rolling pastures? The way it was, imitating natural scenery destroyed? State research indicates that by the second reclamation method with moderately low sodic soils, the land can be made as productive as Class 6 soils; half as productive as Class 4; but only 25 percent as productive as Class 2 soils. (Classes 1 and 2 are good cropland, with 3 and 4 cropped or marginal. Class 6 is limited to grazing.) Since wildlife habitat was undoubtedly destroyed by the mine, conservationists hope some part of each reclamation project will be designated for that purpose. The rugged beauty of butte and badland can never be restored, put perhaps a hill crested with big boulders and sloped with ravines planted to native cedar trees and brush for wildlife can be planned into each restoration.

What happens after the boom?

Boom and bust. North Dakota has experienced these cycles before. This time . . . after the thirty or forty years of mining is over . . . perhaps a better solution can be found than the harsh disruption of countless lives and the familiar discard heap of empty homes, boarded-up schools, run-down businesses.

. . . .

The problems are complex. Some are human problems. Others affect the land for generations to come. It is essential for North Dakota to determine some kind of state policy on timing, controls, and coal development levels without delay. Leadership not grasped will soon be forfeited, and coal is a one time harvest. Consequences of coal decisions on grass, people, crops . . . and the wonderment of the hills . . . will remain long after the coal is gone.

Williston Basin oil well silhouetted against a storm cloud

oil

Oil fever hit Tioga with four gushers in 1951. The vast Williston Basin had been tapped and soon proved to be among the most important oil finds of the quarter century. Much of the Basin is as yet relatively unexplored. Oil is often found near lignite and gas, and the boundaries of the Williston Basin are roughly the same as the lignite areas, extending through the western Dakotas, eastern Montana and Canada.

For 30 years oilmen had sporadically drilled and speculated in the state; natural gas was found in 1907. In the late 1930's a rash of drilling began that continued through the '40's and culminated in the Tioga discovery. Since then nearly 2,000 wells have been brought into production in the state out of 4,000 drilled.

In 1972 North Dakota ranked 13th in crude oil production, 13th in reserves. Estimated proved reserves are 320 million barrels, with indicated reserves of another 60 million.

North Dakota wells average nearly a mile in depth with the deepest over fifteen thousand feet. This is deeper than the national average, but per foot costs are lower here to make a lower total cost.

Crude oil is refined to fuel oils at Mandan and Williston and some is piped out of state to Montana and Minnesota refineries. Natural gas is refined in three plants at Tioga, Lignite, and McGregor. North Dakota ranks 16th in production of natural gas.

Near Medora: No one minds much if the black metal insect crouches in the pasture pumping and sucking away at the earth's fluids.

History
of
North Dakota

> We did not think of the great open plains, the beautiful rolling hills, and winding streams with tangled growth, as "wild." Only to the white man was nature a wilderness and only to him was the land infested with wild animals and savage people. To us it was tame. Earth was bountiful and we were surrounded with the blessing of the Great Mystery. Not until the hairy man from the east came ... was it "wild" for us ... Then it was that the "Wild West" began.

Chief Luther Standing Bear
Oglala Sioux

At first, this was Indian land

Tens of thousands of years ago prehistoric man followed the buffalo from Asia across what was probably a Siberian-Alaskan land bridge. He ranged the northern plains in periodic migrations, increased, was joined by others, and moved out to populate two continents down to the very tip of South America.

In historic times the Mandans were the first known Indians to live in what is now North Dakota. They journeyed up the Missouri River around 1300 to settle rich river-bottom lands as far north as the mouth of the Knife River. Here they built their earth lodge homes, hunted and farmed—raising the native American crops of corn, beans, pumpkins, squash, and sunflowers. Two other agricultural tribes, the Hidatsas and the Arikaras, also established themselves along the Missouri with similar cultures.

Indians continued to move north and west as population pressures grew, intensified by the push of the white man.

On the open plains a new culture was born as lake, forest, and river-dwelling Indians moved into buffalo country. Most of all it was the horse that gave Plains Indians a new style of life.

Three tribes which moved west into North Dakota did not give up entirely their lake-forest living habits. The Assiniboins, Crees, and Chippewas split into forest bands, which settled into wooded areas like the Turtle Mountains, and into plains bands which turned to a nomadic way of life.

The Crow, Cheyenne, and Yanktonai and Teton Sioux embraced wholeheartedly the new culture. They became buffalo hunters, with the horse, the buffalo, and moveable villages as essential factors. Migrating herds of buffalo provided them with abundant food, clothing, shelter. Horses increased their mobility and effectiveness as hunters and warriors in the open country.

Such tribes as the Crow, Cheyenne, and Sioux became powerful on the open Dakota prairies and plains, masters of the fast attack and quick escape. Frequently they were in conflict with each other. Alliances were formed and broken. Enemy tribes hunted and ambushed the buffalo ranges. Bloody skirmishes revenged past violence. But just as likely there was no bloodshed at all. An early fur trader said the Indians did not like to take risks in their fighting.

The Mandans were the first known Indians to live in what is now North Dakota

Five Hidatsa villages at mouth of Knife River, drawn by Sitting Rabbit. Lewis and Clark found Sakakawea here; one of these is scheduled for restoration, with excavation of other sites.

"Most Indian battles consist merely of a whooping and yelling charge, flight of arrows, and precipitate retreat, it being considered disgraceful to lose a warrior," wrote Henry Boller in 1859.

The Revolutionary War and fur trade rivalries between English and French traders intensified Indian conflict as the whites sought alliances with Indian tribes and set them against each other.

But the Indians kept up a continuous trade with each other, the Plains tribes visiting the agricultural tribes annually to trade horses, buffalo meat and hides for corn. The Great Plains was a vast area of light population. People felt comparatively safe in their usual territory, hunting in fairly large bands. But they did not fail to post sentries nor to scan far horizons for smoke signals or sign of enemy.

Bodmer painting: Mandan village and bullboats, made of single buffalo hide stretched over willow frame.

Land ownership ideas of newcomers were foreign to Indian

'To him all days are God's'

The Indians did not have the same concept of land ownership as Europeans did. They lived in close harmony with the land. Their reverence for nature is expressed eloquently by a Sioux, Ohiyesa:

"Whenever, in the course of the daily hunt the red hunter comes upon a scene that is strikingly beautiful or sublime—a black thundercloud with the rainbow's glowing arch above the mountain, a white waterfall in the heart of a green gorge; a vast prairie tinged with the blood-red of sunset—he pauses for an instant in the attitude of worship. He sees no need for setting apart one day in seven as a holy day, since to him all days are God's."

Europeans were quick to establish sovereignty. In 1682 La Salle claimed for France all the land drained by the Mississippi River, including half of what is now North Dakota. Later France also claimed the area south of Hudson Bay and the lands which drained into the Bay, taking in the northeastern half of the state.

In 1713 they had to surrender the Hudson Bay territory to Great Britain. The Mississippi lands they ceded to Spain in 1763—but French traders continued very active in fur trade with the Indians.

Pierre Gaultier de la Verendrye, a French fur trader in command of a post north of Lake Superior, was the first white man in recorded history to come into North Dakota, in 1738. However, old Norse sagas suggest a party of Vikings came from Hudson Bay and up the Red River to Kensington, Minnesota in 1362. Verendrye was following rumors of a race of white Indians—perhaps the lost Welchmen, he thought—and of a westward flowing river extending to the Pacific from this area, which he might claim for France. With his sons he equipped an exploration party and pushed overland from the Red River with Assiniboin Indians as guides.

In mid-winter they arrived at the Mandan earth lodge village, probably near the present site of Bismarck. La Verendrye was disappointed in finding neither the west-

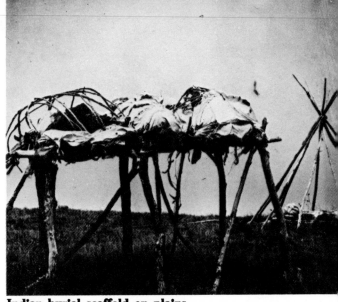

Indian burial scaffold on plains

ward-flowing river nor the lost tribe of Welchmen, but recorded in his journal that this was a mixed tribe: "many of them have blond or fair hair; most of the women do not have the Indian features."

It was 50 years before the plains fur trade became a thriving business with British and Spanish sending traders into the area and eventually setting up trading posts where the Indians could exchange furs for goods they desired. Meanwhile the Indians obtained white trade goods from other tribes and caught the white man's diseases. During the 1780's, smallpox epidemics decimated the tribes of the northern plains, especially those living in permanent villages along the Missouri. Three-fourths of the Mandans and half the Hidatsas were reportedly wiped out. Again in 1837, smallpox epidemics struck northern plains Indians, and again the agricultural tribes were hardest hit.

Hidatsa and Mandans of the Missouri River villages were visited by explorer and mapmaker David Thompson during the winter of 1797. Thompson came by dog sled from trading posts at the mouth of the Souris River.

In 1803 the United States paid France fifteen million dollars for the Louisiana Territory—the Spanish having transferred it back to them shortly before. This was a vast area of 827,987 square miles between the Mississippi River and the Rocky Mountains.

Captains Meriwether Lewis and William Clark set out the following spring from St. Louis up the Missouri with some 46 men in a 55-foot keelboat and two open pirogues, to explore the new U.S. lands.

Signs of a vanished way of life remain in the grass

Teepee rings—rocks placed around the edge of a teepee to hold it down—were once quite common across the state. Turtle effigies and other boulder rings as well as writing rocks have been found. But most of the state's ancient archaelogical history lies near the river beds—especially the Missouri. Much of this history is gone forever, now submerged under Lakes Sakakawea and Oahe.

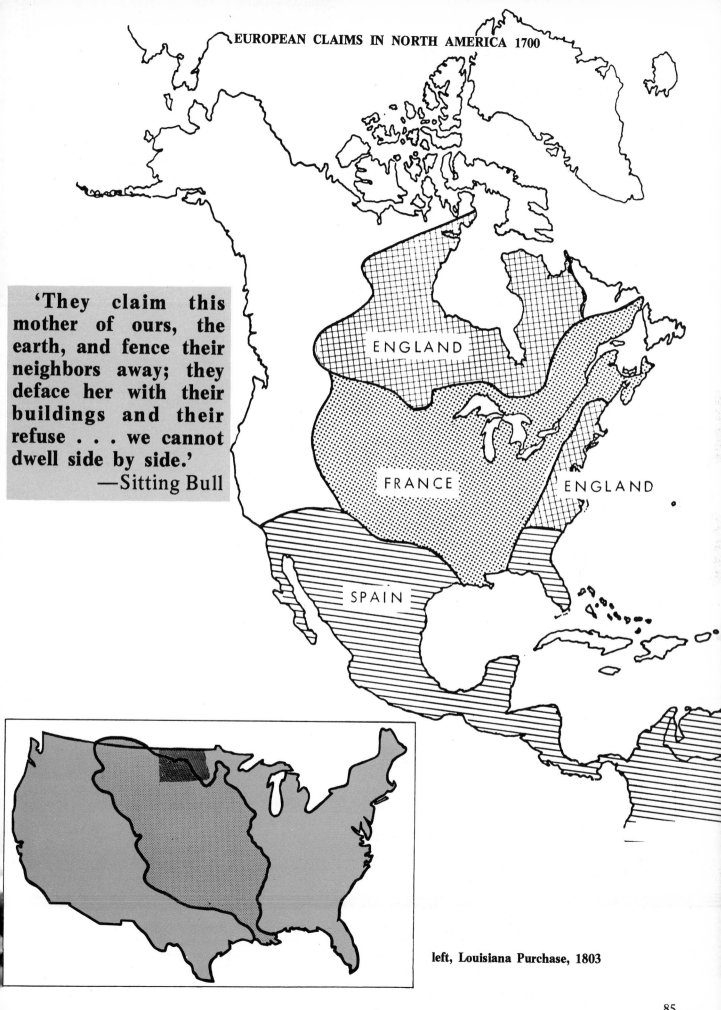

'They claim this mother of ours, the earth, and fence their neighbors away; they deface her with their buildings and their refuse . . . we cannot dwell side by side.'
—Sitting Bull

ENGLAND

FRANCE

ENGLAND

SPAIN

left, Louisiana Purchase, 1803

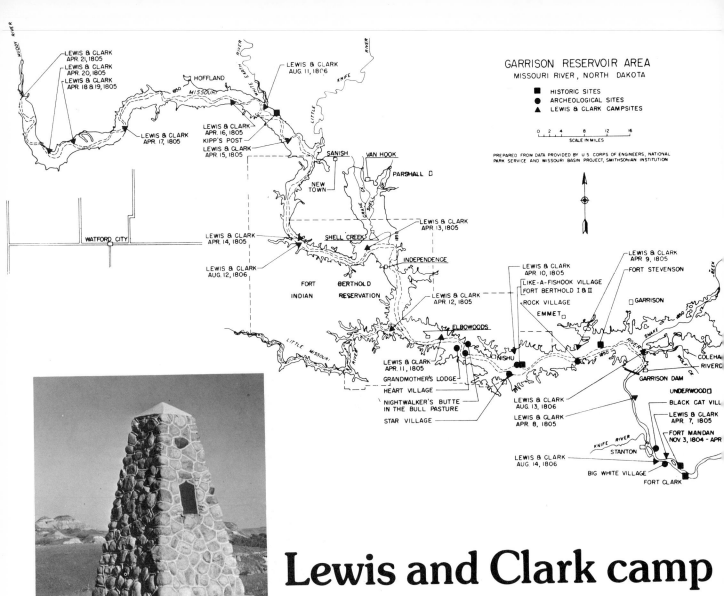

GARRISON RESERVOIR AREA
MISSOURI RIVER, NORTH DAKOTA

■ HISTORIC SITES
● ARCHEOLOGICAL SITES
▲ LEWIS & CLARK CAMPSITES

SCALE IN MILES
0 2 4 8 12 16

PREPARED FROM DATA PROVIDED BY U.S. CORPS OF ENGINEERS, NATIONAL
PARK SERVICE AND MISSOURI BASIN PROJECT, SMITHSONIAN INSTITUTION

**Cairn marks Lewis and Clark camp
near Washburn**

Lewis and Clark camp Ft. Mandan for winter

Lewis and Clark spent nearly six months in what is now North Dakota, making their first winter camp at Fort Mandan. Here—in a stroke of good fortune—they hired Charbonneau, French trader, with his captured Shoshone wife, Sakakawea, to guide them. In February Sakakawea gave birth to a baby called Pompey by the explorers, and a great favorite with them. Lewis recorded some details of the birth:

About five o'clock this evening one of the wives of Charbono was delivered of a fine boy. It is worthy of remark that this was the first child which this woman had boarn, and as is common in such cases her labour was tedious and the pain violent. Mr. Jessome (another fur trader) informed me that he had frequently administered a small portion of the rattle of the rattlesnake, which he assured me had never failed to produce the desired effect, that of hastening the birth of the child. Having the rattle of a snake by me I gave it to him and he administered two rings of it to the woman broken in small pieces with the fingers and added to a small quantity of water. Whether this medicine was truly the cause or not I shall not undertake to determine, but I was informed that she had not taken it more than 10 minutes before she brought forth. [2]

Mandan Indians entertained the explorers with hair-raising accounts of the ferocity of the grizzly bear during the winter. But Lewis, for one, was greatly disappointed at their first grizzly encounter near the mouth of the Yellowstone River. The half-grown bear was too easily killed.

"The Indians may well fear this animal," he wrote. "Equipped as they are with their bows and arrows or indifferent fuzees. But in the hands of skillful riflemen they are by no means as formidable or dangerous as they have

'In an instant this monster ran at them with open mouth.'

been represented."

His patronizing tone soon changed to one of awe and respect. In a few days Clark and George Drewyer killed another grizzly, and he recorded its dimensions:

It was a most tremendous looking animal, and extremely hard to kill. Notwithstanding he had five balls through his lungs and five others in various parts he swam more than half the distance across the river to a sandbar, and it was at least 20 minutes before he died . . . We had no means of weighing this monster. Capt. Clark thought he would weigh 500 lbs. For my own part I think the estimate too small by 100 lbs. He measured 8 feet 7 1/2 inches from the nose to the extremity of the hind feet; 5 ft. 10 1/2 inches around the breast; 1 ft. 11 inches around the middle of the arm. His talons . . . were 4 3/8 inches in length. [3]

The great size of this bear whetted the soldiers' appetites for excitement. A few days later when six men in the last canoe sighted a sleeping grizzly not far from the river, they planned an ambush.

They took advantage of a small (hill) which concealed them and got within 40 paces of him unperceived. Two of them reserved their fire . . . the four others fired nearly at the same time and put each his bullet through him. Two of the balls passed through the bulk of both lobes of his lungs. In an instant this monster ran at them with open mouth. The two who had reserved their fire discharged their pieces at him

as he came towards them. Both of them struck him, one only slightly and the other fortunately broke his shoulder. This, however, only retarded his motion for a moment.

The men, unable to reload their guns took to flight; the bear pursued and had very nearly overtaken them before they reached the river. Two of the party betook themselves to a canoe and the others separated and concealed themselves among the willows, reloaded their pieces. Each discharged his piece at him as they had an opportunity. They struck him several times again but the guns served only to direct the bear to them. In this manner he pursued two of them separately so close that they were obliged to throw aside their guns and pouches and throw themselves into the river although the bank was nearly 20 feet perpendicular.

So enraged was this animal that he plunged into the river only a few feet behind the second man he had compelled to take refuge in the water . . . one of those . . . on shore shot him through the head and finally killed him. [4]

Whitehouse's journal reveals even more dismay for the man in the water. The bear was "near gitting hold of him," he said, before being killed with nine balls in him. The grizzly was pulled to shore and butchered. He measured 9 inches across the ball of his foot, and 13 inches the length of it, according to Whitehouse. "His nails were seven inches long."

Explorers Find Plains of Plenty

The exploration party observed great quantities of wildlife of all kinds in Dakota, along the river and on the open plains. Lewis wrote:

I ascended to the top of the cut bluff this morning, from whence I had a most delightful view of the country, void of timber or underbrush, exposing to the first glance of the spectator immense herds of buffalo, elk, deer and antelope feeding in one common and boundless pasture. We saw a number of beaver feeding on the bark of the trees along the verge of the river, several of which we shot, found them large and fat.

Walking on shore this evening I met with a buffalo calf which attached itself to me and continued to follow close at my heels . . . Capt. Clark informed me that he saw a large drove of buffalo pursued by wolves today, that they at length caught a calf which was unable to keep up with the herd. The cows only defend their young so long as they are able to keep up . . . seldom return any distance in search of them. [5]

At the mouth of the Yellowstone River Lewis again left the boat and climbed the hills.

I had a most pleasing view of the country particularly of the wide and fertile vallies formed by the Missouri and Yellowstone Rivers, which occasionally unmasked by the wood on their borders disclose their meanderings for many miles in their passage through these delightful tracts of country.

The whole face of the country was covered with herds of buffalo, elk and antelope; deer are also abundant, but keep themselves more concealed in the woodland. The buffalo, elk and antelope are so gentle that we pass near them while feeding, without appearing to excite any alarm among them; and when we attract their attention, they frequently approach us more nearly to discover what we are. [6]

In the immediate area the explorers also saw bighorn sheep, coyotes, brown bear, geese, ducks, "brant", swans, and rattlesnakes.

Food was never a serious problem as the travelers crossed the plains; game was plentiful and easy to hunt. Their boats carried a supply of staples such as flour; Sakakawea showed the men how to find and dig edible roots.

The expedition made its way to the source of the Missouri River and there, after anxious searching, they found a band of wary Shoshone Indians. They soon learned, to their delight, that it was Sakakawea's own family band and her brother Cameahwait was chief. It was a happy reunion: Sakakawea pleased her brother with gifts of sugar and helped persuade the Shoshones to sell the explorers good horses from their fine herds. But Sakakawea declined to stay with the poverty-stricken Shoshones. They lived in terror of the powerful plains tribes who came annually to steal horses, and she wanted to see the "great waters and the monstrous fish."

Across the continental divide there was almost no wildlife and the food situation became desperate. The explorers nearly starved before reaching Indian villages where they could get help. Once they had been appalled by the Plains Indians' custom of eating dog. Now—although these river-dwelling Indians were not dog eaters—they remembered the taste of dog from their winter at Ft. Mandan and found themselves purchasing large numbers of dogs for food. Lewis noted in his journal:

I . . . purchased three dogs from them with deerskins. The dog now constitutes a considerable part of our subsistence and with most of the party, has become a favorite food. Certain I am that it is a healthy strong diet, and from habit it has become by no means disagreeable to me. I prefer it to lean venison or elk, and it is very far superior to the horse in any state. [7]

During the long expedition Lewis and Clark met with the Indian tribes on their route, counselling for peace and distributing U.S. flags and presents from the "great father in Washington." They followed President Jefferson's instructions carefully: recording meticulous details of topography, geology, botany, zoology, and anthropology, as well as their own astounding adventures. They named, as they went, great numbers of rivers, mountains, plants, animals. They sketched maps, topographical features.

But when they again reached Ft. Mandan, Clark was saddened to record, "Charbono informed me that our back was scarcely turned before a war party from the two menetarry villages followed on and attacked and killed the Snake (Shoshone) Indians whom we had seen."

Mandan on ceremonial lodge, Crow's Heart

The Fur Trade

The Lewis and Clark expedition strengthened U.S. claims all the way to the Pacific and stimulated interest in the fur trade. But the British continued to trade on the upper Missouri. A major difficulty of American traders was the hostility of Indians, especially Sioux and Arikara, on the lower Missouri, menacing traffic up and down the river. Besides a dislike of white intrusion, these Indians had long enjoyed some of the benefits of middlemen and did not want to lose them to fur traders.

Alexander Henry of the British Northwestern Fur Company built a permanent trading post among the Chippewa at Pembina in 1801. In one season his Red River and Lower Assiniboin posts shipped out nearly 3000 beaver pelts. Competing posts—both company and independent—sprang up along the Red, and Henry sought agreements to eliminate this competition. Under such heavy traffic the beaver trade declined rather rapidly and a major item shipped out of Pembina became the staple Indian food, pemmican.

Kenneth McKenzie built a trading post on the upper Missouri for the Columbia Fur Company in 1822. Columbia competed throughout fur country with John Jacob Astor's American Fur—the nation's first great monopoly. Unable to crush this competition which reduced control and advantage over the Indians, Astor's company negotiated to join forces. McKenzie became a leading partner of

Ft. Clark: 4 cups sugar for a buffalo robe

American Fur.

It was his talents which located Ft. Union, the most important post on the Missouri and perhaps in the entire fur country, at the junction of the Yellowstone and Missouri in 1828. From Ft. Union McKenzie carried on extensive trade up both rivers. He established other forts farther up and Ft. Clark below.

Kenneth McKenzie—"King of the Upper Missouri"—took an Indian wife and lived in grand style in a large two-story house with wallpaper and imported carpets.

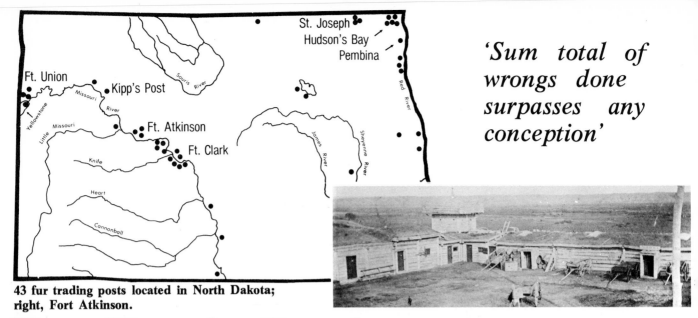

43 fur trading posts located in North Dakota; right, Fort Atkinson.

Fur Trade Exploits Indians

Henry Boller, a young fur trader at Ft. Atkinson near the mouth of the Little Missouri, described his trading post in 1858:

> The store . . . contains the miscellaneous Mdse. which an Indian Trading Post in the wilds of the far North West is supplied: Blankets, all sizes, all colors, calicos, prints, cotton, ticking, blue and scarlet cloth, linsey, blue drilling, guns, fuses, revolvers, and rifles, prepared bullets, shot and abundance of powder, together with flints, perc. caps, powder horns, worms, awls, beads, all sizes and kinds in profusion, hawk bells, gilt buttons, gold and silver lace, sewings, etc., ribbon, fancy bridles, various styles, fancy caps, combs, enough to clear out all the heads in the country; butcher knives, files, shears, vermillion, chrome yellow, cockinal (to dye quills), brass tacks, Jew's Harps, brass kettles, camp do, tin cups, dippers, coffee pots all sizes, small trunks, covered with red morocco and plentifully studded with brass tacks, coffee mills, tin pans; crockery, bowls, mugs, etc., and many other articles to please the tastes of the Indians.
>
> **Sugar, coffee and tea are the most profitable articles of trade; of these we have a fair supply, 20 bbls. sugar, seven sacks coffee, four chests tea, 10 lbs. hard or Pilot bread, and provision for our own use when game or dried meat is scarce.**
>
> Four cups of either sugar, coffee, or tea is the price of a robe (dressed buffalo hide) . . . $1 a cup! . . . We have no money currency up here, **robes** taking its place; for example, you want to buy a horse from an Indian—he will, if a "buffer" horse (buffalo, second only to a war horse) ask 30 robes for him; you pay him in goods from the store, to the value of 30 robes, estimating each at 4 dollars, altho' the actual St. Louis cost of the goods would not be more than 30 or 40 dollars . . . Getting running horses from the Blackfeet and trading them off for robes is one branch of our business.[8]

Boller does not mention liquor in his list of trading post supplies, but it was probably a staple trade item there as elsewhere. Congress banned selling liquor to the Indians, but it was commonly bootlegged into Indian country and used ruthlessly to exploit the fur trade. The American Fur Company had strong political clout and in 1842 they arranged the federal appointment of a company trader as Indian Agent for the Upper Missouri. Their agent immediately stopped the liquor trade of opposition posts, while that of American Fur continued.

The fur trade exploited the Indians from the first—obtaining furs as cheaply as possible, sometimes for trinkets, often with trickery and the liberal use of bad whiskey, watered down more and more as trading progressed, each cupful purchasing ever more fur. Honest traders were caught in the middle, trying to deal fairly with Indians in the face of ruthless competition and at the same time satisfy the profit-greedy fur company.

French traders were most successful in their Indian dealings. Many took Indian wives and lived permanently with the Indians. De Trobriand, U.S. commander at Ft. Stevenson, a Frenchman by birth and a careful observer of the Dakota scene, notes that the Indians let him know they had particular confidence in him because he was French. It was the French who understood Indian nature and kept consistently friendly relations. In contrast, said Tobriand, the Anglo-Saxons and Americans used little else but brute force, demoralization, and oppression in their Indian relationships.

Trobriand invariably took a firm stand in his dealings with Indians, but said that the longer he lived among them and "the more I read the official documents relating to Indian affairs, the more I have modified the ideas I brought with me. The sum total of the wrongs done to these poor redskins surpasses any conception."

Indians in northeastern Dakota, with deeper snow, made much use of dog sleds in winter to haul furs; elsewhere they relied on the travois. Furs were shipped downriver by canoe, raft, and keelboat.

'our country was changing fast—'

Changes came fast for the Indians with the fur trade. On the frontier it was commonly agreed that the intrusion of whites invariably demoralized the Indians. Chief Plenty Coups, although his Crow tribe maintained peace with the whites, voiced his own dissatisfaction:

"... our country was changing fast ... Anybody could now see that soon there would be no buffalo on the plains and everybody was wondering how we could live after they were gone ... White men with their spotted-buffalo were on the plains about us ... We made up our minds to be friendly with them, in spite of all the changes they were bringing. But we found this difficult, because the white men too often promised to do one thing and then ... did another.

"They spoke very loudly when they said their laws were made for everybody; but we soon learned that although they expected us to keep them, they thought nothing of breaking them themselves.

"They told us not to drink whiskey, yet they made it themselves and traded it to us for furs and robes until both were nearly gone. Their Wise Ones said we might have their religion, but when we tried to understand it we found that there were too many kinds of religion among white men for us to understand, and that scarcely any two white men agreed which was the right one to learn. This bothered us a good deal until we saw that the white man did not take his religion any more seriously than he did his laws, and that he kept both of them just behind him, like Helpers, to use when they might do him good in his dealings with strangers.

"These were not our ways. We kept the laws we made and lived our religion. We have never been able to understand the white man, who fools nobody but himself." [9]

With steamboating beginning on the lower Missouri, American Fur—under McKenzie's leadership—built the **Yellowstone.** In 1832 this steamship, 130 feet long, drawing 5 1/2 feet of water, with capacity of 144 tons of freight, steamed up the river all the way to Ft. Union, loaded with Indian trade goods. She returned to St. Louis bearing furs, thus opening a dramatic chapter of steamboating on the upper Missouri. The artist George Catlin rode this first boat to Ft. Union and painted extensively the Indian life he found. Maximilian, German prince, and Karl Bodmer—a young Swiss artist—spent the next winter at Ft. Clark where Bodmer painted and Maximilian wrote. A few years later John James Audubon came and was honored for observations of the Audubon bighorn sheep.

Workshop, church at Pembina, 1818, sketched for Father Lacombe

Early Missionaries

Catholic missionaries sought to bring Christianity to the Indians as early as 1818. Missions were established at Pembina and St. Boniface among French fur traders, their Indian wives and families, and the Metis (French for "mixed breed") who settled in northeastern Dakota and in Canada.

Protestant missionaries Elijah Terry, Baptist, the Rev. Alonzo Barnard, Presbyterian, James Tanner, Baptist, and Mr. and Mrs. David Spencer, Congregationalists, worked in the Pembina-Red River area and set up a church at St. Joseph. But Terry was killed and scalped by hostile Sioux. Mrs. Spencer was also killed in a Sioux attack and Mrs. Barnard died of pneumonia. The three, known as the "Martyrs of St. Joseph," were buried at Walhalla.

Dog teams hauled Red River furs in deep snow— and dignitaries, 1871.

'The vice, injustice, bad treatment sown by whites produced this bloody harvest.'

Painted horses decorate Sioux teepees photographed near Fort Yates

So Pandora's box was opened on the plains

One change of deep concern to whites was the fierce hostility and bitterness they were beginning to meet—especially from the Sioux.

In 1868 General Regis de Trobriand described the changes in hostility which local fur traders told him they had experienced.

There were few whites in Dakota (30 years ago), and all of them came to trade with the Indians, who invariably gave them a warm welcome. Although the tribes did not stop fighting each other, which is an immemorial custom among the redskins, the whites were not involved in their quarrels. They could cross the (plains) in security without weapons, and they were never mistreated. When they met some savages, they sat down together around the fire, smoked the peace pipe, did some trading, exchanged news with each other, and parted as they had met, friends.

At that time, nothing could be more inoffensive to the whites than the plains tribes. From them, they received nothing but hospitality; every promise given was rigorously kept, and as transactions were carried out in good faith, there was the best of feeling between individuals.

If theft, deceit, murder, and war have come since those days, the fault is definitely that of the whites alone . . . The great profits from the trade bred rivalries among the traders; these rivalries resulted in strategems of all sorts . . . each made great efforts to attract the Indians and to turn them away from competitors. So to harm one another, the whites began to stir up the Indians . . . encouraged them to steal . . . Whiskey was introduced among them to encourage them in evil and to despoil them more easily.

So Pandora's box was opened on the plains. And the vice, injustice, bad treatment sown by the whites produced this bloody harvest, which for ten years has cost so much in blood and money.

The discovery of the gold mines in Montana aggravated the situation by bringing a flock of gold seekers, uncontrolled bandits, men on their own, far from the jurisdiction of the law . . .

The Minnesota Massacre in 1862 resulted in the expulsion of the Santees far from their hunting grounds and brought together all the Sioux on the west bank of the Missouri. This concentration of all those at war with the whites produced these hostilities which have increased of late because the treaties concluded with the tribes of the Platte have not been observed by the government. [10]

And finally... buffalo killed for their tongues

Indians were dismayed at the buffalo slaughter and the tons of hides filling steamboats for shipment downriver.

Buffalo were the backbone of Plains Indian culture, their source of independence and wealth. The horse, the other unique Plains Indian feature, enabled them to hunt efficiently and provided the mobility to follow the herds. Only because of the buffalo could they live in bands of great size and power. (And this became, ultimately, one reason for the destruction of the buffalo.)

Other wild game—deer, antelope, elk, bighorns, small animals of many kinds—provided food. But never were they so easy to hunt, nor ranged in such large numbers nor—when killed—provided the sheer quantity of meat as did buffalo.

After a hunt the Indian women dried buffalo meat in thin strips and sheets. Some was further refined into pemmican—dried, pounded with berries, mixed with fat and stored in bags of green buffalo hide. It was an enormous amount of work, but supplied the Indians with staple food for winter camp and travel. Besides meat the buffalo were used in all kinds of ways: their hides for teepees, clothing, blankets, bullboats, rope, drums; horns, hoofs, and bone for utensils, tools, and ornaments.

Buffalo hunting could be dangerous. Boller said in 1869, "Scarcely a Buffalo Hunt takes place without some accident happening to either a horse or rider." He describes the tendency of the wounded buffalo to whirl and try to hook horse and rider when shot. A superb black horse belonging to Poor Wolf was hooked in this way and trod on his own guts, tearing them to pieces before his rider could stop him, made a wide circle and dropped dead, said Boller.

Buffalo jumps were an early method of hunting—and buffalo were quick to charge a man on foot.

Indians killed only for their needs until the fur trade—with finer furs depleted—came to focus on buffalo hides. Buffalo robes became the unit of money, with dressed hides (robes) valued at $4 each; one Indian woman could dress ten robes a year.

Another colorful group, the Metis, launched full-scale hunting forays twice a year into the buffalo country of central North Dakota. These mixed bloods were descendants of French fur traders and Indian women, mostly Chippewa. The Metis sold great quantities of hides, buffalo meat, and pemmican to fur traders as far away as St. Paul. They became famous for their Red River carts, built entirely

Mandans grew corn, squash—killed only what they needed

of wood, with which they hauled buffalo products to market. By 1840 the Metis were taking as many as 1200 Red River carts on their buffalo hunts, killing eight to 10 cows to fill each cart with dried meat. Often they took their local priest along to ensure a successful hunt.

Plains Indians protested: Metis killed too many buffalo.

White hunters, too, began their slaughter as early as the 1850's when wealthy sportsmen came west to hunt. Most notorious was Sir George Gore, Irish "butcher" who killed wantonly for three years, yet lived in luxury, with "a man to bathe and scrub his highness daily." No danger of his coming up again, said one trader, as both Indians and traders were furious with him.

Sir George did not return, but increasing numbers of white buffalo hunters did: they killed for hides, for meat for railroad crews, for sport, sometimes just for the tongue—a noted delicacy valued at 25 cents at the trading post, pickled and sent down to St. Louis.

Red River Carts

The Metis' Red River carts, built entirely of wood, squeaked so loudly as the wheels turned on wooden axles that it was said a caravan of them could be heard for miles. Twice a year the Metis traveled southwest to hunt buffalo, filled their carts with dried meat and hides. Later their caravans turned eastward—all the way to St. Paul—carrying hides and their choice product, pemmican.

ERA of STEAMBOATING

Missouri River not destined for luxury; this steamer, Wyoming, wrecked at Kansas City

It was hardly a voyage of luxury. Two months bucking the muddy Missouri on a journey rife with hidden hazards, cinders, smoke, engine noise, summer heat, lack of fresh food, and hosts of nighttime mosquitoes.

Yet journey by steamship to the northwest was perhaps an easier, pleasanter mode of travel than any other available. Certainly there was, on a steamship, an unmatched air of exotic flamboyance, of rough-and-ready excitement.

Decks were crowded with miners bound for Montana and Black Hills gold fields. Restless troopers heading for military forts in Indian country shared sleeping quarters on the open decks with miners, livestock, and roustabouts. Holds were filled with annuity goods for peaceable Indians, with supplies for merchants and furniture for the fancy homes of gold field barons.

Keen-eyed river pilots—higher paid on the Missouri than any other American river—kept close watch for snags and sawyers that could rip out the ship's bottom, steered for the deep channel, and avoided the sandbars that had shifted position since the last trip. There was the excitement of boat landings with curious Indians crowding close while deckhands drank and fought. There was apprehension—and a careful watch by passengers and crew alike—in hostile Indian country when a stop need be made for woodcutting, or when the ship plied a narrow channel close against cliffs well suited for ambush.

A miner paid $150-$200 fare from St. Louis to Ft. Benton in 1865. Seven years later with an overabundance of steamboats on the Missouri and a new railhead at Sioux City, the going rate was $100. Costs to the North Dakota forts of Stevenson and Buford were then $50 and $65. The army had a special rate of three cents a mile for livestock, three cents for enlisted men, and four cents for officers—who drew cabin quarters.

Business boomed. In 1866 steamboat owners estimated a $10,000 to $40,000 profit from each boat that made it all the way to Ft. Benton. Those returning with gold dust profited most.

Still, the steamboat season was short. A boat could only make one trip to Ft. Benton during the season. The Missouri was shallow, and unique among rivers. Big steamers had to start upriver as soon as the ice broke up in March or April and ride the June raise back down to St. Louis.

Shallow draft was important. Successful boats were flat-bottomed, of lighter weight pine, displacing three or four feet of water when loaded, and cost about $20,000 to build. Stern-wheelers proved more practical than side-wheelers in these snag-filled, narrower channels. Yet nearly every kind of steamboat sooner or later tried her luck on the upper Missouri. Many ran aground, were wrecked by snags and sawyers. A year of high water offered more leeway.

The first steamer to ply the upper Missouri was the **Yellowstone,** an unlikely craft for this river. Built especially to supply trade goods and carry furs from McKenzie's American Fur post at Ft. Union, she was a side-wheeler 160 feet long and drew six feet when loaded to 75 tons. She reached Ft. Union in 1832 and was joined the next year by the **Assiniboine,** which burned two years later near the Heart River with 1100 packs of furs and robes.

Decks were crowded with miners, restless troopers, livestock, roustabouts—

Steamboats also traveled the Red River to Winnipeg for 20 years, after an initial launching in 1859. Railroad connections at Moorhead ended this colorful but expensive mode of moving freight. During the 1880's the **Minnie H** hauled freight, passengers and mail to Devils Lake points. Later she served mainly as a summertime excursion boat and was dismantled in 1908.

The **Yellowstone** took 7000 buffalo robes from Ft. Union in 1833—70,000 went to St. Louis annually between 1834 and 1844. But the 1860's marked a big change in steamboat activity. Gold was discovered in Montana. The Civil War was finally finished. The Minnesota Massacre and westward flight of Santee Sioux sparked national interest in building military forts in Dakota.

Out came civilians by the thousands in search of gold and new opportunities. Out came the military, finished with one war. Steamboat traffic jumped.

Seventy-one steamboats traveled into the upper Missouri in 1867, the peak season; a record 37 went all the way to Ft. Benton. But by 1869 the number was already down nearly half.

A light-draft ship could hit forts between Dakota and St. Louis several times in the season, but only twice did steamships make it to Ft. Benton more than once in the summer. No doubt these were years of high water.

The Army's urgent need to move troops and supply forts stimulated traffic. General Sully used 15 different steamers for his 1864 summer campaign in North Dakota alone.

Government contracts—for military and hauling Indian annuities—were fat plums. River rivalries flourished between companies, crews, and river port towns.

Railroad building sped west, and as each railroad line hit the Missouri farther north a new shipping point was created. First it was St. Louis, then Sioux City. By the mid '70's Bismarck and Yankton were the major rivals.

Bismarck to Ft. Benton took 14 days. The steamer **Red Cloud** in 1877 did it in just under 10 days—and captured the elk horn prize to adorn their "fastest steamship" pilot house. But the next year the prized antlers were lost to a new record: nine days, one hour.

Except for a brief ill-fated attempt, the Missouri never floated the ornate crystal palaces of the Mississippi. Coulson built three luxury steamers, the **Dakotah, Montana,** and **Wyoming,** 250 feet long, elaborately furnished, costing nearly $50,000 each—and drawing six feet of water, loaded.

The **Montana,** damaged by windstorm in Bismarck after one trip to Ft. Benton, had to be towed to St. Louis for repairs and never returned. The **Wyoming** wrecked against the Kansas City railroad bridge. The **Dakotah** also struck the bridge at Kansas City, later struck a snag and sank.

Unequalled in the lore of steamboating are the heroic feats of Captain Grant Marsh and the **Far West** in rescuing wounded from the Battle of the Little Big Horn. Captain Marsh pushed 64 miles up the Big Horn, a narrow shallow river, never before navigated, risking his ship and crew to river dangers as well as possible Indian attack. At 2 a.m. the **Far West** was loaded with Reno and Benteen's wounded and set out for Bismarck. Along with wounded soldiers Captain Marsh brought to the world the shocking news of the annihilation of General Custer and five companies of the Seventh Cavalry.

J. L. Grandin at Fargo levee, 1878

Minnie H on Devils Lake off Rock Island

Going Nowhere

Steamboat Expansion sits high and dry on sandbar

Missouri's a high-hazard run

Missouri River pilots had to know their river. Its waters are muddy and hide under a broad surface the narrow shifting channel and unexpected hazards. Collapsing banks continually dumped large trees into the river where they became snags or sawyers, often not seen until a grinding stop signalled a hull run aground or ripped through. Wind and waves made them difficult to see, and steamships could travel only in daylight hours. Wrecked or burned steamships in the channel were equally dangerous.

Rivermen devised ingenious ways out of their difficulties. Running on a sandbar at full speed, said Tobriand, is "such a shock that it seems as if the whole thing is going to fall apart. The boat literally bends, throws herself right and left, or sticks fast on the bar." They would try to back off, find the proper channel. Grasshoppering, or sparring, was a poling method of pulling the boat over a sandbar. Warping involved tying line to a tree and pulling it up with a steam-powered winch.

On Henry Boller's first trip upriver in 1858, their ship went aground almost hourly. "When the spars won't jump her off," wrote Boller in a letter home, "the freight had to be carried ashore in boats until she floated and then reloaded. We would thus frequently lose from 12 to 24 hours."

Loading onto small boats could also be dangerous in high winds.

The heavy silt of the Missouri water plugged lines and necessitated frequent cleaning of the boilers, or explosions could result. Tobriand commented that the wine for sale on board was so bad that "it is better to drink the yellow, dirty, unpurified, and tepid water of the Missouri." Fortunately it had been proven good for the stomach, he added.

Steamboats required enormous quantities of wood. Crews kept watch for woodyards where daring "woodhawks"—

Western wrecks on ice, Peninah afloat

white, Indian, or half-breed—cut and sold wood for boats at $8 a cord. Cost was $100 a day just for wood. And it was dangerous work: in 1868 seven woodhawks were killed at once above Ft. Union by hostile Indians. If there were no woodyards, boat crews had to stop and gather or cut their own, sometimes green cottonwood.

Hostile Indians were a menace especially during the '60's and '70's. "Sometimes they hide in the brush and fire on the steamboats when they come near the bank," said Tobriand. Most steamers were fully armed, he noted, with howitzers, rifles, and carbines, not to mention revolvers carried by every male passenger.

Railroads seize control of river shipping

Unloading horses at riverboat landing, Bismarck

In 50 years, by 1880, the heydey of steamboating was ended. But river traffic continued another 40 years.

The Northern Pacific railroad was quick to head off river competition as it built west from Bismarck. River shipping depended on railroad cooperation as the source of most freight so the NP was able to negotiate contracts insuring near-monopoly control of all trade above Bismarck. All river freight of cooperating lines had to be channeled through the NP railroad, unless it was local; steamships were not allowed to trade on the Yellowstone River or carry freight to any points on the NP line.

River traffic became mostly local—hauling wheat to elevators on the river. By 1901, 15 of the 26 commercial boats on the Upper Missouri were gas powered.

Interestingly, Congress—long under pressure to appropriate funds for improvement of Missouri River navigation—did so now after most of the steamships were gone. With just 15 steamships left on the river, the government in 1895 operated three snagboats, clearing the channel of logs, snags, sawyers and old hulls of wrecked ships. The snagboats became the butt of river jokes:

"What's that boat out there?" asks a newcomer to Bismarck.

"That's a government snagboat."

"Oh. What's it for?"

"It clears the snags out of the river so the snagboats can run."

The government built, and for 20 years improved, Rock Haven harbor. Five miles upriver from Mandan, it was designed to be a permanent ice-safe harbor, high enough to be safe in spring ice break-up.

Steamboat 'Peninah' at Washburn prepares to unload grain

In two decades Fort Peck dam was under construction, followed by Garrison dam and Oahe, thus ending forever any dreams of recapturing the turbulent era of navigation on the upper Missouri.

Methodist picnickers on Undine, Bismarck

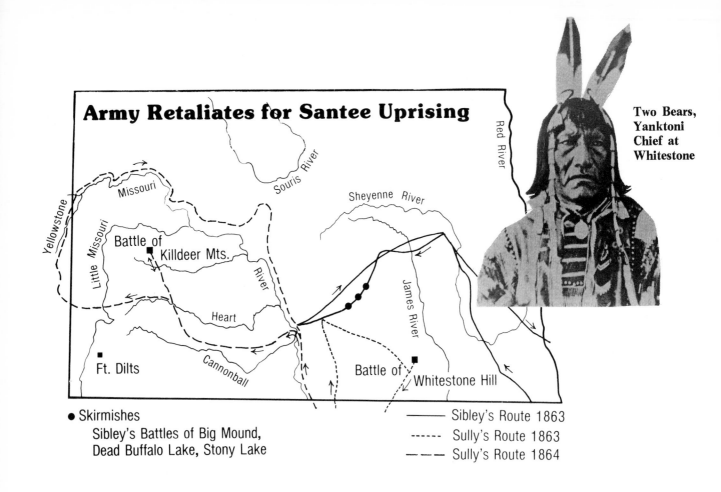

Army Retaliates for Santee Uprising

Two Bears, Yanktoni Chief at Whitestone

● Skirmishes
Sibley's Battles of Big Mound,
Dead Buffalo Lake, Stony Lake

———— Sibley's Route 1863
------ Sully's Route 1863
– – – Sully's Route 1864

Indian Patience Wears Thin

Increasingly the Indians grew restive. They could see their food supply, the buffalo, fast disappearing. Again and again they had made treaties which were not honored. Annuity goods and payments promised were withheld or reduced at an agent's whim, and they knowingly bought their own goods from the post trader. Their people were demoralized by trader whiskey. And they were pushed ever westward, their territory reduced.

War parties were everywhere, reported Boller in 1859. "All the bands of the Dahcotahs and the Riccarees are very much exasperated at the Whites, and upon the slightest encouragement will break out into open war . . . living in Indian country is now more dangerous than it has been for **very many years.**"

Boller explained that the local law was to always avoid meeting Indians on the prairie. "Hide if you see them first, or if too late, and well-mounted, give your horse the whip and try to throw them off your trail."

Then in 1862 a tragic event took place in Minnesota, which had violent repercussions throughout the west for many years to come. The Santee Sioux rose up against an agent who refused them their annuity foods when they were starving. They killed him and for five days went on a rampage up and down the Minnesota Valley killing some 360 whites, burning settler homes, taking women and children prisoners. For many years these prisoners turned up in tribes throughout the west. They were ransomed, rescued, traded, killed deliberately during military attack, or turned in by friendly Indians.

An army of volunteers under Henry Hastings Sibley, former fur trader, moved against them and many of the Santee Sioux fled west into the Devils Lake country. Among them were, no doubt, those most guilty of the Minnesota incidents. But all Indian country soon knew that the remaining Santee were thrown into prison, 303 sentenced to death; 38 actually hanged (after President Lincoln intervened to review the cases); the remaining Santee removed to Crow Creek Agency in South Dakota, their property and annuity money for lands sold, confiscated.

The Santee spread terror and death as they fled west. One hundred sixty settlers fled to Ft. Abercrombie, about 15 miles north of the present city of Wahpeton on the west bank of the Red. The Indians were right on their heels and drove off the government mules and beef cattle from the fort on August 30. Three days later they attacked the fort.

Ft. Abercrombie was but poorly manned with 78 men, later joined by three companies of Minnesota Volunteers, with the remainder of the troops off fighting in the Civil War.

The Santee Sioux forces were so strong that they kept up

Sully's 1864 expedition against Sioux, camped near Ft. Berthold

siege for nearly six weeks. At last they scattered to prepare for winter and various bands joined with other hostile Sioux in the territory.

Next summer the government set out to punish the Sioux. Plans were to move on them from two directions. Sibley marched into Dakota with 2800 men from the east. General Alfred Sully was to come up the Missouri with 2000 cavalrymen to attack from the west. However, Sully was delayed by difficulties with his supply steamers in low water on the Missouri and missed Sibley entirely.

Sibley fought three battles with a big camp of Sioux he found, most of whom had not been in the Minnesota uprising. The battles were at Big Mound, Dead Buffalo Lake, and Stony Lake, near what is now Tappen, Dawson, and Driscoll. The Indian families fled, taking what they could. Sibley's army destroyed their camps, including winter supplies of food and buffalo robes.

When the retreating Sioux came to the Missouri, south of the site of Bismarck, with Sibley's infantry close behind, they left their wagons and plunged into the river and tried to swim. Many were killed or drowned. Sibley did not follow across the river but burned the abandoned wagons and property, waited a few days for Sully, then turned back toward Minnesota.

The Sioux crossed back over the Missouri and traveled east to hunt buffalo and replenish their food supply before winter.

Sully arrived at last and discovered a camp of Sioux on the James River Sept. 3, 1863. After unsuccessful parley, the Indians began to abandon camp and the troopers attacked.

This was the bloodiest battle fought on North Dakota soil: the Battle of Whitestone Hill. Twenty of Sully's men were killed and 50 wounded. Reports vary on Indian losses; according to Robinson about 150 were killed and 156 taken prisoner. The soldiers killed the Indian horses, burned 300 teepees and at least 200 tons of dried buffalo meat.

"The Indians are, and with good reason, utterly sick and disgusted with the 'liars' and 'old women' annually sent by their 'great Father' to soft soap and fool them. The present incumbent (his first trip) possesses every necessary qualification demanded by a Democratic Administration for the responsible office of Indian Agent, as his devotion to the whiskey bottle, and a don't-care-a-damn activeness, sufficiently proves." [11]

Henry Boller, letter to his father
from Ft. Atkinson, 1859

Officer's sketch of Sully's charge at Whitestone

At Battle Tah-kah-o-ku-ty (Place Where They Kill Deer), Killdeer Mountains, Indians "swarmed on every side on their fleet little ponies . . . dashed wildly together or dispersed on signals from their chiefs . . . but the whistle of our shells and long-range rifles taught them the white man had a weapon far superior to any he had yet sold to them," said a soldier in the battle, July 28, 1864.

The following summer Sully was again sent to campaign against the Sioux. On July 28, 1864 he found a large camp in the Killdeer Mountains.

Hundreds of warriors came out to meet him. The sketch above, by a soldier at the battle, shows the contrast between Indian and army styles of fighting. General Custer—in another battle—expressed his admiration for the daring of Indian warriors:

Once a warrior was seen to dash out from the rest in the peculiar act of "circling," which was simply to dash along in front of the line of troopers, receiving their fire and firing in return. Suddenly his pony, while at full speed, fell to the ground, showing that the aim of at least one of the soldiers had been effective. The warrior was thrown over and beyond the pony's head, and his capture by the cavalry seemed a sure and easy matter to be accomplished.

I saw him fall and called to the officer commanding the troop which had remained mounted to gallop forward and secure the Indian.

The troop advanced rapidly, but the comrades of the fallen Indian had also witnessed his mishap and were rushing to his rescue. He was on his feet in a moment, and the next moment another warrior, mounted on the fleetest of ponies, was at his side, and with one leap the dismounted warrior placed himself astride the pony of his companion; and thus doubly burdened, the gallant little steed, with his no less gallant riders, galloped lightly away with about 80 cavalrymen, mounted on strong domestic horses, in full cry after them.

There is no doubt but that by all the laws of chance the cavalry should have been able to soon overhaul and capture the Indians in so unequal a race; but whether from lack of zeal on the part of the officer commanding the pursuit, or from the confusion created by the diversion attempted by the remaining Indians, the pony, doubly weighted as he was, distanced his pursuers and landed his burden in a place of safety.

Although chagrined at the failure of the pursuing party to accomplish the capture of the Indians, I could not wholly suppress a feeling of satisfaction, if not gladness, that for once the Indian had eluded the white man. I need not add that any temporary tenderness of feeling toward the two Indians was prompted by their individual daring and the heroic display of comradeship in the successful attempt to render assistance to a friend in need. [12]

After fierce fighting in the Killdeer Mountains the Sioux retreated into the Little Missouri badlands behind. Again their abandoned camp with winter food supplies and provisions was destroyed by Sully's troops.

The military force then headed for the Yellowstone River where steamboats with supplies awaited them. They pushed through the badlands in a difficult trail with little feed because of drouth and under continual attack from the Indians. A soldier wrote his family that water was very scarce. "The weather very hot . . . a hard road. A great part looks as though it had been burned in a furnace."

General Sully called the badlands, "Hell with the fires out."

The two big campaigns of 1863 and 1864 against the Sioux actually accomplished little but to increase Indian bitterness at the injustice of punishing many who were innocent for the crimes of a few. They tended to stir up even more trouble in Indian country.

Besieged wagons hold out behind ramparts of sod

Before Sully arrived back at Ft. Rice he was called to help Captain James Fisk who was escorting an 80-wagon immigrant train bound for Montana gold fields through Dakota with a cavalry escort. The train was under attack by a band of Hunkpapa Sioux near what is now Rhame.

The attack began September 1 when a wagon overturned in a creek bottom. Instead of halting the entire party, Fisk left another wagon and eight troopers to set it upright while the wagon train continued west.

Watching, the Indians dashed down on the two wagons killing 12 men. Fisk heard shots, turned back and the Indians retreated. Jefferson Dilts—a scout for whom the site is named—was returning from scouting the badlands and unluckily rode right into the path of the retreating Sioux. He was badly wounded, later died and was buried with others under the sod wall of the fort Fisk's party built.

The immigrant train continued about 10 miles under fire from a big war party of Indians, and made camp. Before breaking camp next morning they left out a box of hardtack laced with poison, hoping to discourage further attack. They moved on three miles where they plowed sod and built a defensive fort with walls six feet high, large enough to encircle their wagons and livestock.

The Indians kept up their attack, but volunteers were able to escape by night and rode to Ft. Rice for help. At one point the Indians set up a flag of truce with a note from a captive they held, Mrs. Kelly, stating they wished 40 head of cattle, that many had died of the poison, and a personal plea to "try to free me for mercy's sake."

On September 17 additional troops arrived, but the Indians had already gone, seeing the immigrant train defenses were too strong for easy victory.

Makatunke says he will not fight wagons, but they have been fighting two days. They had many men killed by the goods (poisoned hardtack) . . . They say for the soldiers to give forty head of cattle . . . Be kind to them, and try to free me for mercy's sake.

Fanny Kelly

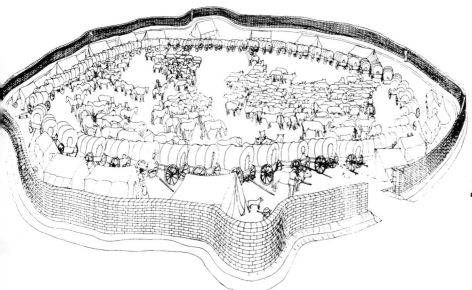

'A hard road... hell with the fires out.'

Trapped immigrants built sod wall around wagons and animals at Fort Dilts

Army seeks control of Indian matters

The government built ever more forts to control the Indians, to protect steamboat traffic and overland wagon trains. Sitting Bull's band of Hunkpapas (of Teton Sioux) led resistance and tried to induce peaceful bands to join them. They killed mail carriers, ambushed hunters and small parties of soldiers and miners, fired on steamboats, harrassed wood details near the forts and stole cattle and horses, but did not directly attack the forts.

In 1868 the Ft. Laramie treaty was signed—"to settle the Indian problem for all time." The Sioux were given full rights to a vast area roughly bounded by the Missouri, North Platte, and Yellowstone. No white man was allowed to trespass and the U.S. agreed to destroy three military forts in the area in exchange for peace. It was a triumph for the Sioux and illustrated General John Pope's contention that the Indian bureau policy was to reward hostile Indians but not peaceful ones. "It is a common saying with the Sioux, that whenever they are poor, and need powder and lead, they have only to go down to the overland routes and murder a few white men and they will have a treaty to supply their wants."

Dr. Best, agency doctor at Ft. Berthold, believed the Indians were well equal to the challenge of meeting whites in council. "The Indian is an attentive listener," he said. "Noting carefully every word spoken to him. His remarks are brief, concise and directly to the point . . . Some of them are really orators and astonish you with their logic. One of the best speakers in the councils here is Good Bear, second chief of the Gros Ventres. He is a fluent speaker, his black eyes sparkling, words falling from his lips quick and fast, and his logic is good. He can recall any promises the whites ever made them, even quoting their own language."

General Pope, commander of the Division of the Missouri, was convinced the treaty system and other Indian bureau policies benefited neither white nor Indian, attracting as they did the worst elements of white society—the whiskey seller, crooked Indian agents in league with greedy post traders—and nearly unlimited opportunities for graft and exploitation of the Indian. His recommendations for switching Indian affairs to the war department were laid before Congress.

Fort Berthold became the military outpost longest in use in state, occupied for 28 years.

Most other military leaders agreed. De Trobriand said, "There is only one remedy for this evil; transfer all the administration of Indian affairs to the war department; replace the agents with quartermasters from the frontier posts under control of higher authorities, and then the government will save millions and will easily live in peace with the Indians . . . Living by corruption, the Indian Bureau maintains itself by corruption, and God only knows when Congress will shake loose from its venal influence and put an end to its career of spoilation."

The policy was strongly supported and argued in Congress, but the lobby, which General Custer called the third house of Congress, had more influence. "The lobby," said Custer, "is so powerful that almost any measure it is interested in becomes law." One of the strongest lobbies was assembled, in his belief, when the question of interfering with the system of civilian superintendents, agents and traders for the Indians arose.

"Why this determined opposition? I made this inquiry years ago and the answer then, equally applicable now: 'There is too much money in the Indian question to allow it to pass into other hands.'

Fort Totten, established as Indian agency and military fort in 1867, still serves as reservation agency

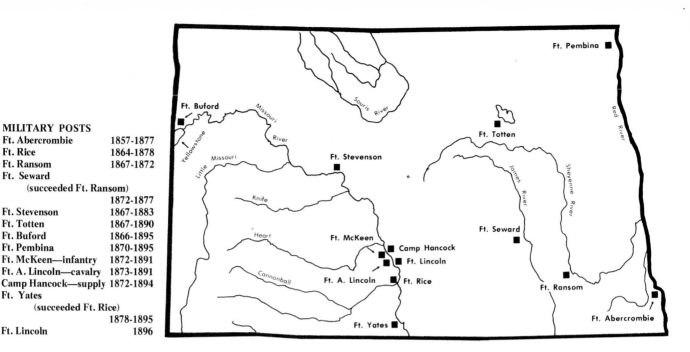

"It seems almost incredible that a policy which is claimed and represented to be based on sympathy for the red man and a desire to secure to him his rights, is shaped in reality and manipulated behind the scenes with the distinct and sole object of reaping a rich harvest by plundering both the government and the Indians. To do away with the vast army of agents, traders, and civilian employees which is a necessary appendage of the civilian policy, would be to deprive many members of Congress of a vast deal of patronage which they now enjoy. There are few more comfortable or desirable places of disposing of a friend who has rendered valuable political service or electioneering aid, than to secure for him the appointment of Indian agent. The salary of an agent is comparatively small. Men without means, however, eagerly accept the position; and in a few years, at furthest, they almost invariably retire in wealth . . . How do they realize fortunes upon so small a salary?"

The military were unable to prevent the acts of injustice and exploitation they observed because they had authority to act only against Indian hostilities. The civil officers had control of the Indians in peace; the army in war. Observed Custer, "While the army is fighting the Indians at one end of the line, Indian agents are making treaties and furnishing supplies at the other end." Further, he said, agents were eager to make treaties since the more treaties an Indian agent could negotiate, the larger the appropriation of money and goods that passed through his hands; the agent would like nothing better than an Indian war every other day with treaty-making on intermediate days.

Custer and other officers insisted that the Indians preferred to deal with the military since they could believe what the commanders told them, and understood that the army had power to fulfill promises.

But for their part, the army, too, had problems. They had a difficult and critical public. When they failed to catch and punish Indians who raided the frontier the settlers were angry; when they did, they were attacked by humanitarians throughout the country. But accusations that the army and the frontiersmen were anxious to get up an Indian war were totally false, said Custer: No one had more dread of an Indian war or was more willing to sacrifice to avoid its horrors.

The military did not have a clean record for competency. Trobriand took to task his officers at both Ft. Totten and Ft. Buford for drunkenness and their petty charges of assault and counter-assault. Despite his recommendations these officers were able to maintain their positions. "And it is thus that justice is sacrificed to favor," he said.

The Ft. Laramie treaty quickly became impossible to honor. The Civil War was ended; people were on the move west, reaching for new frontiers and new opportunities. There were constant violations of trespass. Indians retaliated.

A herd of 250 beef cattle under guard near Ft. Buford was swooped down upon and stampeded into the Missouri breaks. The infantry marched out to the rescue and fought Indians for three hours, but could not turn back more than about 50 of the beeves. Three soldiers were killed and three wounded. Next day three companies of infantry and a party on horseback searched the breaks east as far as the mouth of the Little Missouri to recapture their cattle, but only 57 could be found, most of them wounded. Today's ranchers may find it inconceivable that 200 head of cattle could disappear so quickly, even hardy grown-out steers. But most of the pursuers were on foot and the mounted men were too few to range far in advance of the infantry in hostile country. Also, and probably most telling, was the incompetent and quarrelsome leadership at Ft. Buford. Several officers were under court martial and one of them, Major Little, had to be released from arrest so he could command the infantry that scoured the Missouri breaks for the cattle.

Dakota Territory was no place for the careless. Daring mail couriers, often Metis, carried the mail between the forts every two weeks. Periodically they were ambushed, hacked to pieces, scalped. Sometimes the military sent armed escort. De Trobriand describes, in some annoyance, the ambush of an escorted mail wagon in which three soldiers were killed west of Ft. Totten.

"The men had unhitched the mules from the wagon . . . at midday at Big Coulee . . . and with the blind imprudence which is characteristic of the soldier left to himself where there is no danger evident, they had left their weapons in the wagon. The sergeant had not placed any sentinel, thus disobeying the orders given him. That disobedience cost him his life, as well as those of his two men.

"Six Indians ambushed near there, seeing how our men neglected to protect themselves . . . had slipped up the slope and then crawled behind a large rock. From this point they fired at a distance of 20 paces on the group of soldiers who were nonchalantly eating their dinner, sitting on the ground near the unhitched wagon. Not one of them had his gun. The arms were all in the wagon.

"One of the couriers who had just gone to water his horse at the neighboring spring and who had taken his carbine with him had, for this act, been the butt of the soldiers' jokes. 'So he's afraid the Indians are coming to attack him?'. . . Scarcely five minutes had passed before three of the jokers were struck dead by Indian bullets.

"If the sergeant had only placed a man on watch at the edge of the plateau, not an Indian could have approached without being seen, for the ravine is as bare as your hand, and there is not a bush where a rabbit could hide.

"But the Indians . . . saw right away that our men did not have their weapons and that they were not keeping watch . . . it is probable that they figured they would come up as friends to exchange handshakes and beg some bits of provisions if they were discovered. But everything going as they wished, they fired their shots and fled, running away with the mules.

"The other three ran for their arms, but it was too late. They could fire only from a distance on the assailants, who fled, taking advantage of the depressions in the ground." [13]

Tobriand felt most Indians were tired of war and ready to make peace by 1868, except for a few who were continually trying to involve the peaceful Indians in hostilities. "This band of incorrigible Unkpapahs is led by four or five chiefs, such as Dark Moon, Red Horn, Four Horns and Sitting Bull."

Tobriand was right: Sitting Bull was not ready to come in and make peace.

"We cannot dwell side by side," he told his followers. "These people claim this mother of ours, the earth, for their own and fence their neighbors away; they deface her with their buildings and their refuse. Their nation is like a spring freshet that overruns its banks and destroys all who are in its path." He was on the warpath almost continuously from 1868 through 1876 when he made medicine at the battle of the Little Big Horn, and did not surrender until 1881.

'Ye Can't Fight Injuns in an Ambulance'

"SEE H'YAR, GENERAL, in order that we hev no misonderstandin', I'd jest like to ask ye a few questions . . . Are you an ambulance man ur a hoss man? Do you b'leve in catchin' Injuns in ambulances or on horseback?"

"Well, Joe, I believe in catching Indians wherever we can find them, whether they are found in ambulances or on horseback."

This did not satisfy the scout. "That ain't what I'm drivin' at. S'pose you're after Injuns and really wanted to hev a tussle with 'em, would ye start after 'em on hossback, or would ye climb into an ambulance and be haulded after 'em? That's the pint I'm headin' fur."

Gen. Custer answered that he would prefer the method on horseback "provided I really desired to catch the Indians—but if I wished them to catch me, I would adopt the ambulance system of attack."

"You've hit the nail squar on the hed. I've bin with 'em on the plains whar they started out after the Injuns on wheels, jist as ef they war goin' to a town funeral in the States, an' they stood 'bout as many chances uv catchin' Injuns az a six-mule team wud uv catchin' a pack of thievin' ki-o-tees, jist as much. Why that sort uv work is only fun fur the Injuns; they don't want anything better. Ye ort to've seen how they peppered it to us, an' we a doin' nuthin' a' the time. Sum uv 'em wuz 'fraid the mules war goin' to stampede and run off with the train an' all our forage and grub, but that wuz impossible; fur besides the big loads uv corn an' bacon an' baggage, thar war from eight to a dozen infantry men piled into the wagons besides. Ye ort to hev heard the quartermaster in charge uv the train tryin' to drive the infantry men out of the wagons and git them into the fight."

from **My Life On the Plains**, George A. Custer

"Count me in for the Black Hills!

There ain't bed room enough for the people who will come . . . nor has Uncle Sam military enough to stop them."

Custer's Seventh Cavalry sets out for the Black Hills with 150 wagons

Custer's charisma led to death on a high knoll

Fort Abraham Lincoln was built for a cavalry post with George A. Custer in command and his wife, Libby, as charming hostess. Ft. Lincoln was a lively and gracious center of activity. One newspaper reporter expressed surprise that, despite what he had heard, the Custer home was one of a "cultured gentleman, instead of a roystering cavalryman, as is generally supposed." General Custer, said the reporter, does not drink, smoke nor swear—in spite of the prevailing belief in his intemperance. Instead, "he believes in and practices total abstinence. The good temperance teachers of the day can use him as an example rather than an object of regret."

Custer's actual rank during his Indian fighting days was Lieutenant Colonel. During the Civil War he had become major general; after the war with a surplus of military officers, his rank was reduced. However, according to custom, he was called general by his men, fellow officers, newspapers and the public.

Custer was an effective military leader, a long-time veteran of Indian war. But he was a controversial figure—opinionated, vain, publicity-seeking. Frequently he was in trouble with the administration, acting without proper authority, and severely and publicly criticizing federal Indian policies.

A Chicago reporter, captivated by the charisma of General Custer, posed the question, "What are his vices?" And the answer, "His soldiers will tell you he has none, unless it is his inordinate love for . . . the best dogs . . . horses . . . and hunting. He has the reputation of being the best sportsman and the most accurate shot in the army." Much of Custer's charisma was his devotion to his men, his enthusiasm and vitality. He spent a great deal of time in writing.

In 1874 Custer was sent with 1200 troopers of the Seventh Cavalry and an enormous retinue of wagons, mules, cattle to investigate reports of gold in the Black Hills and violence between the Sioux and illegal gold miners.

This campaign was a clear violation of Sioux rights as established by the 1868 Ft. Laramie treaty. The government was under pressure to permit gold-seekers and home-seekers into the lovely Black Hills country. The Sioux were

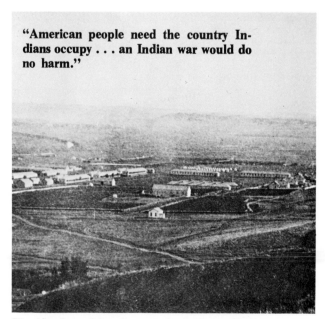

"American people need the country Indians occupy . . . an Indian war would do no harm."

Ft. Abraham Lincoln as it looked in 1876

Custer camped on Hiddenwood Creek, right, in 1874. Site as it is today, left, renamed Flat Creek by railroad, seen in background bordering grain fields.

'What are Custer's vices? His soldiers will tell you he has none.'

adamant—this was their religious home and they did not intend to give it up. The military had attempted to keep miners out but this was not too successful and many had already been attacked and killed. Resultant publicity had the nation in an uproar: On the one hand were forces violently defending the Indian rights; on the other were those in an outrage at the bloody attacks on whites. Gold fever added excitement and urgency.

Bismarck newspapers were highly vocal in support of the miners. The town saw itself as the jumping-off place for the Black Hills, with much to gain by a gold rush.

"This is God's country," proclaimed the Bismarck Tribune. "He peopled it with red men and planted it with wild grasses and permitted the white man to gain a foothold; and as the wild grasses disappear when the white clover gain a footing, so the Indian disappears before the advance of the white man . . . The American people need the country the Indians now occupy; many of our people are out of employment: the masses need some new excitement. The war is over, and the era of railroad building has been brought to a termination by the greed of capitalists . . . and depression prevails on every hand. An Indian war would do no harm, for it must come, sooner or later."

Gen. George Custer

At the same time the newspapers encouraged the miners. "Today there is forming on the banks of the Missouri an expedition consisting of from 75 to 100 of as brave boys as ever drew bead on a red-skin, to be led by the redoubtable Chris Gilson, and sworn to visit the Black Hills and report . . . Those who wish to go with Gilson should apply to him at once at Bismarck." [14]

The Custer expedition to the Black Hills was no small operation:

"A train of 150 wagons . . . each drawn by six mules, making a mule herd of no less than 900. The cavalry battalion requires about 1000 horses, and a herd of 300 beeves, which will be driven with the train . . . and 2000 men, including civilians."

It moved slowly, sometimes through difficult terrain as in the Little Missouri badlands after turning west from Hiddenwood Creek.

"General Custer is a famous road maker, and to him . . . as to the great Napoleon, nothing is impassable. Reaching a place that has to be bridged, the General selects the most available point and with a shovel in his hand he directs and assists at the work himself. If cobblestones and sod or willow branches and rushes will not make a roadbed the train master cries 'poles,' and every teamster brings the extra wagon tongue he always carries with him and lays it devotedly down at the General's feet." [15]

WE HAVE SUFFERED and panted through a march of 20 miles to enjoy this balmy evening and beautiful spot—the most beautiful in varied scenery of any we have yet seen. This place, the only timber in a radius of 30 miles, is called Pahachechacha, or Hidden Wood, by the Indians, because the hills so cluster around it that the trees cannot be seen two miles away—one of the few shady oases in this desert of prairie land, and very grateful after a week's marching. For a background a sunset as gorgeously beautiful as any that ever glowed . . . and a high, jagged bluff, covered with clusters of trees, with a clear stream of water running at its base; in the foreground a smooth grassy plain covered with tents, hooded wagons, and grazing horses; a band in the center playing familiar airs, and an atmosphere cool, fresh, and bracing—and you have a picture of our camp to-night. 16

Custer sent back reports of gold. The flood of prospectors could no longer be stemmed. There was some doubt as to how much gold was in fact there, but the Chicago Inter-Ocean stated the general acceptance of gold rush, "The Sioux must leave their hunting grounds in the Black Hills . . . There is gold in the hills and rivers of the region, and the white man desires to take possession of it. What, to the roaming Yankee, are the links that bind the red man to the home of his fathers? He is but an episode in the advance of the Caucasian. He must decrease that the newcomers may grow in wealth."

For three years gold seekers scoured the Black Hills before the gold fever died out. The Bismarck Tribune repeatedly warned people from entering the Hills from a southern route, "as they would be compelled to pass through a country swarming with Indians, and beset with dangers on every hand. Below will be found an article clipped from the last Sioux City Journal in which is detailed the troubles of Frank Stone and party . . . one of whom was killed, one mortally wounded, and the remainder bruised and wounded."

When thousands of miners and others overran the Black Hills the government attempted to get the Sioux to cede their lands. They refused and many fled westward. Fearing an outbreak of Indian war, the Commissioner of Indian Affairs in December 1875, ordered all Sioux to report to their agencies by the end of January. This was an impossibility for peaceful Indians in the middle of winter; many barely got the message by that time and the Indians customarily made winter camp and traveled little until spring. Hostile bands made no attempt to comply.

This was the final decisive year of Indian resistance. In early June, 1876, a force of Sioux and Cheyenne routed General Crook on Rosebud Creek in eastern Montana. A bigger force of military might was already on the way and did not learn of Crook's defeat until much later.

In May General Terry set forth from Fort Lincoln with 1000 cavalrymen (600 of them seventh cavalrymen under the command of Custer), infantrymen, and a Gatling gun detachment, and plans to meet up with another large force of infantry on the Yellowstone River.

Custer almost missed the Battle of the Little Big Horn—which would have undoubtedly been a bitter disappointment for him. In deep trouble with President Grant, he had testified at a Congressional investigation in Washington against the graft that involved members of Grant's family and administration. Grant attempted to remove him from his command, but Custer pleaded with his superior officers to intervene and was sent back to Ft. Lincoln.

Libby Custer rode out from Ft. Lincoln with the Seventh Cavalry. "The general could scarcely restrain his recurring joy at being again with his regiment, from which he had feared he might be separated by being detained on other duty," she said. "At every bend of the road, as the column wound its way round and round the low hills, my husband glanced back to admire his men . . . The soldiers, inured to many years of hardship, were the perfection of physical manhood. Their resolute faces, brave and confident, inspired one with the feeling that they were going out aware of the momentous hours awaiting them, but inwardly assured of their capability to meet them."

The wives did not share this confidence. "When our band struck up 'The Girl I Left Behind Me,' the most despairing hour seemed to have come. All the sad-faced wives of the officers who had forced themselves to their doors to try and wave a courageous farewell, and smile bravely to keep the one they loved from knowing the anguish of their breaking hearts, gave up the struggle at the sound of the music . . ."[17]

The expedition halted for a day near the Little Missouri. Custer breakfasted at 4 a.m., took four companies of cavalry and a group of scouts and rode 50 miles up the river to investigate rumors of a big band of hostile Indians gathered there. It was no doubt during this halt that two seventh cavalrymen left a record of their fateful march by carving their names in the sandstone rock.

That evening Custer wrote his wife. "I am determined to sit up, even though it is ten o'clock and write to you, notwithstanding I have had a tremendous day's work . . . we marched the 50 miles and got back before dark, having settled the question beyond doubt that all stories about large bodies of Indians being here are the merest bosh. None have been here for six months . . . We found the Little Missouri River so crooked and the Bad Lands so impassable that in marching 50 miles today we forded the river 34 times. The bottom is quicksand. Many of the horses went down, frequently tumbling their riders into the water; but

all were in good spirits, and every one laughed at everyone else's mishaps . . . I have about made up my mind that when I go on expeditions like this you are to go, too. You could have endured this as well as not."

"I now have some Crow scouts with me as they are familiar with the country." wrote Custer **on June 12.** "They are magnificent-looking men and so jolly and sportive . . . They have formally given themselves to me, after the usual talk. In their speech they said they had heard that I never abandoned a trail; that when my food gave out I ate mule. That was the kind of a man they wanted to fight under; they were willing to eat mule, too."

On June 22 he wrote what was to be his last letter to his wife:

Do not be anxious about me. You would be surprised to know how closely I obey your instructions about keeping with the column. I hope to have a good report to send you by the next mail—A success will start us all towards Lincoln . . .[18]

Three days later, on June 25, Custer's scouts reported a large camp of Indians ahead. Without waiting the two or three days needed for Terry and Gibbon's infantry forces to come up the river to join them, as planned, Custer decided to attack. Dividing his forces to attack from three points in a strategy he'd used with success before, Custer led some 200 men down a long draw right into the hands of hundreds of Sioux and Cheyenne warriors ready and waiting for him. Too late he realized his mistake, sent back a messenger with a desperate call for help, attempted to take command of the crest of a knoll.

The battle was brief. Fort Lincoln's daring yellow-haired general met and was quickly vanquished by superior forces marshalled by—among others—Dakota's most famous native son, Sitting Bull. Sitting Bull was no longer a war chief but a powerful medicine maker and had seen his own vision of the battle's outcome.

Much has been written of the Battle of the Little Big Horn. Major Reno was severely censured for not coming to Custer's rescue, though under Indian attack himself. Custer has been called an incompetent soldier, a glory-hunter, needlessly risking his men.

Undoubtedly one of Custer's main concerns in deciding not to wait for the slow-moving infantry, aside from the possibility of gaining personal glory, was a fear that the Indian camp would disperse into dozens of small parties traveling swiftly in separate directions. Like most military men he had had the experience of observing even large Indian camps disappear as if by magic at the distant approach of soldiers, not to be seen again. But his poor use of scouts is difficult to understand in a leader of his experience.

Certain it is that had Custer been an "ambulance man" instead of a "hoss man" the battle would not have been fought in the way that it was.

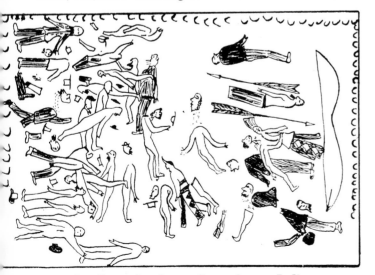

After the Custer battle, as drawn by an Indian witness. Horseshoe framing indicates it was a cavalry division.

'The red man is but an episode in the advance of the Caucasian. He must decrease that the newcomers may grow in wealth.'

Indians return from a pow-wow, colorful feather bustle at rear of wagon. Top photo shows a reservation home, tent behind; mission church.

On the reservation there was disease, poverty

Indian victory at Little Big Horn was short-lived. The Indians scattered. Sitting Bull and his bands fled to Canada. The U.S. Army, both cavalry and infantry, launched all-out assault and the non-submissive Indians were beaten decisively in a series of skirmishes. Starving, desperate, disheartened, they straggled back to their now-shrunken reservations.

There they lost most of their traditional freedoms and had to live under the fickle thumb of government and the Indian agent. Guns and horses were taken from them and every effort was made to induce them to farm and to forego Indian ways. Children were sent to live—sometimes for an entire year—at mission schools where "talking Indian" was forbidden. So began another era: reservation life.

Not until 1881 did Sitting Bull and his followers return from Canada to surrender. James McLaughlin who had distinguished himself as an Indian agent at Ft. Totten was transferred to Standing Rock to deal with them. McLaughlin writes:

> On the day that I arrived, Sept. 8, 1881, Sitting Bull and 146 of the more turbulent of his followers were taken down the Missouri River to be held prisoners at Fort Randall . . . and I was left to deal with nearly 6000 Indians, over half of whom had been out with Sitting Bull in active hostility for several years . . . [19]

It was a hard year for Sitting Bull's people, said McLaughlin. They were far gone with poverty and disease when they came in, and died at a high rate. They were fed "as well as the means provided would allow," but did not accept white man's medicine.

The next year McLaughlin accompanied his Sioux charges on their last great buffalo hunt, on the banks of Hiddenwood Creek, some 100 miles west, where an estimated 50,000 buffalo—the last of the vast northern herd—were ranging.

Two thousand Indians, with 600 of them hunters, all dressed in their finest clothing and decorations went on the hunt. "The plains of Dakota had not for many years seen so resplendent a gathering of these people as that which moved out of Standing Rock just after dawn on the tenth of June, 1882," said McLaughlin.

On the first day 2000 buffalo were killed, on the second they were butchered, and on the third 3000 more were killed. "The slaughter had been awful but not wanton," said the agent. "I was impressed with the fact that the Indian displays more restraint in hunting, even though his desire to kill makes his blood boil, than the white man. I never have known an Indian to kill a game animal that he did not require for his needs. And I have known few white hunters to stop while there was game to kill. The hunt stopped when 5000 buffalo had been slain."

It was a time of feasting and rejoicing. "The great hunters . . . head men of the Sioux Nation . . . were all in that hunt and at peace on the banks of the Hidden Wood Creek that night."[20]

But all was not well with the reservation Indians. They were helpless in the face of disease, living in a closed-up house instead of the airy teepees without proper sanitation, forced to change to an unfamiliar diet. Tuberculosis and other diseases became common.

McLaughlin believed that the Indian bureau policy of holding all the purse strings—still a policy today—was a poor one. "I believe (the task of improving life for the Indian) will be accomplished soonest by giving the Indian his portion and letting him solve the problem himself . . . the government became his banker for the enormous amount of wealth that **is his curse today**—a veritable mine from which he may take only enough to keep body and soul

Instead of hunting wild game, Indians were issued beef, as in photo of beef issue day on Standing Rock reservation (right).

together while loafing between payments . . . These immense holdings are being doled out to the Indians by a pauperizing system in sums inadequate to their needs, yet sufficient to give the sense of being provided for."

And there were still treaties that had to be made.

Then came a new religion, Ghost dancing, which spread rapidly through the reservations and gave hope to the Indians that the whites would pass away and the earth be made new with sweet grass and herds of buffalo for God's chosen people: the Indians. The message was not of violence, but whites who watched the constant trancelike Ghost dancing were struck with fear that this was a new kind of war dance. McLaughlin and others feared a general uprising, and especially feared Sitting Bull who took up the new religion wholeheartedly and had a great influence on his people.

Sitting Bull, perhaps Dakota's most famous son, was a great spiritual leader of the Sioux. He had led resistance against white encroachment longer than any other and submitted only when his people were starving to death. He made a tour with Buffalo Bill's Wild West Show, to an often-unfriendly audience. Now it was decided he must be arrested and imprisoned again. Forty Indian policemen were sent to bring him in before daylight on Dec. 15, 1890. At first Sitting Bull submitted, then he shouted to his

people and shots rang out. When it was over Sitting Bull, five policemen, and seven other Indians were dead.

McLaughlin, who was much criticized for his handling of the arrest, had Sitting Bull buried in the Ft. Yates cemetery not far from the Indian policemen killed at the same time.

But Sitting Bull remained a tragic, controversial figure in death as in life. In 1953 a group of white Mobridge, South Dakota citizens came in the night and removed his bones to a new tourist-oriented site near Mobridge. The grave was not well-tended at Ft. Yates, they claimed. According to Sitting Bull's great-grandson, two cement trucks stood ready and the coffin was lowered to a wooden platform so concrete would flow freely above and below, encasing it permanently.

"They should not have done that," the grandson says. "They should have left his bones alone—not used them for a tourist attraction."

As a final irony, the Oahe dam floodwaters forced relocation of the bridge leading to the Mobridge gravesite and it is no longer of easy access for tourists.

Today's Reservations

Turtle Mt.

Ft. Berthold

Ft. Totten

Standing Rock

Sisseton

Indian lands established in North Dakota by treaties

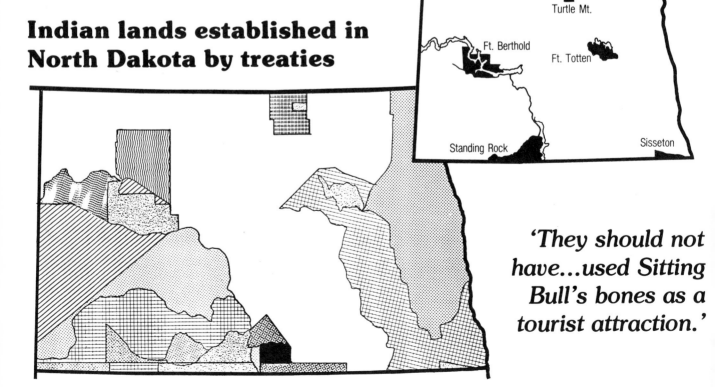

'They should not have...used Sitting Bull's bones as a tourist attraction.'

110

He could neither Understand nor cope...

Girls in 'white' dress at teepee

With all these unknown and unnamed ills beating them into the earth, the Indians sat supine, waiting for the coming of that day in which they would live and thrive as the white man lived and throve. They had been told that they would be as white men if they obeyed the agents of the Great Father . . . the Indian . . . came to know that just before he reached the fatal point in the process of starvation, the government would come to his rescue and, if he was not content, he was passive under conditions he could neither understand nor cope with . . . He was by turns browbeaten and cajoled, bribed and punished, threatened and rewarded, and all of the worst elements in his character developed for want of firm, consistent, and honest treatment.

—James McLaughlin

Indian Treaties involving North Dakota land

1851—Sioux, Cheyenne, Arapaho, Crow, Assiniboine, Gros Ventre (Hidatsa), Mandan, Arikara
1863—Chippewa (Red Lake and Pembina)
1867—Sioux (Sisseton and Wahpeton)
    Acts of Congress: 1872, 1873, 1874
1868—Sioux
1870—Arikara, Gros Ventre, Mandan
1872—Sioux (Wahpeton, Sisseton)
1875—Sioux
1876—Sioux, Northern Cheyenne, Arapaho
1876—Sioux
1879—Sioux
1880—Arikara, Gros Ventre, Mandan
1882—Chippewa (Turtle Mt.)
1883—Sioux
1884—Chippewa (Turtle Mt.)
1889—Standing Rock Sioux
1891—Gros Ventre and Mandan
1891—Sioux (Sisseton, Wahpeton)

Sitting Bull, a tragic figure, here with Buffalo Bill

Legend says Standing Rock, left, is kneeling woman with child abandoned in camp

Right, Mission School: 'talking Indian' was forbidden

Dakota Territory and the Making of a State

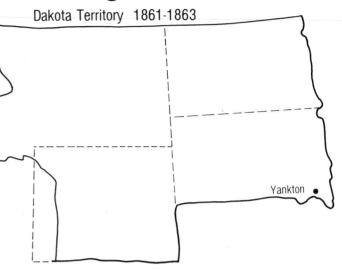

Dakota Territory 1861-1863

Yankton

Dakota Territory, 1861: it was later cropped and in 1889 cut into four states.

Dakota Territory was organized in 1861. The new governor ventured west for the first time, took census and discovered 76 whites living in what is now North Dakota. Over 1000 whites lived in the southeastern corner of the new territory, so he chose the settlement of Yankton as territorial capital.

But when Bismarck got the railroad and vied with Yankton for river traffic, she also began a campaign to get the capital moved. Working to this end were two powerful forces: Alexander McKenzie, master politician, and the Northern Pacific Railroad, coveting the capital for its main line. Besides, Yankton was located down in one corner: southern Dakotans were not entirely satisfied; northern Dakota territorial delegates most often had to go there by way of St. Paul.

Under vigorous Yankton protest, a nine-man commission was organized to consider nine towns. Each had to promise $100,000 and 160 acres of land. With McKenzie leadership, Bismarck mustered the political power to wrest the capital away from Yankton, and began at once to build the new capitol building. The first territorial convention held there voted to move the capital to Pierre, but the governor vetoed the bill.

The distance was too great for southern Dakotans and, wearied with being held under control of federal appointees, they pushed for statehood. Populations grew well past the required minimums but statehood was blocked politically until 1889, when Congress admitted four states together: North Dakota, South Dakota, Montana, and Washington.

A constitutional convention was called in Bismarck to determine organization of the new state. The major struggle was between the Dakota Farmers' Alliance, trying to limit corporation powers, and the corporation interests, strongly represented by McKenzie. McKenzie continued for many years to be a figure of political power and controversy in the state. A former railroad construction worker, he died a millionaire, but spent one term in federal prison for political manipulations in Alaska.

The convention did four things in creating North Dakota's constitution, according to historian Elwyn Robinson:

● Constructed a defective framework for state government;
● Provided wisely for management of state lands;
● Tried unsuccessfully to control corporations in the public interest;
● Guaranteed amply a free and democratic society.

The constitution gave only cautious power to the governor, with executive branch heads to be elected, not appointed. Some of the checks imposed on the legislature, especially on taxation and debt, have hampered its effectiveness.

Bismarck retained the capital—fortunately, since it is centrally located, though that reason was only incidental. The "spoils"—14 institutions—were scattered expensively throughout the state.

Prohibition passed separately by a slim margin and North Dakota went dry, though bootlegging and "blind pig" activity flourished in many communities.

Bismarck in 1880 . . . a few false-front stores

Aerial view of Capitol, 1925, as it was 1883-1930

Cowboys camped with herd in McKenzie County

Branding big stock in 1911

By 1916 chutes made branding easier

Cattle soon stocked rich north ranges

First trainload of cattle from Reeder stockyards, 1908

Beef cattle first came to Dakota in the '60's to supply military forts. Daily they were taken out to graze, under constant guard, lest a quick swoop by Hunkpapa Sioux steal them away. These were never cow-calf operations; when the beeves were all butchered, one after the other to supply the mess, a new herd of 300 or so was requisitioned and driven up from Kansas or booked passage on a Missouri River steamer.

Buffalo by the tens of thousands had fattened on the tough nutritious northern grasses; with their near-extinction the vast grasslands lay vacant. But not for long.

Hoofbeats soon pounded up the Texas Trail on the Long Drive. Thousands upon thousands of cattle trailed north until they perhaps equalled the buffalo herds of old. These were not cow-calf operations either at first, but big herds of steers, yearlings or two-year-olds, coming north to grow out and fatten for market. Northern winters were considered too cold for cows.

Several famous old trails cut into western North Dakota, branched out, and spread onto new cattle ranges. One of the first Texas herds into North Dakota was trail-bossed by J. H. Cook in 1876, moving 2500 longhorn steers from the Nueces of southern Texas through western Dakota up to Missouri River country, according to Bowman County history. Others soon followed: Hashknife of the Continental Land and Cattle Company, the Mill Iron, the Long X, the Deffenbach brothers, the Dickeys, M. C. Connors.

The grass may have seemed scant to the newcomers.

Bill Sewall, visiting the badlands, wrote home, "You would think the cattle would starve here, but all the cattle that have wintered here are fat now and they say that cattle brought here from any other part will improve in size and quality."

Texas steers did indeed begin to grow when they hit hardy northern ranges. Southern cattlemen were enthusiastic and soon agreed that the longhorn brought here as a yearling, or even a two, grew out 200 pounds heavier when ready for market at five or six years old, than did those which stayed south. Northern plains grasses also cured on the stem for grazing all winter, except in years of deep snow.

The steers needed little care. They could be trailed north in herds of a thousand or more—sometimes in sight of the dust of other trail herds ahead and behind them—turned loose on free grass with a few cowboys posted in line camps to keep them thrown into the general range which was the owner's by prior right and common consent. When grown out and fat they were trailed to the nearest railroad town and shipped to market.

Montana cattlemen were trailing their beef to Bismarck by 1879. By then eastern cattle, "pilgrims" as they were called, were coming in by rail to stock Dakota ranges—and it was discovered that a cow could survive northern winters on the range and raise a healthy calf come spring.

The Texas outfits which trailed north were usually financed by eastern or foreign investors, and were big operations. Hashknife ran 60,000 head of cattle. The OX and the Long X each ran 15,000. Texans established about three-fourths of the open-range spreads in North Dakota, according to historian Erling Rolfsrud. There were big losses, big expenses, big profits.

Smaller ranches, too, began to multiply. Cattle from the east often stocked small-sized ranches of 200 to 300 cows. Cowboys who came north on the Long Drive often stayed to build up their own ranches.

One of these cowboys was Tom Stevens of Arkansas. He left Texas in 1895 with 15 other cowboys and 3200 head of

Driving cattle in a blizzard, Einar A. Olstad painting; disastrous winter of 1886-1887 broke many cattlemen.

longhorns for the Reynolds Cattle Company. They were trailed to the railroad, loaded on stock cars and shipped to Oran Junction, Wyoming, where they were unloaded and trailed on to the company ranch 80 miles north of Dickinson. Many of these cattle, dehorned before the drive, died on the way from maggots. Stevens stayed with the North Dakota herd for three years, then returned to marry a Texas girl. Tom and Mollie returned to the Cedar River country south of Dickinson where they went into partnership on the 66 Bar and ran cattle until 1905—when the homesteaders came. Then they, too, took a homestead as there was no longer any range for their cattle.

Ranching boomed throughout the western half of North Dakota during the early '80's. Some stockmen bought railroad sections in checkerboard fashion to alternate with public lands they used and—since it was not practical to fence around single sections—when they were forced into fencing, they fenced in the public lands with the private. To the north the Mouse River Horse and Cattle Company was one of the largest; the big Diamond C ran south of the Killdeer Mountains; the biggest cow outfit on the range, the Turkey Track, extended up into southern North Dakota along the Grand River.

Theodore Roosevelt established his ranching career here in 1883 with two ranches—Chimney Butte (branding Maltese Cross) and the Elkhorn. Although he owned no land at all, he ran up to 5000 cattle. Roosevelt had come west to hunt buffalo that fall and purchased a ranching

Roundup camp in western North Dakota.

interest with 400 head of cattle. In February both his wife and his mother died in the same night and, disheartened, he came west again and threw himself into the ranching business.

Later he said, "I never would have been President if it had not been for my experiences in North Dakota."

Years later local ranchers remembered with affection his game attempts to learn the cowboying business and his modest claim: "I can now do cowboy work pretty well." Not everyone agreed with that, but ranch country was used to dudes, tenderfeet, and foreign or eastern owners who arrived on rare occasions to inspect their cattle enterprises and Roosevelt was respected for his energy, enthusiasm, and efforts on behalf of the cattle industry. He in turn respected the men he worked with, called them brave and hospitable, but "there is no use in trying to be overbearing with them for they won't stand the least assumption of superiority."

Roosevelt made a valuable contribution to local ranching by helping create the Little Missouri Stockmen's Association to seek solutions to pressing problems of the range. Most urgent problems were overgrazing, rustling, the ravages of wolves and coyotes, and organizing the fall round-ups.

The Marquis de Mores, a young French aristocrat married to the daughter of a wealthy New York banker, also came west in 1883 and immediately plunged into a series of expensive business ventures. He built a meat packing plant at a cost of $250,000, invested in thousands of cattle and sheep, ran a stagecoach from Medora to Deadwood, and founded a town across the river from Little Missouri which he named for his wife, Medora.

Overstocking continued to be a problem as more and more ranchers sought to crowd into the free range. Drouths in the south caused Texas outfits to move even more of their cattle up to northern ranges. By the summer of 1886 the Mandan Pioneer said:

"In certain sections of the West the losses this year are enormous, owing to the drouth and overstocking. Each steer needs from 15 to 25 acres, but they are crowded on very much thicker, and the cattlemen this season have paid the penalty . . . The days of excessive profits are over."

Then came the disastrous winter of 1886-1887 which began in November with heavy snow. Part of the snow melted in December, then froze back and formed a crust,

T Cross horse ranch operated by Harry Hadley

sealing off the grasses below. Thousands of cattle literally starved to death in the months of heavy snow and cold temperatures that followed. An estimated three-fourths of all the cattle in the northern plains were wiped out in that single winter. Many of the big cattle companies went broke and eastern financiers put their money into other investments. Roosevelt hung onto his ranching operation another 11 years trying to recoup a part of his losses. The De Mores packing plant closed for good that summer.

But the hard winter made Pierre Wibaux king of the range. He borrowed money to buy out surviving cattle until he reportedly owned 146 brands and 40,000 head of cattle. His range was along the Montana-North Dakota line, most of it in North Dakota.

A strong horse market developed to the east with heavy settlement throughout Minnesota and eastern Dakotas. Many western stockmen turned to raising horses. A. C. Huidekoper changed to horses, purchased Northern Pacific lands by the township, invested in Percheron stallions. Soon his HT ranch was raising the greatest number of purebred Percherons in the U.S. Other big horse ranches grew up with the need for good work horses, a market that did not decline until the increased use of machinery after World War II.

Wolves were a particular menace to horse ranching. Some years they took the entire colt crop of horse herds that ranged near rough country. Badlands offered good protection for wolves. They raised big litters and hunted in family bands of up to 12 or 15.

Sheep ranching was never as extensive in North Dakota as cattle and horse raising. But bands of sheep were herded in most parts of western Dakota except for the very rough country where the danger from predators was too great.

Wool wagons driven to Hettinger market, left; below, sheep band is moved to new camp southwest of Dickinson.

"Danger from coyotes and wolves was too great"

115

Few white hunters Stopped Shooting Until game was gone

Successful deer hunt on Maverick Flat, Dunn County, 1886, Frank Brennen and Robert Fisher

Big game hunting was big time in early-day North Dakota. When the railroad reached the town of Little Missouri, hunters poured in from all over. The country was a hunter's paradise. Local ranchers, too, gathered their winter supply of meat by the wagonload.

By this time the elk and the grizzlies were gone. Mountain lions, black bear, and wolves were rarely seen but still ravaged cattle and horse herds. The Audubon bighorn sheep, most prized of game animals, found capering the highest steepest bluffs—had only a few remaining years until total extinction. The last one in existence was killed near the Killdeer Mountains in 1905. Big rams, wrote Roosevelt, reached the weight of a small cow elk. Deer and antelope were abundant, but soon only remnant bunches of buffalo were left—and these were sitting ducks for whatever lean homesteader or line camp cowboy happened to sight them. They couldn't hide and they didn't try.

The bulk of the buffalo slaughter was done in the dozen years from 1872 to 1883. Bleached skeletons lay thick on the prairies. Said Roosevelt, "No sight is more common on the plains than that of a bleached buffalo skull." His friend who traveled a thousand miles across the northern plains reported that he had never been out of sight of a dead buffalo—nor had seen a live one—the entire distance.

The last buffalo hunt in Wells County was on a Sunday in late July 1882. Mr. Harris was holding religious services at the Sykes and Hughs ranch headquarters dining hall, when in rode the herder at a high gallop. "There's a buffalo grazing with the oxen," he announced to the worshipers.

Mr. Hughs quickly left the meeting and formed a party of buffalo hunters, all sportsmen and big game hunters.

They mounted their mustangs and soon had the buffalo, an old male, singled out from the oxen. They took the first shot as they raced over the present townsite of Sykeston. This infuriated the buffalo who, when they reached a firebreak, suddenly stopped and charged back at the hunters and succeeded in unhorsing several of them. Ever afterward each hunter stoutly proclaimed that the buffalo was right at his heels, although each one was running in a different direction. [21]

Two buffalo, a bull and cow, came nearly into the town of Ashley in October 1891. A number of Ashley and surrounding area residents took chase with pitchforks, whips and small-bore guns—much to the anguish of others who were rooting for the buffalo. Only the sheriff was armed for shooting big game, but he refused to fire, saying he had come out with his wife and son to see a buffalo in its natural state. The chase ended when it grew dark.

This pair was probably the last remnant of the North Dakota buffalo herds, reported the McIntosh County Republican. "Indeed it was thought that for years none could be found east of the Missouri, and that this small herd should remain in a county even as sparsely settled as McIntosh is almost beyond belief. Let us hope they may remain unmolested and allowed to live to the end of their times without being slaughtered by the hunter's bullet."

only bleached skeletons by 1883

Ranching Refined— Not Killed

In line camp, cowboys 'take grub'

Ranching seemed doomed when land promotion followed on the heels of government survey cutting the land neatly into quarter sections, enticing homesteaders by the trainload.

Nationally it **was** programmed for termination. Congress never considered the stockman as more than a trespasser or, at best, as a forerunner of civilization. Plains historian Walter P. Webb has charged that never until 1916, after most rangeland had been plowed, seeded to thistles and deserted, was the rancher considered of any importance to Congress.

Teddy Roosevelt expressed the common attitude:

> It is scarcely a figure of speech to say that the tide of white settlement during the last few years has risen over the West like a flood; and the cattlemen are but the spray from the crest of the wave; thrown far in advance but soon to be overtaken.

Ranchers could only purchase the alternate railroad sections; intervening sections of public lands had to be open for homestead. Sometimes ranchers fenced in these public lands with their own; fencing around each section was impractical because of water, lay of the land, and amount of barbed wire required.

But this practice caused trouble as homesteaders, when they dared, simply cut the fences and moved in. They themselves fenced off necessary trails and water holes customarily used by range cattle. There were acts of retaliation on both sides.

An Adams County pioneer had his beautiful garden and strawberry patch invaded by a trail drive of hundreds of cattle. "Dad told the man to get his cattle off but the big man put his rifle against Dad, made him raise his hands and back into the house while the garden, small haystack and all the forage disappeared," recalls his daughter. "Dad said he would have killed or been killed that day, but he had no gun."

Fortunately North Dakota had few serious rancher-homesteader conflicts. Instead, ranchers and cowboys usually proved helpful; ranch wives were generally delighted to see women and families move into the community. Changes were not always welcome—"we began to hear, with dismay, rumors of a coming railroad"—but they were accepted.

Said a southwestern pioneer, "We all had praise and respect for the ranchers we found here. These old-timers were always willing and anxious to be of help."

Many newcomers worked for the ranchers to get their start; ranchers discovered in the homesteaders a rapidly growing market for horses and cattle. Schools were a great advantage to ranch families; social life was more interesting—and, the cowboys quickly noted, there were more available girls.

Western hospitality was broad enough to include the hosts of new settlers. Strangers were welcome to stop for the night, eat, feed their horses at any ranch even if no one were home. Homesteaders learned to expect to provide the same kind of hospitality.

"It was not uncommon," said one homesteader, "for me to come home and find Zahl's cowboys had shared my shack and supplies and left a quarter of beef hanging in my cellar."

Ed Lemmon, famed cowman of the Hettinger area, helped homesteaders when they needed it. Nat Pierce recalls being sent to his ranch as a boy to buy bacon and potatoes. "An elderly man with a crooked stick opened the door and I told him my name, where my homestead was and explained to him about cutting some hay before we went to Dickinson for food and asked him to sell me some bacon and potatoes. For a moment he said not a word, only stood there looking at me, then said, 'Boy, we haul our provisions a long ways and have nothing to sell.' My heart went down into my shoes. Then he looked at me with the most kindly smile I had ever seen and with his crooked stick pointed to a shed saying, 'There are bacon and hams hanging in that shed and a hook to take them down—there is a cellar there with potatoes in it. Help yourself to whatever you want but don't forget to return whatever you take.'" Later Lemmon sold his cattle and went into the land business.

In time of blizzard, neighboring ranchers and homesteaders checked on each other. A family who lived their first winter in a tent survived a three-day blizzard. Next day a rancher rode in from the southwest, "expecting to find us all frozen to death. He was dressed in a big sheepskin coat and my husband, being quite a joker, put more coal in the four-hole laundry stove and opened it up. It wasn't long before the rancher had to take off his heavy coat. He said that now he could go home and have a good night's sleep as he hadn't slept much during the blizzard because he had been so worried about us."

Ranchers in level open country were mostly forced out of business. In the badlands it was possible to continue running cattle on small scale even at the peak of homestead activity. Ranchers and cowboys alike took up their own homesteads and began to build back herds, leasing and purchasing grazing lands from departing investors. Serious-minded settlers often did the same and became indistinguishable from old-time cattlemen.

But it was uneven business. Available parcels of land were scattered here and there; getting them together in a workable ranch unit has been a critical problem of range country ever since.

on foot
on the prairie

stories
of danger

Range cattle, especially the wild Texas longhorns, were dangerous to anyone crossing the open prairie on foot. Intensely curious, on the fight in an instant—just as ready to stampede—the longhorns were wholly unpredictable. They could rip apart a haystack, tumble down a sod shanty, or attack man, woman, or child caught without protection. They could even kill wolves, gathering in a ring to toss the hapless victim from horn to horn as if in furious play. Settlers in eastern North Dakota passed a law limiting Texas longhorns to ranges west of the river.

I had to carry my water from a spring in the hills two and a half miles away and used two shiny tin buckets. I would go out on a hill and look for cattle before making the trip. This time I was coming back and was about a half-mile from the shack when I heard a bawling and there they were coming out of the hills, a thundering herd. I set down the buckets and made that half-mile in nothing flat. They bawled around the shack most of the night, but had disappeared in the morning. My buckets were only scraps of battered tin and, lucky for me, it snowed that night and the cattle disappeared forever from the grasslands. Thirty miles was a long way to walk for my mail and new tin buckets.

A young lady homesteading west of me was living alone in her claim shack. One hot summer evening the range cattle came, fighting mosquitoes, and started rubbing against the corners of the house, pushing it off the rocks on which it rested. It started to roll downhill. Finally she gathered courage enough to open a window and fire shots into the air, frightening the cattle away. Shortly after, she sold her relinquishment and moved away.

In Traill County all the land was already taken up, and we continued west in covered wagons with ox teams in May 1887. There were days when we did not see either town or farmers. When large herds of cattle were sighted we would circle around the hills to keep them from seeing us, or the oxen from seeing them as the oxen would begin bellowing and attract the cattle. We had heard that sometimes when herds came upon covered wagons drawn by oxen, they would force the oxen to run away leaving the wagons and belongings scattered on the prairies.

Nina Farley Wishek

We had to watch out for range cattle. When Hans and I were digging my well, I was down in the well and we struck a rock so Hans walked home for more tools. While he was gone, I kept on working and the range cattle came. Discovering the mound of fresh-dug dirt, they pawed in it, bellowing, and fought, throwing dirt down on me. Their weight caused the walls of the well to start caving and I thought my end had surely come, but finally they wandered off again. I was grateful when Hans returned and helped me out.

They had to herd our cattle as there were range cattle all over. Mother broke her leg while herding so Dad had to pile a bunch of rocks by her so she could protect herself until he came with the oxen and stoneboat to haul her home, and no doctor. They set the leg with splints and wrapped it.

One day when Paul was on his way home from a trip on his bicycle, a herd of range cattle spied him. In full stampede, they took after him. Paul started pedaling like he had never pedaled before, hoping and praying that the wheels would hang together. He made it just in time to get himself and the bike into the shack and the door closed before his pursuers arrived. Once inside, he remained perfectly quiet, as he was afraid if they could hear there was someone inside, they would tear the shack down.

A cowboy rode up one day when Inga was drawing water from the well. He warned her never to get caught in a ranch herd. He said if her cow ever got into the herd he would bring it back, but she must never go into the herd after it. Inga awoke one night to find her shack surrounded by range cattle, rubbing against the corners till the shack shook.

Railroads 'opened up' the west

Railroads were fast pushing west. Northern Pacific engineered through Congress a land grant more generous than any yet granted to a railroad and—because of adverse public reaction—virtually ended the era of land grants.

In 1872 Northern Pacific tracks crossed the Red River and the following year reached the Missouri. But by this time the company tottered on bankruptcy. They continued track building west of the river, but the million dollar bridge at Bismarck was not built for ten years. In winter tracks were laid down on the ice and trains could travel.

Within the decade Great Northern crossed the northern part of the state reaching Minot in 1886. During the '80's a great boom in track-building laced the eastern part of the state with numerous branch lines—with a total for the state of over 2000 miles of railroad track.

It was too much track. As settlement extended westward the networks continued to multiply until even some of the smaller towns, such as Mott, were served by special branch lines of two railroads.

Railroads "opened up" the west for settlement, and became the most aggressive boosters of any western region. But they were caught up in a treadmill effect. They advertised and brought in hosts of new settlers; the more distant settlers and the boom spirit of the times demanded more railroad service—hauling farm products long distances to market by horse and wagon was too laborous and time-consuming. They built more track, but once the tracks were laid the railroads needed more traffic, more freight. They demanded more people, and they knew how to get them.

These forces worked simultaneously to cause overbuilding and boom times that could not last.

North Dakota's Railway Systems

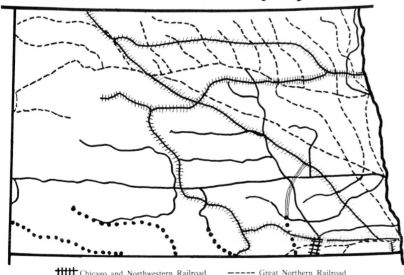

▥ Chicago and Northwestern Railroad	- - - - Great Northern Railroad
●●●● Chicago-Milwaukee Railroad	──── Northern Pacific Railroad
▥▥ Soo Line Railroad	≡≡≡ Midland Continental Railroad

THE TRACK LAYING west began and I hurried out and was put on the tie gang. There were supposed to be 12 men but there never were more than eight, so my fingerprints were on the end of every fourth tie, and we laid two miles of track a day. The ties were of oak and very heavy.

The foremen were big rough men with laced boots to their knees and stalked about cussing and ready to put the boots to anyone found shirking his job. At the end of the month the forty dollars looked pretty small so I quit.

"Sir, we have already given an empire to this monopoly. A grand empire!"

from Senate hearing on 10-mile indemnity to NP

Above map shows extreme outer limits of railroad land grants.

Granted: North Dakota Lands

The Northern Pacific became deeply involved in the land business. Their grant plus a narrow strip along the Red River Valley included 24 per cent of the state of North Dakota, 10,697,490 acres, the highest percentage of any state. (Although Minnesota and Iowa appear nearly solid black in the map above, percentage of grant lands in these states is 18.5 per cent and 13.1 per cent.)

Dakota was still a territory—the land considered of little value. Grants were doubled when they reached the territories. In North Dakota the grant was in alternate sections 40 miles out on each side of the track, with a 10-mile indemnity allowance when the 20 sections per mile could not be met within the 40-mile limit due to settlement or other reasons. Sometimes the indemnity was used to make up for grant lands which could not be met in another state. Thus control of the NP lay in a belt 120 miles wide across the state of North Dakota, with actual ownership of 40 or more square miles for each mile of track.

Northern Pacific sold its first grant lands in eastern Dakota to large-scale investors and speculators. This began the era of bonanza farming in that area; the first bonanza farm in North Dakota was of more than 20 sections of NP land sowed to wheat. These spectacular farming operations employed much labor and were profitable but they did little to develop the community.

By the time settlement reached the Missouri, NP had decided to sell their lands directly to the small farmers, bypassing speculators and land companies when possible. They found the speculators often hampered settlement by inflating prices. For example, lands purchased from the railroad at $1.35 per acre in western North Dakota were resold at $3 to $20. This could put settlers deeply in debt and often caused their failure. Sometimes speculators sold, as tillable, lands which were classified by the railroad as grazing lands only.

Much of the grazing land went to established ranchers in the area—some to large cattle companies. In 1902 the Golden Valley Land and Cattle Company bought a strip 30 miles long and nine to 15 miles wide of the alternate sections. Grazing lands became difficult to sell. In south-

'Both you and your company are doing much good for our state, and we who are on the firing line recognize and appreciate it.'

Letter from North Dakota's immigration agent to Bricker of the Northern Pacific

This map is a fairly accurate indication of amount of land actually given railroads.

'We need the right kind of colonists'

western North Dakota a million and a quarter acres were sold for $1 per acre on speculation, a sale NP president Charles S. Mellen regarded as advantageous for the company.

"I regard the sale as an extremely favorable one, if the parties pay us the price agreed upon, even if they utterly fail to colonize the lands, as I have no doubt they will, owing to their character."

Meanwhile, to the north, the flamboyant Jim Hill of the Great Northern—with no grant lands to sell, but a wide country to populate—was vigorously promoting and colonizing. In 1894 he brought in 350 German Baptist Brethren from Indiana to settle at Cando. The special train consisted of 38 freight cars and nine passenger cars. Large banners festooned the outside of the cars:

> From Indiana to the Rich, Free Government Lands in North Dakota, via the Famous Red River Valley, the Bread Basket of America!

The train was scheduled to travel only in daylight so that all could see and perhaps catch the fever of the westward movement.

The railroads opened promotional offices in Britain, Norway, Sweden, Denmark, Holland, Switzerland, and Germany and advertised in dozens of newspapers, including foreign-language newspapers, throughout the United States and Canada. They competed at the immigration centers at Ellis Island and bribed steamship officers to entice newcomers west on their railroad lines. At the same time Union Pacific and Canadian railroads—promoting their own areas—were casting venomous publicity toward the "waste lands of Dakota—rampant with howling blizzards, scorching drouth, hail and grasshoppers."

Foreign immigrants were considered choice colonists by the railroads. They were most likely to stay put and they worked hard.

Northern Pacific's land commissioner wrote approvingly:

> I think also we should make special effort to secure the right kind of settlers . . . we saw colonies of Russian-Germans and Hungarians doing well on lands similar to those in the Cannonball District. Being frugal and industrious and not afraid of hardship, people of these nationalities, who have had some agricultural training in their old homes, make excellent pioneers. I have no doubt we can dispose of these lands at prices which will average on the entire tract about $4 per acre.

Local newspapers had praise for the railroad efforts. Said the Adams County Record, "One force has been more largely responsible for the peopling of the fertile prairies here than any other . . . the Chicago, Milwaukee and St. Paul Railway . . .

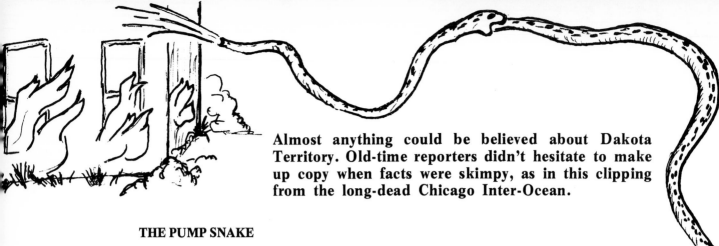

Almost anything could be believed about Dakota Territory. Old-time reporters didn't hesitate to make up copy when facts were skimpy, as in this clipping from the long-dead Chicago Inter-Ocean.

THE PUMP SNAKE

A Reptile Who is of Great Use in Dakota They Say

In central North Dakota, on the "Missouri Bottoms," there exists one of nature's strangest freaks. The settlers term it the "pump snake." How it came there or where it came from is yet unknown. It first made its appearance in Emmons County in the spring of 1886.

A full grown pump snake measures about 16 feet in length and about three inches in diameter. They are of gregarious habits, roaming the prairies in large herds, as many as 300 having been counted in a single flock. In dissecting one of these reptiles there is found a tube which extends from the roof of the jaw to the extremity of the tail, and terminating in an opening.

This tube is about two inches in diameter and lined with a tough, yielding substance, similar to rubber.

The pump snake is easily trained to answer the call of man. The inhabitants in this section trap them in large numbers. A farmer in Cat Tail Creek has a flock of 20 pump snakes trained to a remarkable degree of proficiency. At the blast of a whistle the snakes assemble on the banks of the creek. The leader (there is always a leader to a herd of these snakes, who is elected by two-thirds majority) dashes into the water of the creek, leaving only the extremity of its tail on the bank. Another snake immediately grasps the end of the leader's tail in its jaws, a third snake takes hold of the second snake's tail in a similar manner, and so on until there is a continuous line of snakes joined end-on, extending to the water troughs in the cattle yards, 300 feet away.

The leading snake commences to swallow or pump the waters of the creek, which passes through the long line of snakes as it would through a hose and falls in a heavy stream into this trough. This agriculturist told of an extraordinary circumstance which occurred a short time ago. While working in the field near his home he observed flames issuing from the roof of his house. Wild with excitement, he hurried to the burning building, only to find that it was a hopeless task for himself to attempt to extinguish the flames.

In despair he gazed on the work of destruction; suddenly he heard a loud rustling in the tall grass, whence issued his herd of pump snakes on the run. The leader hurried himself into the creek, the rest instantly adjusting themselves, heads and tails, from the creek to the burning building.

The last snake, standing on its head, waved its long flexible body, from the tail end of which issued a stream of water that was thrown with terrific force on the burning building. Back and forth dashed the tail end of that living hose, squirting the water where it would do the most good, while the loud pumping of the leader could be heard above the roar of the conflagration.

Within 15 minutes the last spark was out. Then, and not until then, did the pump snakes quit work. They were completely exhausted, the leader having fainted away. The main part of the building and its contents were saved, thanks to the presence of mind of these wonderful snakes.

The territorial government is becoming awakened to the extreme usefulness of these interesting creatures, and laws are to be enacted to protect the pump snakes.

Promotion created magic

First train pulls into Reeder, 1907

The get-rich-quick people who came as a result of railroad promotion became in turn boomers themselves. Advertising was the sure cure for local setbacks and towns could live on their boom until something more solid developed.

The story is told of a stranger visiting a boom town and inquiring how such a small town could keep up four newspapers.

"The town's not supporting the papers," he was told. "Rather, it takes four newspapers to keep up this town."

Promotion magic was often created in the style of Col. Pat Donan of Fargo, a well-known Dakota boomer:

> Oh, Dakota is a splendid, magnificent, hunkidorious domain—a land of majestic dimensions, a land of gold and silver mountains, of fruit trees and vineyards, of lowing kine and golden grain . . . God and Nature have made her, in many respects, the garden spot of all its imperial domain . . . On all the beauteous, pendant globe, no fairer richer realm unfolds itself to tempt the angels down . . .

The commissioner of Agriculture and Labor pushed for state-financed promotion. He told the 1897 state legislature, "The various railroad companies and local land agents are sending out valuable information, and doing good work, but if the same advertising matter and information was endorsed by or issued under the authority of the head of this department, much more credence would be given it by those who are sought to be influenced."

The state did push five kinds of promotion including traveling exhibits, brochures, and a North Dakota promotion magazine. But there were protests of such use of state funds.

"Who except the railroads and those who gamble in farmlands at the expense of the tiller of the soil, and of every businessman dependent upon that tiller, can hope to benefit by such appropriation? Those gamblers, and our governor is one of the largest of them, hope to profit by it through being enabled thereby to inflate the value or water the stocks of the farm lands which they hold or control," challenged J. S. Gogin of Osnabrock in 1915.

Settlers sometimes did not stay. Canada directed strong promotion efforts at the North Dakota settlers.

Commissioner Galbreath complained that North Dakota could not successfully compete with that because of Canada's closed corporation of espionage, evolution and resources. "That government is taking annually thousands of our best American farmers . . . The settler is a very important factor . . . and we can ill afford to permit him to escape."

Great Northern's Max Bass scolded the legislators: "For Lord's sake why do you gentlemen not stop the Canadians from coming over here and taking your citizens away?"

Bishop Shanley of Fargo protested against priests who were luring entire congregations away to Canada.

Yet every day came trainloads of new settlers into the farthest reaches of North Dakota.

Harvest hands swarm over bonanza farm belonging to R. C. Cooper, 1882

Bonanzas reaped big profits

Bonanza farming got its start in the Red River Valley around 1875 when real estate dealers and out-of-state financers began purchasing railroad sections, plowing them up and seeding wheat. The price of wheat was high; so were profits.

Huge wheat farms in operation were spectacular. Twenty or 30 men on breaking plows, each behind teams of horses, would break into a level section of land and finish it in a week; later, gang plows turned up eight furrows at once. In harvest six to 12 horse-drawn binders followed each other in diagonal unison through the ripe wheat. Just behind them were hundreds of hired men, scattered through the field shocking bundles.

Pennsylvania bankers, the Grandin brothers, were the largest landowners with over 40 sections of rich land near Mayville. In harvest they worked 400 horses and mules, 400 hired men, and 115 binders.

Big farming operations like these had never before been seen in the United States, perhaps not in the world. Foreign visitors, eastern tourists, even President Hayes, came to see for themselves and watched in amazement. A two-cent postage stamp honored the North Dakota wheat farms and the area was quickly dubbed the nation's bread basket.

Bonanza farm owners had many advantages over the small farmers whose homesteads lay on the alternate sections in the middle of the big farms. They paid low prices for land in quantity, bought equipment wholesale, had big capital to work with, even obtained railroad discounts for shipping their wheat to market. They raised one crop only—wheat—and it was in high demand. Local farmers often hired out to the bonanza farms in busy season. Some took over as managers.

A critical problem for the owners was hiring good managers for their operation. The big sprawling farms required good management. There were dry years and the price of wheat dropped. After the financial panic of 1893, which ruined many, most of the big land holdings were broken up and sold.

One Wisconsin real estate dealer, George Baldwin, who purchased many of these dispersements, by 1907 owned 69,000 acres in North Dakota—only a fourth of his total land holdings. He kept his farms more diversified as he notes in the following letter:

Cattle, hogs, corn and alfalfa is our motto . . . just returned from a six-week trip up to the Dakotas. We're putting up some farm buildings out there which require a great deal of attention . . . we are glad to do it if we can make a success and do something for Dickey County.

The Baldwin plan was to rent out the lands where possible. Later he broke them into smaller-sized farms and hired a foreman at $60 a month and the wife for $30 to manage each. The Baldwins clung to their big farm holdings for 50 years before liquidating.

Wagonloads of corn lined up at another bonanza farm

They came—to get a new start

New Lands!

Out came the homesteaders, the home-seekers, the speculators, the adventurers, the honest, the naive, the dishonest, the swindlers. All in response to the promotion and half-truths, the dream and the boom. Some came in desperation to make it work—others came just for the lark. Entire communities migrated from the old country—to settle together in Dakota where they were joined by others of their nationality. And sometimes they looked with deep suspicion on neighbors of even slightly different background.

The new settlers mostly obtained their land in one—or a combination—of four ways:

1. By homestead—proved up, or commuted in shorter residence time
2. Relinquishment—taking over someone else's homestead
3. Purchase of Northern Pacific land
4. Purchase from land companies, speculators, or homestead owners

Often the new homesteaders were bona fide settlers. But just as frequently they were themselves speculators who hoped to make a quick buck by getting free land and selling it later to the big operators or neighbors who'd want to expand.

They were soon to discover that the lands were not strictly "free." Five years' residence could stretch interminably through drouth, blizzard, and hard luck as well as through profitable wheat crops.

The Homestead Act of 1862 granted 160 acres to the man or woman (head of household) over 21 who would build a house on it, live there five years, dig a well, and cultivate a specified acreage. The Homestead Act was modified many times. It became complicated and tied with so many requirements—some quite impossible under existing conditions—that many land agents just looked the other way and accepted any claim the proving-up settler made. For a time "timber" and "stone" quarters were allowed,

Alfred did just enough on his homestead to prove claim on it. When he went for his final papers, he was asked if he had a well on his homestead. He said, "Yes." "Is there any water in it?" He replied, "There ought to be because I poured a pail of water in it this morning."

They came—for a lark, or to get rich

125

FREE HOMESTEADS

until much fraudulent use of this law was exposed. The five-year residence requirement was finally dropped to three toward the end of homesteading and, as if in retaliation for this good deal, mineral rights were withheld from later settlers—principally in western North Dakota.

Homesteads could be commuted after 14 months residence by paying $1.25 per acre ($2.50 an acre if it lay within the Northern Pacific land grant as did nearly half the state of North Dakota). Residence of seven months out of each year, instead of the entire year, was later allowed.

Those who settled before government survey were known as "squatters." In the lake region the settlers crowded in before surveying, claimed pieces of land they judged to be about 160 acres, but did not know where the section lines would be. When the land was surveyed, it was found there were not enough quarters for all the squatters. First squatter had prior rights so there were many contests before the U.S. Land Office as to who had first claim. Some of these also ended up with less than 160 acres.

When the Land Office was distant, the problem of claim jumpers was increased, as the first to file claim became owner. When new townships or reservation lands were "opened up" for filing there would be a rush on the land office to forestall any dispute. Crowds waited outside the door all night.

Non-citizens had first to declare their intention to become citizens before filing. Veterans could deduct military time—from required residence—as long as they lived on the homestead at least one year.

Homesteading worked well enough in the more humid areas of the nation including the Red River Valley where a family could make a living on one quarter of land. But it soon became obvious it could not work in the Great Plains. More land was needed.

Congress had the report of Major Powell stating that in the western plains, the farm unit should not be less than 2,560 acres. Land should be surveyed, not by the township—six sections square—system, but by the topographic features so that each place had some water, pasture, and the possibility of some irrigable or hayland.

Eastern lawmakers were appalled. They were certain all this land could be farmed intensively, one way or another; they believed cattlemen were only forerunners of the settler; and they could not understand any but a rectangular division of the land which ignored the difference between rocky ridge and rich, level bottoms. They did make adaptations of the law, but with each concession they tied on additional limiting strings.

The Enlarged Homestead Act, for example, of 320 acres allowed the homesteader to live within 20 miles of his land if there was no possibility of water for domestic purposes, but he had to cultivate half the land instead of one-fourth. Says historian Walter Webb, "The absurdity of requiring cultivation of 160 acres of land on a tract so destitute of water that none could be had for domestic purposes evidently did not occur to the legislators, who seemed determined to have the land farmed whether or no."

Sonderall does land office business on open range where Hettinger grew

and so they came—

by ox team, by wagon, horseback, on foot, in immigrant cars...

Missouri Settlement

The two men from Missouri set out from Grand Forks with team and covered wagon in August 1882 to go to Wells County and locate claims. They arrived at the township line between townships 149 and 150 and, confusing township 149 with range 69, continued on west. When they reached the Sheyenne River at Harvey they discovered their mistake and turned and traveled southeasterly for many miles and late at night reached a settler's home, two and one-half miles northwest of Sykeston. They drove 65 miles during that day and never saw any sign of civilization except the surveyor's stakes marking the township lines. They squatted on land ahead of the U.S. survey. Next year friends and relatives came and this became known as the "Missouri Settlement."

Walter Spokesfield

WE CROSSED THE Missouri River at Evart, S.D., on a pontoon bridge and got along all right until we came into the path of a prairie fire on the Cedar River. We burned off a space on the prairie and put the horses and wagons in the center of it. The fire swept around us and we soon were able to start out again.

We came by covered wagon in 1889 from Loyola, S.D., to New England. My father drove a yoke of oxen hitched to a lumber wagon, covered with canvas cloth. Inside the wagon besides six children were two trunks loaded with clothing and bedding, the cooking utensils and other articles. South of Ft. Yates we met up with some Indians who surrounded the wagon, lifted the canvas and peeked in all around not doing any harm but satisfying their curiosity. This worried my mother dreadfully as she was much afraid of Indians. As for us children, it was fun! They were much interested in Grace's long beautiful hair which hung down below her waist, touched it and slid their hands down on it.

We crossed the Missouri River on the Standing Rock Reservation. My father offered two dollars to the Indians standing around watching us, to carry the small children across the river. The Indians were very happy to accept this money and were anxious to do it. They rushed to the small children and hurriedly got them across, then came back for others. My oldest sister Grace, about 16, flatly refused to let them carry her across. After crossing the river with the wagon, the wagon tipped over because of the misbehavior of one of the oxen. Luckily no one was hurt but everything had to be reloaded.

Anything on wheels could become a covered wagon.

THERE WERE 96 immigrant cars on that train and they wouldn't switch so that we could unload the stock. We carried the unloading ramp from one car to the next and unloaded the whole train that way, just carrying the ramp around, up and down the track. The machinery we just dumped out.

Immigrant train unloads at Hettinger, 1908—new settlers and all their worldly goods. Many then hitched up ox teams like in photo at bottom.

DAD HAD THE milk cows in his car and Henry and I each had four horses in our car. Dad had the lunch box so we were eating in his car when I decided I should go to my car and check on a young horse. The train seemed to be going real slow so I decided I could easily get to my car, which was ahead of Dad's. But I was fooled as I could not even keep up with Dad's car. Luckily our friend's car was behind Dad's and he was standing in the door and reached out his hand and pulled me into his car. I did not try such a stunt again.

SOREN AND HIS son Sigval boarded an immigrant car on November 1. It was packed so full there was hardly room for the animals to lay down, with cows, horses, equipment, machinery, seed, furniture, and three large half wooden barrels of salt pork. Sigval had to remain in hiding since only one was allowed to ride in the car. The only available place to sleep was the cow manger. One day the train was switching and one car bumped another and the cows all came falling in on him and also the barrels of salt pork. A cow gave birth to a calf and Sigval had to share his bed then with the calf.

It snowed all the way from Fergus Falls to Minot and the train was delayed so many times they began running short of hay. In Minot Soren took a twine rope and started out to buy some hay north of the depot. Just as he was returning with the hay slung over his shoulder the train started out. Soren waved and shouted and Sigval got excited and forgot

he was not to be seen but anyway they drew the railroad men's attention and they slowed down enough so Sigval got hold of the bundle of hay and Soren climbed on. When they got to Rival they were getting snowbound and the men got off and shoveled, but it filled in as fast as they shoveled it out. Then the train ran out of water and they were stranded there a whole week. The railroad had to feed the passengers so everyone walked up to the small eating place and at first living was pretty good but they soon ran out of supplies. The restaurant operator had a few small skinny pigs and so the railroad men talked him into butchering one. A fancy job, Sigval said, of skinning a hog by inexperienced railroad men.

Finally they had to unload the animals and chase them through the snow to a farm nearby. The trip from Fergus Falls took nearly three weeks.

AFTER UNLOADING THE freight cars it was necessary to decide what was needed most for the first loads, the rest would require several trips to take the 60 miles home. Dad decided to sell the pigs then and there. We had our hands full herding the cattle and sheep. It took three days to make the trip to our new homesite. We found some kind and hospitable homesteaders along the way who gave us water, food and a place to sleep. Milking was done evenings and the stock turned out to graze and again in the morning before pushing on. The milk we left with the kind friends in partial repayment of their hospitality. Many in those early days had no stock yet.

THEY BOUGHT HIS sister's claim rights and moved west by immigrant car with a friend stowed away in the freight car. At one point a trainman who had become suspicious investigated. The stowaway quickly dived under a wagon box which had been turned upside down and blocked the open end with sacks of grain. The trainman took up the pitchfork and began to jab it into the hay stacked in the car. He pushed on the piled grain sacks in the end of the wagon box but as the stowaway was pushing back from the other side, the sacks didn't budge and he finally left.

Tent Town: before the lot sale. In background is tent hotel

ANNE CAME IN 1909 with her sister-in-law. They came on the Great Northern and stayed overnight between trains down the line, but the only sleeping room was above a pool hall. It was noisy, as they played pool all night downstairs, and the bedbugs were so terrible they had to keep the kerosene lamp burning all night. There was hardly any water to drink and it was in the heat of September.

WE UNLOADED IN Gladstone, put all our belongings in the hayrack and wagons with lumber for the claim shack, climbed on top of the load and the long 75-mile trek began. It took us 2 1/2 days and my dad walked most of those miles, herding the cattle along. One cow was tied to the wagon so the rest would follow better. Tired and weary we arrived at the homestead on the third day. Mother and Aunt Helge prepared supper by walking two miles to a bachelor's shack to cook the evening meal, then carrying the kettles back. For lodging the men unloaded the hayrack, turned it upside down, covered the sides with horse blankets, and we had a first class hotel.

Off to the homestead, these settlers ford the muddy Little Missouri

Locator takes prospects for a ride

THE FIVE MEN went threshing near Mohall and heard about more homestead land farther west. When their threshing was finished they set out for the Minot Land Office where they learned of vacant plots of land. Then without a locator they continued northwest looking for their promised land. They learned to read the government markings and used a little white cloth tied on the buggy wheel for their surveyor's chain.

Thousands were located

"Locating" took several forms. Ideally the prospective settler scouted the area by horseback or wagon, took his time, searched out the land which would have those qualities important to him. He found the government survey stakes in the grass, wrote down the identifying numbers and hurried to the nearest land office to file claim.

"They stopped here and there to examine the soil, digging with a spade to see the depth of the humus. Short detours were made to some high vantage point to obtain a better view of the surrounding country. Camp was always made early in order that the animals might graze either loose or at the end of picket ropes.

A peculiar thing about the pushing west of settlements from year to year was the advice by many not to go any further out as the lands there were arid . . . but in every instance the so-called desert was made to bloom and yield in abundance.

The six original settlers of the Viking settlement south of Maddock selected their lands this way. Says a son, Levard Quarve:

"They bent the bows on the wagon box and covered them with canvas. Inside were stowed all their belongings, bedding, provisions, cooking utensils and feed for the team. They struck off due west to Broken Bone (Rugby) and the Mouse River Valley. To the one schooner was hitched a team of horses, to the other a yoke of oxen, and behind it two milk cows were led.

"They found most desirable land had already been staked or settled. Finally they turned around and began retracing their journey.

"By now the party had decided that the most likely place was farther east, near Sheyenne. The first night camp was made five to six miles after they left the Mouse River. The next morning brought dismay, for their cattle had strayed back to the river. The day was far spent before they could proceed.

Where is the square quarter? SCS land classification in picture at left shows the differences in potential between Class VII gumbo bluffs and Class VI grassy bottoms. But U.S. survey system took no notice of such features. Major Powell recommended great plains homesteads be surveyed along the lay of the land so that each would include creek frontage, bottom hay or farm lands and higher pasture. But his voice was not heeded in Congress.

WE RAN OUT OF money and had to borrow. A few weeks later a locator came to our house with a load of men to file on claims. He asked to spend the night. Dee filled a stall with hay in the barn and made them a bed there. The next morning he asked to hire Dee's horses. Dee replied that he wouldn't let his horses out, but would drive them on that trip. That day he learned to locate. The next day he went to the railroad, found a bunch of men waiting to file on land, so he had a job. He located lots of people after that and was soon able to pay our debt.

Tarpaper store on the prairie at Gascoyne, 1907

"They camped for three days west of Sheyenne, examining the countryside, decided to locate about 20 miles farther east—where they located their individual claims. Then they built their claim shacks. This was in June 1886."

First settlers could be more choosy. They could ride a little farther west, a greater distance north or south of the railroad, and seek out the better lands. One season later it became a wild scramble to beat the crowd to good claims. Finally it was only a question of taking what the locator offered before someone else did.

Real estate locators soon had it down to a system. They met the immigrant train filling a wagon with eager land-seekers who each paid his $25 or $50 (depending on distance to go by wagon and competition). Each worked his own territory out at the limits of the land already taken up. A. O. Brown, Hettinger pioneer, recalls his trip with the locator.

He loaded the 24 of us into six wagons . . . first night we slept in a haystack . . . late next day we found a surveyor's monument and started right down the township line. After we'd gone awhile he pointed, "This is the last quarter filed on. The next one we can take."

We didn't waste any time. We all hunted in the grass for the stone marker. When we found it, he tied a red rag on the wagon wheel. We counted the revolutions and when he thought it was about right we'd all get down and hunt for the next stone.

He asked who wanted the first quarter to the south. One fellow said he'd take it. Another fellow said he'd take the one on the north side. Then we started out again, east down the township line, counting revolutions of that red rag on the wagon wheel.

Some of the quarters were flat enough, but some had a big gravel hill right through the middle. I don't know how anyone could have ever farmed them. We didn't know any better. We each took a quarter as he pointed them out to us. We didn't know there was lots of good land farther south, across that ridge of hills. Even if we had, we still wouldn't have known which quarters had been filed on and which hadn't . . . the only one who knew anything about the country was that locator. So we took what he offered like everyone else. He made pretty good—$600 for that two-day trip. By fall they had the whole country solid homesteaders.

Information passed by word of mouth where better lands could still be had. Relatives notified each other to come out quick to take adjacent quarters before someone else did. Immigrants sought settlements where their native tongue was spoken.

Most often the father came out ahead of his family, selected the homestead, filed, built some kind of habitation—dugout, shanty, or sod house—for them to live in. Then he returned east for the winter and brought out his family in the spring. An immigrant father perhaps came alone to the United States and sent for his family when he earned enough money working off his claim for steamship tickets.

When Ole first came out it was a winter when there was a lot of snow and he picked out a quarter that looked nice and flat. But in the spring he found the quarter was sloughs which had been level full of snow that winter.

We came from Iowa. There were 11 children and Father died before Loretta and I were in school. Mike was the first to come west and take a claim. Shortly afterwards John, Ed, Nody, Nelly and Agnes came. Mike married, sold his land and moved over and proved up his wife's claim. Mother filed on land farther west and north. As soon as I reached 21 I, too, took up a claim. But by the time Loretta was 21 the land in that area was all taken.

They came—from everywhere

New settlers poured in from every state in the Union and from far across the Atlantic. At first the immigrants came mostly from Scandinavian countries, particularly Norway, often after a Minnesota stopover. They settled the eastern and later the northern tiers of counties. Somewhat later the German Russians came into the central and southern portions of the state. This movement was largely begun by enterprising real estate agents such as J. H. Wishek of Ashley.

A November 1886 item in the Bismarck Tribune notes that Wishek "will go to Odessa, Russia, during the winter and organize a colony for McIntosh County, which already has been favored by the location of several colonies. Mr. Wishek is a genuine Dakota hustler and has done much for this promising young town and if successful in his winter venture, expects to bring back 1000 families in the spring."

In 1910 a little less than one-third of North Dakotans were from older American stock. The other two-thirds were immigrants, or the children of immigrants. About 21 per cent were Norwegian and 20 per cent German-Russian and German. Twelve percent were English and Canadians of British stock; five per cent were Swedish.

Czechs came to Richland County in 1871 and established settlements. Danish people brought dairy to Cass County, settling along the Sheyenne and Red Rivers. The Swedish came first to Harwood and the Fargo area. Icelandic settlements sprang up around Pembina in 1878.

The record year for immigrants to enter the United States was 1907. That year 1,285,349 new citizens came in the greatest mass movement of human history. An average of

IN BURLEIGH COUNTY we have a Jewish settlement, Russian refugees, people who commenced their pioneer life by digging up the prairie with a spade and carrying water from the river in buckets to irrigate their crops. In McIntosh County there is a large settlement of Russians who sign their names as they were taught and live in solid dirt houses, whitewashed within and without. They are as permanent as the hills. Not less fixed or less thrifty are the Hollanders who have moved into southern Emmons County.

Bismarck Tribune 1887

HAAKON'S FAMILY IN Norway decided they wanted to come to America but did not have money for all. So they sent Haakon, the oldest son, first in 1904. Next year by working out threshing he was able to send money for his next oldest brother, who also filed a homestead. In 1907 they sent for their father and a sister, Julia. It was three years before they were able to send for the rest of the family, their mother and four brothers and sisters.

5000 a day passed through the immigration center at Ellis Island, New York. On April 7, 1907—a record day—nearly 12,000 were admitted.

Many were Dakota-bound.

Their reasons for leaving ancestral homes varied.

"No more working for someone else without hope of getting ahead."

"There was so little to eat in the old country—and so many mouths to feed."

"The Russians were drafting our young men—we didn't want to fight for them."

"An exciting adventure—it all sounded wonderful when the agent told us about this new fertile land, the free country."

Paul Hjelm, a journalist, came to Dakota in 1868 with a wagon train. He wrote about Dakota in Norwegian newspapers and encouraged many of his countrymen to come.

The German-Russians had lived in Russia for a hundred years but never assimilated. When their sons began to be drafted into the Russian army, many of them began to leave. These were the only ones of North Dakota's immigrants who had lived in semi-arid country and understood the problems of periodic drouth.

Still it was not easy to break old ties of family, country, home and friends. Many, such as Scandinavians of the fjord country had left towering mountains, green trees, rushing waters to come to the most flat, treeless areas of North Dakota. Perhaps they longed for the green mountains at times, but the farmer in them must have rejoiced—no clearing of the land, no odd-shaped, steep little plots. Instead a man could plow an entire quarter, almost, corner to corner and square with the world, with fields and roads laid in as precise as a chessboard.

"The day we got our citizenship papers!" at Adams County Courthouse.

THEY WENT

Das Vaterland was very dear to them
And generations loved their Deutschland home,
But evil times begat the stratagem
That laid them low, thus forcing them to roam.

They wandered to a strange and lonely land
And settled Russia's wide and rolling plains.
And German-Russians came to understand
Great promises transmuted into chains.
· · · · · ·
Das Land der Freiheit warmly welcomed them.
She promised refuge to the homeless and deprived.
They grasped the flame, more precious than a gem,
And "durch die Gnade Gottes" they arrived. [23]

Arnold Marzolf

GERMAN-RUSSIAN WOMEN bore large families and in seeding or harvest could scarce spare the time for childbirth. Nina Farley Wishek, who taught in homes among them, said she heard many unbelievable stories of the endurance of the women. "For instance, there was the mother who came in from the field, gave birth to a child and cared for it alone, and then prepared the meal in time for the workers when they came.

"Instead of coats the women wore heavy woolen shawls in cold weather, folded and wrapped about themselves with the babies inside next to their own bodies and the shawl tucked tightly around. So secure was the baby within this peculiar twist that the mother could walk easily with arms swinging. On their heads they wore small square fringed head shawls called Tuechles. The fact that I never saw them with uncovered heads led me to wonder if it were not an old Biblical custom."

THE WEEK BEFORE Christmas Mother was busy baking Jule-kage, fattigman, and lefse. The latter, spread with butter and sprinkled with brown sugar, then rolled up like a cigar, was most delightful to the hungry children coming in from a scuffle in the snow or the long tramp from school. Ludefisk in the form of bone-dry codfish, Mother had secured weeks before. To prepare it required two weeks of soaking in lye and later watering out with a change of clean, fresh water every day . . . There were plenty of nice frozen roasts and steaks, in addition to pork sausage, mincemeat, meat balls, blood sausage and "klub."

Viking Settlement

German-Russian immigrant

Stage arrives at Leff from Dickinson, making two trips weekly

A town is born

Leff sprang up quite naturally on the prairie—the way you'd imagine a town **would** spring up.

Albert Leff, founding father, dug a coal mine on his ranch to supply the new settlers coming in. There was need for a restaurant, hotel, and general store—so he built them, too. Before long Leff was a real town with bank, post office, two-story hotel, and the WESTERN CALL newspaper. The little western town had its occasional excitement with a shoot-up in the cafe or on the street.

Albert Leff even ran a stagecoach 60 miles north to Dickinson for mail and settlers, many of whom had no other means of transportation than walking. The stagecoach had a runaway its first trip with a bank cashier perched nervously on the high seat guarding his suitcase with $10,000 in it for the new bank and eyeing the four half-broken broncs on the hitch and a driver who had hit the bottle too heavily. Suddenly as they careened too fast around a curve, a front wheel dropped into a buffalo wallow. The stage tipped and both cashier and driver landed hard. The horses ran wildly

off, dragging the stage. The bank cashier jumped up and followed into the gathering dark. A heavy fog was settling in and he couldn't see the stage but imagined his money scattered all over the rough ground. At last he found the stage with the money safe—and the new bank opened on schedule next morning.

With rumors of a railroad coming, Albert Leff hoped to have a depot and siding located in his town. But in this hope he was naive. Instead, the coming of the railroad spelled its doom.

This was not the way a town on the railroad could begin. Not in the west where railroads had long understood the profits to be made from townsites. Instead, the Northwest Townsite Company (also known as Milwaukee Land Co.) bought land a mile west of Leff, had it surveyed and platted for town lots. Northwest was a special company of railroad officials with inside knowledge and limited distribution of profits. They chose the name of Reeder to honor a railroad engineer. (Who was he? Did he ever see "his" town? Did he care? No one knows.)

Squatter businesses were permitted to locate at the Reeder site and soon a thriving Main Street developed facing the tracks—east and west.

REEDER N·D
APRIL '08

Squatter's Reeder grew typically, photo at left, with Main Street paralleling railroad. After townlot sale Main Street was turned at right angles to tracks.

The townsite company chose May 14, 1908 as townlot sale day—and a gala day it was, much like a 4th of July celebration. A special train came in loaded with speculators and prospective merchants; there was a cornet band, speeches, sporting events, the auction sale itself, a rodeo,

Great Northern had a standing offer to businessmen of Kermit to move their buildings to Noonan as well as furnish them a lot without cost. With this proposition, every now and then someone would sell out or move, so Kermit gradually dwindled and Noonan started to grow.

dance, and special entertainment. Towards evening the Leff stagecoach came tearing into town from around a hill, chased by a band of road agents and whooping "Indians."

During the next few days the squatter businesses were snaked around to their purchased locations with chain and log rollers. Main Street was now positioned to run north and south down to the tracks in the way of Milwaukee Railroad towns. The railway offered to move the Leff businesses. Philosophically, Albert Leff took them up on it and opened his general store in the new town of Reeder.

The Leff-Reeder story is not at all unusual in the annals of North Dakota. It is remembered, in some variation, on every railroad and branch line throughout the state.

Fargo's official name—that of a Northern Pacific director—was sent by telegram from New York in September 1871. Minot was a Boston Great Northern railroad backer who never made it west. Bismarck was named in honor of the German Chancellor in the hope of bringing German capital to the rescue of the financially stricken NP railroad. Nearly all the Soo Line towns were platted by the Minnesota Loan and Trust Company, a holding company for the railroad.

One railroad agent, A. C. Bovay, used more imagination in naming Glen Ullin. He took it from his favorite Scottish ballad: **Lord Ullin's Daughter.**

Towns didn't spring up casually in the west. They were schemed, surveyed, platted, promoted, advertised and sold at auction; then they boomed or died. A single venture could mean big profits for some, financial ruin for others.

Independent townsite companies also mushroomed as soon as railroads began a survey into the state, or contemplated a new branch line, and the race was on.

Most railroads had their own offshoot townsite land companies that bypassed regular stockholders. They grew secretive and tried to outwit the independents. NP used false survey stakes and various deceptive moves to mislead would-be squatters.

In Fargo the battle was a close and exciting one. Independents were keeping a watchful eye on the Puget Sound Land Company—which denied any connection with NP but whose directors and officers were identical with those of the NP. Three men—Lowell, Back, and McHench—rode the banks of the Red River from Wild Rice River to the mouth of the Sheyenne every day for nearly three months before Lowell came upon one "Farmer Brown," dressed in worn overalls and holding onto a plow, but who didn't quite ring true as a farmer.

Lowell and his friends, plus a host of others, hastened to stake claims at the site, and their hunch was right. This was still Indian land not yet legally open for homestead and endless complications ensued: lawsuits, claim jumping, and the growth of two rival camps called Fargo-on-the-Prairie and Fargo-in-the-Timber.

But the townsite battles were unequally joined. The railroad invariably won. They had only to build their siding a half-mile down the road from a beginning town, drop a boxcar on the spot for a depot, name the place in someone's honor and write his name on the maps, advertise and wait for the population to come. Businesses did come because the depot was where the action was. The alternate site soon withered.

Main Street of typical North Dakota town, like Sheyenne at left, is one-sided, facing the railroad tracks

$2400 for the choice lot of bare prairie

McIntosh County Democrat, May 7, 1887 —

It is reported from Aberdeen that more than 500 teams are at work on the line between that city and Bismarck. Chief engineer and right-of-way agent for the railway company have been in this neighborhood for several days and it is supposed that the two gentlemen have been definitely settling the location of a station and townsite near here.

One day in 1886 Mr. and Mrs. Erik Ramstad were honored in their homestead shack by a visit from James J. Hill, president of Great Northern. The city of Burlington, the county seat, was not far off: but Hill wanted his own town and requested the Ramstads to sell him land for a townsite. He pledged them to secrecy.

Ramstad has been called the father of Minot; later he donated other lands to the city. But the honor of naming the town went instead to another man.

Bypassed, Burlington dwindled, though with a tip of Jim Hill's hat it could just as well have been Great Northern's busy switchpoint. Perhaps there is irony in the fact that Jim Hill's town, subject to flooding, may be rescued only by a dam which floods part of the Burlington community. Almost immediately after the railroad came through a county election, reportedly well lubricated by whiskey and illegal votes by non-resident "rails," swung the county seat away from Burlington and gave it to Minot.

This is a common story of Dakota towns, named on paper in St. Paul railway offices instead of by local pioneers. Some which had descriptive local names were summarily changed as were other landmarks such as historic Hiddenwood Creek of southwestern North Dakota which the railroad officially dubbed Flat Creek.

Old Crosby was left out

The Soo had come through in 1906 and the Great Northern was on its way in 1907, and old Crosby on the prairie was to be left out. There was no choice for the squatters in old Crosby. They must move. The only question was whether they should move to the Soo Line townsite of Imperial a mile east or to the townsite laid out by the Great Northern. Some of the building owners moved to Imperial. Others chose the new townsite of the Great Northern which was to perpetuate the name of Crosby's founder. All would probably have moved to the new Crosby, but for the fact some feared that the Great Northern might not come through, true to their promise. This set the stage for a bitter rivalry between Imperial and Crosby. There was a little over a mile distance between them, so close that both could not possibly exist. Trade eventually seemed to flow to Crosby. Before the railroads pronounced its death sentence, old Crosby had two newspapers and two banks.

Hettinger's townlot sale day in October 1907. Watching horse races from on top of boxcars was part of the entertainment. The event was advertised with posters up and down the Milwaukee line and brought crowds early in the week. A special train came in the night before with sleepers for speculators and prospective merchants from Minneapolis and points east. Bidding was brisk and competition was keen with the choice corner lot of bare prairie going for $2400. Total income for Northwest Townsite Company that day in Hettinger was $54,000.

Dwelling of prairie sod often shocked women from the east

The Law Required...
a habitable dwelling

The sod house—an innovation of the grasslands—was cool in summer, warm in winter and tight against howling winds or blizzard.

Each was of unique design depending on the know-how and imagination of the builder. Most often sod strips about one and one-half to two feet wide and two to four feet long were plowed and stacked one on top of the other, brick fashion, for the walls. The strips were about four inches thick and held together with grass roots which might grow for a time to interlock the strips. Heavy clay soils were best.

Roofs were of poles or branches filled in with brush and covered with a thick layer of more sod. But leaky roofs were a common problem in heavy rain. Floors were usually dirt, sprinkled with water and packed until floor boards could be purchased and laid. The sod shanties were plastered inside and out with native clays and sometimes wallpapered or whitewashed.

Besides having a leaky roof the soddie tended to be dark, dirty, and infested with mice and bedbugs, since there were unlimited hiding places in walls and ceiling. When the homestead mother rocked the baby she took care not to knock out chinks of sod. Cattle rubbed on the corners, weakening them and sometimes the roof fell in.

Grass grew on the roofs and the north walls and they could be gay with wildflowers.

When we got there Olin asked, "Where is the house?" When told it was the little sod house, he said, "That's not a house, it's a chicken coop."

Lacey worked hard building four sod walls. Then before he was able to get the roof in place the rains came. Down came the sod walls in sodden muddy masses. He couldn't plow wet sod anymore so he took the lumber meant for roof and floor and he built a small wooden building with a dirt floor.

WHEN THE NEIGHBORS heard my wife and children were coming five men came to help build a house. By noon the third day the floor was laid, windows were in, sod all smoothed and plastered with white lime we got near the coal mine. We also rounded the outside door and window frames, put in the door and steps. Then we moved in the stove to help dry the plaster. The children loved the "dirt house," as they called it.

Sod houses: warm in winter, cool in summer

The tarpaper shack

Hard winds and hail whipped tarpaper to tatters, blew through cracks

Frame box looked naked on plain, as yet untarpapered

The tarpaper shack was the most common type dwelling built by those who wished only to satisfy minimum requirements and sell out as quickly as possible. They were not intended as winter homes. But it often happened that destitute families ended up by living in them year around.

The tarpaper shacks were built as cheap as possible, usually of poor lumber nailed across 2x4 studdings. They did not have inner walls or partitions although these were sometimes added later. In hot sun, rain and hail, the green lumber would shrink and twist leaving open cracks in the walls.

Tarpaper was tacked on the outside with lath as protection against the weather. But the shacks were baking hot in summer, difficult to heat in winter, and often sprung leaks through both walls and roof. Fire was a constant threat as these shacks would burn quickly.

Sod often winterized tarpaper homes

Log houses were considered permanent. They were built in timbered northeastern areas of North Dakota, along the Missouri and tributaries where big cottonwoods were available, and in pine tree areas of the southwest. In the west, roofs were frequently of red scoria rock. On the inside logs could be left natural or hewed flat, then chinked and plastered or papered.

A danger was the heavy ridgepole which could break and come crashing down from the weight of the roof.

Solid log houses were considered permanent, but logs could be scarce

LOG HOUSES
When there was timber

Near the woods log houses were built. The roofs were dirt supported with poplar poles; you had to have about 18 inches of dirt well settled before it would shed rain. I know of a family who pitched a tent in their log house to sleep in. After the dirt was settled it would shed any ordinary rain if not too prolonged.

A Devils Lake pioneer

Crude chinking kept out wind, also provided a secure home for generations of bedbugs

Our house was a family project. It was built of stone and gumbo built partly in a sidehill. Dad and Mother did the masonry while Marion and Joe hauled rocks from a nearby stone hill on the rented quarter. Wanda carried the water and I did the mixing of the gumbo with my bare feet for smoothness and right consistency of clay. When the house was completed we had two rooms on ground floor and two rooms upstairs under the roof. A great convenience was a drilled well in the kitchen. As the years went by a wooden floor was put in, and a screened-in porch across the front of the house.

Dugout could be cozy

Stone houses were permanent, though if small, might be replaced later by a bigger house and used for chicken house or granary.

Temporary homes took many forms. The new settlers often slept in their wagons while the house was built. Some turned their hayrack upside down, hung blankets around, and lived there months. They lived in tents, even through the winter. One family living in a tent shared it with their chickens. The hens laid their eggs under the cook stove but during winter the eggs often froze.

Dugouts were commonly dug into a sidehill and roofed over with branches and hay, as in sketch at right. Or a six-foot hole could be dug in flat ground with one side sodded up higher to make a sloping roof with window and doorway dug down into it—dark, but quite comfortable if cattle or horses didn't come crashing down through the roof. The Johnson family of Bowman County was cramped for room in their dugout: parents and baby slept on a three-quarter size bed and the children on trunks which were carried out each morning to make room. One night a big rain caved in a wall of the dugout on the sleeping children.

Homestead girl feeds bum lambs

Their first home was a hole about 12 feet square, boarded over. When it rained they all crawled into the hole, sharing it with calves and the family dogs.

A stone granary was built with much hard labor, some of the rocks being 100-125 pounds. A stone boat was pulled by two horses west a half-mile to a stony knoll where stones were most plentiful. These were loaded on the stone boat and pulled home, and once again lifted into place for the granary walls. Later Lewis built a stone barn, half dug out of a bank.

Stove like above was a luxury, as was wallpaper. Woman in inset photo spins her own cloth.

My dear sister Carrie—

Well, Carrie, if you could step inside our house for a few moments you wouldn't think we were roughing it. You would think it a millionaire's cozy corner. From the outside it looks like a sod house, I must admit. The house is 17x23 built of the best sod three feet thick at the bottom and two feet thick at the top. Inside it has pegs drove in the wall and strips nailed on and a heavy blue cardboard nailed on it. The windows and doors are made rounded which gives it the appearance of fine architect work. The roof is covered with one layer of thin sod and then a coat of clay one inch thick to shed the water. On the floor we have our wolf rug, with head mounted and our badger skin.

We have a cellar with 35 bushels of spuds, canned goods, 700 pounds of flour with other grub. Tomorrow I am going to get a quarter of beef as I go after coal. We have already got seven loads of coal hauled and are going to get 15 more that will last a year or more.

I suppose Dad told you about us putting up about 300 tons of hay this summer and selling it for $1.25 a ton. Well, if we had that hay now we could get $2000 for it.

Well, we had an awful prairie fire one night about twelve o'clock and burned most of it left (80 loads). And we had fire guards plowed around it, too. The lead fire came through this bottom at the rate of 40 miles an hour. When it was five miles away everything was as light as day. I had an awful time keeping Dad and Bessie quiet, but I have been in prairie fires before so I kept quiet. I had good fire guards around the whole place so I wasn't worried after the lead fire was past as side fire is easily headed off.

Don't breathe this to anyone so Ma will find out or she won't come.

I suppose you wonder if it is settled much here, well along the road one-half mile west of here in two miles there are 11 houses. There is a rumor of building a town a half-mile from Dad and Oscar's place.

I remain your
Loving brother,
Henry Flamme

Bachelor grinds coffee, cooks on stove without oven

Homestead girl framed her sod

The homestead shanty was improved as soon as possible. When Julia Klovdahl came at 20 to homestead near Bucyrus, she lived in a sod house with tarpaper roof. Hail damaged the roof and her brother shingled it to stop leaking. But Julia didn't like the mice that lived in the sod walls and longed for a frame house. So under the good roof and outside the sod walls, her brother built new walls of wood and, when they were finished, the sod was removed. When Julia married, her husband moved his homestead shack over to this one to enlarge the house.

Visitor is entertained in refined interior of home below

Bachelor girl Julia Klovdahl (right) began with sod home; her brother built another around it.

Those who intended to stay...

Old home often became a barn

The settlers who stayed improved their homes or built new when they could afford it. They added on rooms of the same or different kinds of materials; they added flooring; inside walls were insulated slightly with building paper and wall-papered; they partitioned off bedrooms.

But the goal was usually to build a new home and consign the old to barn or chicken house. The most typical house was a one-and-a-half or two-story white frame home with a front porch. In some areas large cement block homes were put up by builders who made the blocks on the spot with special forms.

Three-story house of cement blocks, poured and cured in barn of Norwegian pioneer

Typical permanent homes: 1 1/2-story white frame

Cornering the claims

Cornering was a common practice. Three or four homesteaders built at a corner where the claims came together, sharing barn and well. They were close enough to help each other, eat together if they liked, exchange stories and play cards to pass the long winter months. Family members tried building over the line with each a bed to sleep over his own claim, but the law was changed forbidding this practice and every homesteader had to have a separate house.

Water—they were

Homestead law required a well, but finding water in the dug hole was not so easy. Early wells were dug by hand with homemade windlass with rope, bucket and crank and one man always down in the well. They went down amazingly deep. One pioneer says bachelor neighbors dug their well about 40 inches in diameter and were lucky to strike water at 84 feet. "The well had a good flow and was semi-hard, clear and excellent for drinking and for livestock. Many neighbors had troubles with dry holes, colored water, alkali and poor flow." A later method used horses to dig the well by walking them around in a circle.

When the diggers did strike water, they sometimes brought up disappointment: water of a rich rust color or black from coal veins or strong alkali unfit to drink.

Well digging tragedies were not uncommon. Lack of oxygen in deep wells caused a number of deaths. Buckets loaded with mud or rock sometimes fell on the man down in the hole when a rope broke or slipped.

The simplest way to get water from the well was to drop a

Water lifted by bucket, above. At left, earliest wells were dug with shovel, dirt excavated by bucket.

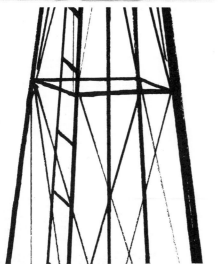

A well digging tragedy

Dynamite was used to blast rock down in the well. Then George, one of the boys, was lowered down in the well after the blast to start work again. When he didn't respond to calls, Adam, another son, was lowered to see what was wrong. He didn't answer either and the neighbors had to physically restrain the father from going down in the well after his

desperate for it

Our water was hauled in a barrel on a stoneboat from a reservoir about a half-mile away. The water sloshed over the top of the barrel as the stoneboat lurched forward pulled by one horse.

Every quarter section had a dug well on it, sometimes three to four feet across, often abandoned. One day a neighbor's cow disappeared; after several days she was found and rescued from one of these wells.

Water hauled by stoneboat

pail with a rope tied to it, let it fill, and bring it up hand-over-hand or with a crank windlass, but this required great effort for each pailful. Pumps were probably most common and children spent hours pumping water for livestock and household use. If the well was slow-filling or deep, a lot of pumping might be needed just to get it to the surface. Windmills were a most welcome convenience when there was wind to do the work.

Says one old-timer, "Many people have complained about the wind in North Dakota but we boys complained most when the wind didn't blow. Then we had to use the hand pump and my arms still ache just thinking about it."

Fights in the water tank between brothers and sisters cooled off many a hot summer day, but culminated with having to pump the empty tank full again before Dad came home with the thirsty team from the field.

There was danger from boarded-over abandoned wells left from dry holes or deserted homesteads. The wells grew over with weeds to make a trap for grazing livestock or even wandering children. Many pioneer mothers ran first to check abandoned wells when a child was lost.

One night a 15-year-old boy disappeared walking the four or five miles home from Reeder. The entire community searched weeks and it was at last believed he was stolen or ran away. But 20 years later his bones were discovered at the bottom of a forgotten well.

THE "WATER WITCH" walked slowly and stealthily across the homestead claim grasping two tines of a willow fork. When the tail of the willow began to bend, it pointed out the spot to dig, and for a water witch with the right "feel" the branch actually bent in half in his hands, straining toward underground water. A man who had dug six or eight deep dry holes became a believer in a hurry when he drilled at the witched spot and struck good water.

Pumping water: 'My arms still ache . . .'

sons. Both died. Probably not enough time had elapsed after the dynamite blast—not enough oxygen. After that anyone digging a well would hang a lighted lantern down in the well to see if it would remain lighted before going down in the hole. All the well digging work was done by hand and a hand windlass was used to lift and lower men and working material by rope.

Drilling grew more sophisticated

THE FARMERS SAVED all their cow manure and piled it at least a foot thick. To this they added used straw bedding and after a rain, they packed it with a team of horses or oxen. Then they left it to age for about six weeks. Then the bed was cut into blocks of about one foot by one or two feet. These blocks were left to dry a few days and then were stacked into cocks much like bundle shocks. When they felt the blocks were dry enough, they stacked them into a mound and coated it with fresh manure mixture. This coat protected it from rain and snow. It is surprising how well this stuff burned and how warm it kept the shanty; it was much used among German-Russian pioneers.

Bricks of manure and straw piled, left, for winter fuel

When you were cold, you burned anything

Dakota pioneers burned a variety of fuels. Twisted slough hay was probably least satisfactory; it burned quickly and took a lot of time in twisting of the 50 pounds a day needed for heating the kitchen. People who spent half their waking hours at this tedious chore may not have enjoyed it as much as a light-hearted Ellendale journalist of the 1880's suggested, when he wrote this:

The average farmer on the frontier has but little to do in the winter, and he can afford to put in half his time at the menial occupation of twisting hay. When the young men of the neighborhood go a-courting there is neither cornhusking or sleigh-riding for amusement. They help the objects of their adoration to twist hay. And it is said that no form of occupation affords better opportunities for hand-squeezing!

'Within 60 miles of Ellendale there are 300 families with no fuel this winter but twisted hay.'

Corncobs made quick fire for summer cooking. Dead trees and branches were first choice for starting fires and summer cooking, but scarce in many localities. Western Dakota coal was dug out by hand; small underground coal mines became common. Elsewhere settlers purchased coal at the railroad.

Buffalo chips and cow chips were the unique fuel of the treeless prairie, and German-Russians made manure into a kind of brick for fuel. To the uninitiated it was a strange custom. Recalls one pioneer, "The first time my mother came home with cow chips, we children weren't going to eat the food that was cooked with them. But it wasn't long before all of us were out picking cow chips, too, and it wasn't half bad. Everybody else used them, too."

Good coal could be had for digging

They scoured the hills and creek bottoms for wood

146

One-bottom walking plows began breaking up the prairie sod

Breaking the sod

Corn planter behind team of horses

Homesteaders were required to break the sod, whether soils were tillable or not. One would-be farmer testified that he plowed "around six acres"—and that's what he'd done, one long furrow around a good-sized patch of ground.

Two horses or oxen, or a combination of horses and oxen, pulled the 14-inch breaking plow which was held steady in the ground by a man walking. Eight or 10 rounds down to the end of his quarter and back in the forenoon and the same in the afternoon for a total of 16 to 20 miles a day walked was considered a good day's work.

Just before World War I came the big steam tractors pulling gang plows with three to 10 bottoms and turning up to 20 acres a day, causing wholesale plow-up of tough native grasses.

News item: James Joyce is a partner of Mr. George Sager in his big Jumbo steam breaker. Their intention is to break night and day, carrying two crews. Later they will break for anyone wishing good work done at a reasonable price which is $3 an acre. The engine is a monster 35-horsepower and is drawing nine 16-inch plows. They claim the native coal is unsurpassable in its ability to keep up steam.

In 1916 grain drill, tractor made work easier

With coming of huge steam tractor, several furrows plowed at once

Foundering

Cut in the wart of the fetlock of each front leg; take 1 teaspoonful of blood each. Give to swallow 1 tsp. dry Alum.

Remedies

Draw 1 gallon of blood from the horse's neck, drench with 1 quart linseed oil. Rub forelegs long and well with very hot water.

Livestock was vital

Horses, cattle and the other stock were of vital importance to the new settlers. They were needed for field work, transportation and food. A working animal going lame or getting sick was a serious loss and pioneers had their own special remedies.

Horses were first choice for field work and transportation. Mules were used

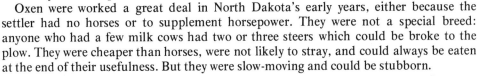

Homesteaders brought hogs to plains

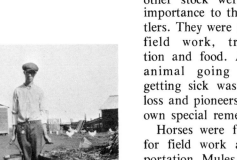

Chickens were food

to some extent, though mostly on the large bonanza farms. They were expensive and, since they did not reproduce themselves, were usually dead-end for the small farmer.

Oxen were worked a great deal in North Dakota's early years, either because the settler had no horses or to supplement horsepower. They were not a special breed: anyone who had a few milk cows had two or three steers which could be broke to the plow. They were cheaper than horses, were not likely to stray, and could always be eaten at the end of their usefulness. But they were slow-moving and could be stubborn.

Milk cows brought in some cash—or at least trade at the grocery store. One man who had 26 milk cows in 1908, separated, and made butter, claimed that any good milk cow would clear $40 in milk and cream during the year plus produce a $10 calf.

At first there were no fences so horses and cows had to be kept on picket ropes or herded. Horse thieves were fairly common and horses were easily driven or led to another part of the country for sale. So a close watch was kept: a handsome team or saddle horse was a great source of pride to the owner, besides its economic value. Children usually got the chore of herding. Townspeople could throw their milk cow into the town herd which was taken each day out to graze. One rancher got his start the spring of 1901 by herding settlers' cattle from the Lefor community on a per head basis. He collected 350 head which he grazed farther west from May 1 to November at $1 each.

Sheep were always herded—even on the large sheep ranches. Coyotes were thick and wolves were a menace almost into the '20's.

A druggist who located with his family had never farmed but needed milk for his small children. When he heard that a man had come from Iowa with a herd of cows he rode on his pony 12 miles, bought a cow and led her home on the end of a rope. He arrived home and found that neither he nor his wife could milk and that there was no one within two miles who did know how. So it was up to him to learn. The cow was a pet or he would never have gotten her home, let alone get her milked.

OXEN WERE SLOW. In warm weather you rose at 3 a.m., found your oxen wherever they may have wandered, and worked until 10 a.m. Then they rested until 4 p.m. and you worked them again until 10. While the oxen rested you dug out rocks. I broke up 80 acres this way. To keep my oxen from wandering so far, I used to tie them together in pairs. Oxen were easy keepers; they scrounged the prairie and needed no oats or ground feed.

They broke steers to harness for ox teams

Oxen made good draft animals in the field but were not always so easy to handle on the road.

August Anderson, a new homesteader in the Swede settlement to the west of us was using oxen to haul lumber from Oberon. He had started from home before daylight and in mid-afternoon was returning past the open door of our schoolhouse. We heard the rattle of chains and rumble of the load passing and became so interested the teacher called recess.

A few rods past the school the road crossed a slough which, at this time of year, was full of water. There was a narrow dirt grade thrown up through the center, but it was soft and a treacherous roadbed for the heavy load. The driver, afraid his load might sink in and get stalled, tried to hurry across. He lashed the oxen into a run, hoping the momentum of the load would carry through the worst places.

But the oxen as usual had a mind of their own. They were tired, hot and so thirsty that their tongues were hanging out. With one accord, they swung off the road and a dozen drivers could not have stopped them from making right for the middle of that water, dragging the load of lumber in after them, the wagon sinking down to the hubs in soft mud. As the water came up to their bellies they laid down to cool off and drink their fill.

The driver realized it would be useless to try to pull the load out, so set to work to unload the lumber piece by piece, carrying it up on dry land. We boys rolled up our trousers and waded in, barefoot, and helped him.

We unhitched the oxen, took the wagon apart, rolled the rear section back on the road and then the fore section, and reloaded the lumber. By that time the oxen were feeding on green grass along the edge of the slough. He hooked them to the wagon again, got on the load and we watched as he gave the command, reinforced by sharp lashings of his ox whip.

The load started across the grade, but the off ox gave another look at that cool pool of water and jerked his fellow out with him. In an instant the load was out in the ditch again hopelessly stuck. We were glad the teacher rang the bell to call us back into the schoolhouse.

Levard Quarve

Forenoon lunch: a must with Norwegian settlers

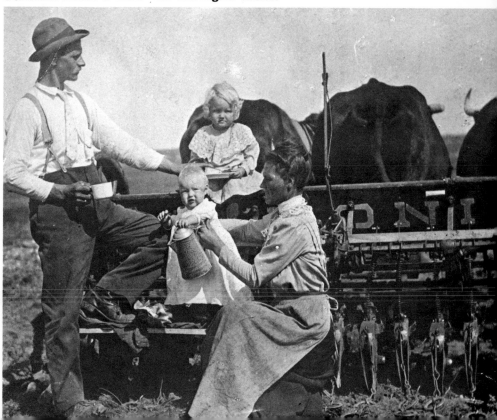

One winter we had six fine big black and white steers, ready to be broken for spring's work. It was great fun—the men would get two of these wild fellows yoked up together under the heavy wooden yoke attached to a log chain and flat jumper sled. The driver got on the sleigh, yelled and cracked the whip; the men who had been holding the oxen by the nose let go and with another whoop and a good lap on their flanks the steers started out in a wild rush. After half a mile of loping, they settled down to a trot and later a walk. Now the driver began training, "Gee" to the right and "haw" to the left, using the whip vigorously on the ox ahead so he turned in as the driver called that direction.

Shocking oats before threshing

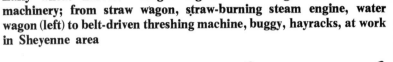

Early wheat harvest brought together a strange assortment of machinery; from straw wagon, straw-burning steam engine, water wagon (left) to belt-driven threshing machine, buggy, hayracks, at work in Sheyenne area

Harvest hazards

Threshing day started in the dark with the screeching of the steam whistle from the gigantic steam engine which could be heard for miles. The bundle haulers crawled from their bedrolls in the straw pile or hayloft when they heard the whistle. They fed and groomed their horses. Then they came to the kitchen table to eat breakfast by kerosene lamp. The table was set for 15 or 20 men. The cooks were already preparing the noon meal, and the same work started following dinner for the evening meal. Supper was eaten by lamplight and the kitchen chores continued until nearly midnight before the women could retire to rest.

Prairie Pioneers

Fire was always a hazard since sparks were being hurled into the air by the engine and these would float through the air and light into straw, bundle loads and also on the

ONCE DAD LEFT me to fire the engine, but with no instructions. I felt pretty important but the more I fired the lower the pressure went and the harder I fired. I was really forking in the straw, tears rolling down my cheeks, when the engineer came and asked how I was doing. I pointed to the pressure gauge, "I can't keep the pressure up." He took the fork from me, reached in the firebox, stirred up the straw and told me I had it choked to death by feeding too large bunches at a time.

Header cut only wheat heads

Men pitch bundles, separator man stayed with thresher

Wagons line up at threshing machine operated by steam engine

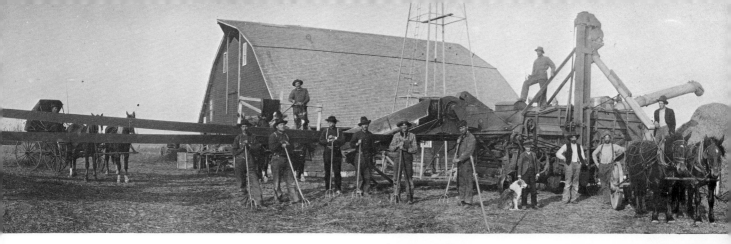

brought suspense

separator and start fire. A steam engine could be blown to bits by a careless operator; many cases of this happened. Parts of the engine could be found hundreds of yards away and anyone close was fortunate to escape death or injury. Water of good quality for the boiler was sometimes a problem—there was foam and scale with bad water. The fireman had to start firing the boiler at 3 or 4 a.m. to have steam on the boiler when the engineer and crew arrived at 4 to 6 a.m. Bundle crews were sometimes in the fields to get bundles when it was so dark they couldn't find the shocks.

Owners of the threshing outfit had to be good managers and operators to be successful. Many farmers could not get their outfits paid for and consequently lost their land and everything through foreclosure.

Divide County

Hungry crew lines up for dinner

IF A RAINY spell came during threshing it turned into a big problem to feed the crew and horses. Often the farmer had to dig into his new oats crop to feed the horses and might have very little left to thresh. Enormous amounts of food were prepared even though the men were not working. Two or three neighbor women might come to help.

Cook shack traveled with some crews

WHEN 14 I WAS threshing for a neighbor with a big rig. I enjoyed myself but had lots of work to do. I was water boy for that steam tractor and was it thirsty! The tank wagon held 700 gallons and some days I would have to make as many as six trips to the creek, pumping water in by a double acting pump, which if working right pulled about a half-gallon to the stroke. But sometimes it would get dirt in it and would have to be taken apart a couple times a day. Then I had to pump it into the two tanks at the rear of the firebox and the third tank on top of the boiler.

Women brought boilers of food for dinner in the field

Hayloft, needed in damp eastern climates, was found less necessary here

Rake dropped hay in heaps; horse blanketed against flies

Danger rode the hay rake

Dallas was haying three miles from home so he would be gone all day. One afternoon I saw the team coming over the hill and Dallas was riding one horse. I thought this was very strange for him to be coming so early. Then I saw his face looked dark and as I went out to meet him I saw he was covered with blood. He told me he had hooked the team to the rake, one older well-broken horse and a four-year-old. The horse flies were bad and they were fighting flies and stomping their feet. The young horse kicked and caught her leg in between the double rake tongue. Dallas got off to see if he could get her leg out, but they got frightened and began to run. He was knocked down and dragged by the rake. There were depressions on the hillside we called buffalo dugouts, or wallows, where the buffalo were supposed to have rubbed their heads for relief from flies and mosquitoes long ago. When Dallas came to, he was lying in one of these depressions. The team was standing on the hilltop a half-mile away without the rake which was broken against the new haystack. It was a terrible experience—it all happened so fast and by some miracle the horses had run across this low place so he was dropped out.

In 1912 there was no hay for the stock because of drouth. In late summer we hauled Russian thistles for feed from 12 miles away. As we unloaded them we salted and tramped them down. A prickly job it was but it was very good and nourishing food for the cattle.

Many men did work of today's single farmer

I WAS MUCH frightened once when I went to the field and found our son Leonard lying across the whippletrees in front of the disk and right behind the horses' heels. He was caught there and was afraid to move for fear the horses would kick him. He had fallen from the seat after being bounced over rough ground. Luckily the horses stood still until I could get Charlie from another part of the field to help me. I was afraid to yell or go near the horses for fear I would scare them and set them running. We got Leonard out with only a few scratches and bruises.

Grain elevators rising against the skyline punctuated towns in wheat country. Sometimes they exploded into flame. Dams and water towers were built to provide water for steam locomotives on the railroad.

Community store was gathering place for families and neighbors

Town life was lively

The town merchants had come, like the homesteaders, from every walk of life, from everywhere. They, too, filed claims, but most were quickly commuted and sold after minimum residence.

Town life was lively with social affairs, visiting, and baseball games. There were always talented and trained people among the town's elite as well as in the nearby tarpaper claim shanties to organize musical and literary groups.

Main Street was often filled with saddle horses, horses hitched to buggies or wagons—sleighs or bobsleds in wintertime, tied to hitching rings or hitching racks. Livery barns did big business especially on Saturdays when the settlers came to town. A team of horses could be fed and left all afternoon at the Hettinger livery barn for 10 cents.

Fire was always a danger—it could quickly raze a town of small frame buildings. Elevators sometimes burned from heating grain. A livery barn which burned in one small town killed 16 horses. Two men sleeping in the loft were never found and the puzzle baffled townsfolk until a man came to town 35 years later and said, "I was one of the men sleeping in the livery barn when it burned—we didn't want to be blamed." When the local hotel burned it was said two million bedbugs died in the fire.

Reeder boasted a single rare board sidewalk by 1909

Many towns had no sidewalks; horses hitched in front of stores or tied to wagons

AT FIRST THERE were only a few wooden sidewalks on Main Street and those were very uneven but at least they kept one out of the mud. Several of us young mothers used to take our babies out for rides in the evening. The men called it the Baby Buggy Parade. With all the rain there were hordes of mosquitoes, so we put netting over the carriages.

The bumpy rides pleased the babies and gave us mothers a chance to visit.

At cobbler's bench worked the bootmaker

Banks sprouted everywhere; interest was 12 per cent and up.

Winter boxing matches held

My father had a kind of gymnasium in the basement of his drugstore. On certain evenings in the winter he would allow some townspeople to attend the boxing matches in the basement, and would lock the doors of the store. We youngsters fought in the preliminaries while the older generation fought in the so-called main attraction. The main attraction would involve my father boxing Dr. Odou, the veterinarian; Dr. Johns, the medical doctor, boxing Pat Norton, the U.S. Senator; or Leon Tank boxing Nick Gahr. Later they converted the old livery stable into a gym with a ring where boxing matches and wrestling matches were held.

Lemmon was a border town with the depot almost on the line between North and South Dakota. A prime reason for border towns were the state liquor laws. North Dakota came in dry, but both South Dakota and Montana were wet until Prohibition. Saloons were sometimes built with the door in North Dakota and the bar and stools across the line. Ed Lemmon, boss cowman of the big L7 and one of the few local people able to influence railroad policy, envisioned two county seats for Lemmon.

Depot was focal point of most towns

But livery barn was the heart of local transportation

BILL RUN THE dray line which was a big operation in these days as all the merchandise to supply the town and country came in by railroad. Then in connection with that, there were deliveries of coal in the wintertime and ice in the summer and as was the usual custom in the pioneer days the dray man usually maintained a livery barn where rigs could be hired with a driver. Boarding accommodations were provided for the farmers' horses when they came to town if they desired such service.

Mrs. Marchant loved her flowers. They bloomed even in drouth years. She watered them as long as the wells held out. In 1911 both wells were nearly dry and she was expected to leave the flowers die. The menfolk hauled water from the Grand River in barrels and one barrel sat by the kitchen door for dishes and washing. Her flowers kept blooming all summer, but it was several years before she dared tell the men why. She simply carried a pail of water in the back door and, when nobody was looking, sneaked out the front door and watered her flowers.

A balanced diet, when she could

Mother's realm was family and home

Women knew heartache and loneliness

Life for women was challenging, but often filled with hardship. They were accustomed to that, most of them, and yet for the woman who sought beauty in close familiar sights it was difficult to get used to the wide blue skies, open spaces where she could see for miles, the scarcity of trees. Neither could she find much beauty in the claim shanty, its stark lines and makeshift furniture. A man took pride in his wide acres, waving crops and fine livestock—when times were good. His wife was proud of these, too, but her personal accomplishments lay mostly in the realm of family and home, and sometimes there was little to do with except a new baby each year. She did her best and reared her children for better things. In them she could instill a love of beauty, of great ideals, of nature—finally even the beauty of the prairies and not just that which she had left behind.

Women could not vote in North Dakota until 1917; many church congregations forbid them the vote for another 30 or 40 years. Yet they exerted a steady influence on decisions at all levels.

Emerging from eastern Victorian standards many expressed amazement at the women's freedom in the west. "The girls here all ride horseback, and most of them astride," they wrote to shocked friends. Widows with children found it a good place to start over, and even unmarried mothers could begin a new life far from the suffocating influence of disapproval.

But always there was endless work and worry over children, sickness, finances, pregnancy. For many a deep homesickness persisted for friends and family left behind; only by long expensive journey could they ever hope to see them again. The claim could be lonely, too, with no other women for miles. Frequently mothers were left for months at a time alone with small children while the father was out working.

When I came from Minnesota to teach school, I was met at the train by my brother. As I stepped off the train, there was a young girl there, handcuffed. My brother said, "Just another homesteader who can't take living on the prairie." They were committing her to a mental institution.

A Prairie Mother

The prairie's little five-foot-two
Could pack an awful whap.
Her hair was gray, her eyes were blue
And she could cut a swap.

"We got to have a Sunday School,"
She told the church's board.
"I may be slow, but not a fool."
And there was one, by Lord!

"We got to have a P.T.A.,"
She told the County Seat;
"We want to have our rightful say,"
And one began to meet!

"We got to have good government,"
She told the councilmen.
"We won't pay you another cent."
The mayor left his den!
. . . . .
"We got to have more city light,"
She told the neighborhood.
"Our children will not walk the night."
And soon the streetlights stood!

"We got to have a future goal,"
She said before she died.
"We also have a living soul."
And where does she abide?

The prairie's little five-foot-two
Could pack an awful whap.
Her hair was gray, her eyes were blue
And she could cut a swap. [24]

Arnold Marzolf

Refinements, as most had known them, were few in this harsh environment

THIS WAS HOW THEY LIVED
'A peddler brought us the queen's jewels'

The peddlers made their rounds regularly and sold everything a farmer and his family needed or dreamed of owning. I remember one who gave my sister and I a string of glass beads for his night's lodging. To us, the queen's jewels were no more beautiful.

Marge Erickson

Wall decor: postcards from home

> The sound of the foot powered sewing machine was a familiar one. Mother made all our clothes. It must have been almost impossible to sew by the feeble flicker of a kerosene lamp. Another distasteful job was keeping the kerosene lamps and lantern clean and filled, also cleaning and polishing lamp chimneys. What a great day it was when gasoline lights were available. Mother did all her baking, churning butter, and canning—and what delicious meat came from those jars cooked in the oven. Every child took his turn bringing in the night's supply of coal and filling the reservoir on the back of the stove for a supply of warm water.

WASHDAY WAS ALWAYS a very tiring day for Mabel, and Josephine remembers her mother was more apt to be cranky on that day. Barrels of water were filled from a spring an eighth of a mile away and hauled by stoneboat behind the team. This was actually a sled with runners and it was very hard for the team to drag those barrels of water.

She lifted water by bucket from the barrel, carried it into the house and filled a boiler on the range. Then the hot water was dipped into a pail and carried to the galvanized wash tub. Another tub was filled with cold water for rinsing. Mabel did all her washing by rubbing the clothes up and down over a washboard. After the washing and rinsing, the clothes were carried out to the clothesline and hung. John helped all he could with carrying water for washing, but he often had his own field work starting early in the morning.

One of Eva's outstanding memories was when she went to the outdoor toilet, shut the door and hearing a peculiar sound, looked down. There was a large rattlesnake all coiled behind the door. She screamed and Hank came to her rescue. After that she said she never forgot to look before shutting the door.

Flour barrel stood nearby

One day Aunt Kari wanted to bake bread in the stovepipe oven, which is just an oval shaped metal oven that fits in the stovepipe. She made the loaf of bread too big—and could not get it out when it was baked. It had to be cut in pieces to get it out. They had lots of laughs over that.

Often they were well-read

156

You're the doctor

Corn sweat for pneumonia: put 20 ears of corn into a boiler, boil half an hour, wrap in 5 large towels with four ears in a towel. Put an ear in end of towel, wrap next ear, until you have a pack. Put one pack at feet, two at hips, one under each arm. Cover patient up to neck. Stay by bed and hold covers up if necessary. . . . .

Pneumonia is the most fatal of all diseases. Under 1 year of age most cases are fatal, after age 60 the death rate is 60-80%.

. . . as soon as the head is born, clean the mouth and at the same time see if the cord is around the neck of the child. If it is, it should be removed. Caution: In case the attendants discover birthmarks or any deformity of the child they should use every precaution to prevent the mother's knowing as it may grieve her to the extent of causing convulsions and consequent injury.

Child-bed fever: After 3-4 days there is a rise in temperature to 103 degrees or more with increasing discharge. A doctor should always be called for treatment. Very serious. The usual cause is dirty hands of doctor or midwife.

Diptheria: membrane forms in throat which causes very difficult breathing attended by hoarseness and a harsh cough with a metallic sound. This is followed by constant whistling, harsh breathing, much restlessness and anxious breathing. The child may grasp the throat with its hands and as it becomes bluish it often grinds its teeth and looks piteously from side to side for relief. As the disease advances the child becomes more and more limp and struggles less for breath and unless relief is quickly obtained suffocation will result.

Care of the body after death: Straighten limbs, placing arms at side or across chest. Close eyelids and keep closed with fingers or place something on them. Place false teeth in place, if not already. Close mouth and tie handkerchief under jaw. Tie on top of head, tight enough to make the mouth close and look natural. Comb hair. Wash and dress, change bed linens. Tie knees and ankles together, make look natural and cover with sheet.

When a neighbor died of diphtheria no one could come close for fear of the disease. A coffin was brought within shouting distance and someone else dragged the coffin to the door with horse and lariat. The widow put her dead husband in the coffin. The grave was dug by two Norwegian neighbors and two others hitched a pair of broncs to a wagon and carried the coffin to the cemetery. The broncs bolted and had to be unhitched to unload the coffin.

Keeping them alive wasn't easy

Illness, accident and death were close at hand for the pioneers and often had to be handled without professional help. The midwife was a cherished person in the community and dealt not only with childbirth, but with all kinds of illness and trouble. Usually she fell into her trade naturally because she was so desperately needed. Most homesteaders were young, often newly married, so before long the babies began coming. Death of the mother during childbirth was not uncommon, and loss of the newborn baby was not unusual at all.

Typical is this report from Adams County: "The eighth child, a boy, was buried with Mother. John, the oldest child, was about nine and the baby 16 months. Our grandmother stayed with we seven children until father married Kathrine and then they had eight children of their own. The first two babies died in infancy."

Epidemics took a terrible toll: diphtheria, scarlet fever, complications of measles, and later, the Spanish influenza.

"During the diphtheria epidemic in November 1907, both boys, Per, age four and Halvor, two, were taken, bringing great sorrow to their parents."

"We went through a hard ordeal when we had scarlet fever and were quarantined for seven weeks. Five children out of seven were sick and we lost one daughter, Verna, age seven. We had to hold an outdoor funeral at the graveyard with scarcely any help in severe cold weather. No one could come near to help us during the seven weeks. The big job of fumigation and cleaning up afterwards was strenuous and very tiring."

The Spanish Influenza in 1918 was worst of all and ravaged the entire nation. A Wells County historian says there were 16 deaths in that county in October from the flu, 29 in November, seven in December, and one in January, 1919 for a total of 53 flu victims during the epidemic. He says an estimated one-third of the state's population caught the flu, with 2971 deaths reported to the North Dakota Board of Health. Neighbors did all they could to help each other, with chores, bringing coal and groceries. Public meetings were stopped and schools closed at Thanksgiving.

With death came the necessity of laying out the body and arranging burial. One pioneer remembers the emergency when her father died in August, 1905, of appendicitis. "It was 40 miles to the closest place to get a coffin and a minister. With the hot summer how to keep a body was a problem. Then mother thought of alcohol and camphor; she mixed it and bathed the body in that to preserve it."

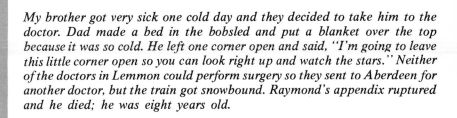

My brother got very sick one cold day and they decided to take him to the doctor. Dad made a bed in the bobsled and put a blanket over the top because it was so cold. He left one corner open and said, "I'm going to leave this little corner open so you can look right up and watch the stars." Neither of the doctors in Lemmon could perform surgery so they sent to Aberdeen for another doctor, but the train got snowbound. Raymond's appendix ruptured and he died; he was eight years old.

Some used bicycles to ride the range

He hauled out my lumber and supplies, unloaded them and left. It was a gray melancholy October afternoon. Beside me was my lumber. There were miles of lifeless brown prairie grass—and silence. I felt I was sitting in the middle of nowhere, suspended in time and space, and I wondered: "How in the world can I stay here for nine months?"

Last Homesteader

He cast an eye at brooding clouds
Afraid they would pass him by;
He guarded his acres with jealous pride,
Suspicious of passers-by.

He lived alone in his little shack
For almost fifty years—
Through blizzard and calm and sunny days,
Nursing his hopes and fears.

And he grew old, a little queer—
At least so neighbors said;
And he grew sick, nigh unto death—
Still he clung to his homestead bed.

His acres sold, his keepsakes strewed
Upon the cabin floor;
The North wind moans a requiem
Through the sagging, open door.

Divide County

One cannot live in a small shack over winter without really knowing one's companion. Johnnie was the best and there was not one instant when there were any ill feelings between us. I came to love him like a brother.

'Batching it'

IN CANADA, LATER, I saw many that went wrong through loneliness and I understand why. The silence will grow on you, become thicker and thicker until some morning you will spring from your bunk shouting and yelling, striking your fists against the wall and jumping about, and the tension is broken and you whistle and sing and return to normal. I had two or three such spells that winter. Sister Jennie had given me a Bible before I left home, that was all I had to read. I read it from beginning to end and parts of it several times. It was very seldom that anyone came.

Christmas was the hardest part of that long lonesome winter. It was as if there was no such thing as Christmas. Self-pity was getting the best of me. I found a few dried peaches in my cracker box cupboard and put them to soak. Knowing nothing whatever about pie making, I started my peach pie. I had no pie tin but used a can cover and the pie was baked in my stovepipe oven. What a pie! As soon as it was cooled I overturned it on my plate, picked it up in my hands and started gnawing on it. It really wasn't fit for a pig, but I devoured it, then my feelings overcame me and I laid my head on that little table and cried like a baby from homesickness.

And I was cured for never again have I been homesick in my life. Having heard that smoking was a great relief from loneliness, I bought a corncob pipe and a package of tobacco, but it only made me sick so I put it up in the eaves of the shack. The long cold lonesome winter finally ended and the homesteaders returned.

BEFORE WE WERE married my husband had a store and post office on his claim. The store was of boxes, cardboard and wood, the floor was dirt. The post office had homemade pigeonholes in a little corner of the building. His bed was a shelf under a counter in the back of the store. We were married in my shack and left on our honeymoon—a trip across the prairie to his claim. That night a cyclone came along and blew my homestead shack away. End of that experiment.

Bachelors yearned for wives

Homesteaders were young people and the majority single, most of them men. Life on the claim for the bachelor could be a pleasant round of visiting, playing cards, playing practical jokes on other homesteaders. One married woman had six bachelor neighbors she baked bread for; other neighbor women were enlisted for laundry help. Some bachelors were good cooks and prided themselves on their pies and biscuits, but most were delighted to be invited to the married families' homes for real home cooking.

Single girls over 21 had their claims, too, most often coming west with relatives or family. They taught school, or had jobs in town. When young people married they moved their claim shacks together. But it was necessary to prove up, or commute, the wife's homestead before marriage—or lose it—as a claim was allowed only to the head of the house.

A FAVORITE PASTIME when the bachelors got together was trying to marry each other off. Several practical jokers went so far as to send for a mail-order wife for a young Bowman-area homesteader. When the girl arrived at the young man's shack she was accompanied by her aunt as chaperone. The friends, hearing word of the arrival, rode over to his claim where they found him some distance off in a field. They explained the joke and all sneaked up to the shack to peek through the window. There they saw a white-haired lady with a long nose. The bachelor's friends rode off laughing at the great success of their joke— leaving him to try to get rid of the unwanted bride. But around the front of his shanty he met a pretty and charming girl. He was delighted. They soon married and the last laugh was on his friends at the wedding.

Many bachelors went east, or back to the old country for their wives. Others never married.

Lucky was the bridegroom

The Little Old Sod Shanty

O when I left my eastern home, a bachelor so gay,
To try and win my way to wealth and fame,
I little thought that I'd come down to burning twisted hay
In my little old sod shanty on the claim.
My clothes are plastered o'er with dough and I'm looking like a fright,
And everything is scattered 'round the room.
But I wouldn't give the freedom that I have out in the West
For the table of the Eastern man's old home.

Still I wish that some kindhearted miss would pity on me take
And extricate me from the mess that I am in.
The angel, how I'd bless her if this her home she'd make
In my little old sod shanty on the claim.
And we would make our fortunes on the prairies of the West,
Just as happy as two lovers we'd remain.
We'd forget our trials and troubles as we rest
In our little old sod shanty on the claim.

4th of July: Parades and races

Prairie lasses proved they were fleet

The happiest days

Homesteaders brought a love of music

"The most happy days were the homestead days. Everyone was friendly and no one had much money at that time, but all seemed to enjoy life. I think they were the happiest days of our life. But I don't think I'd want to go through them again."

Early rodeos: Out in the open

Boating on a Sunday afternoon

The neighborhood boys went camping

Community picnic

'Baseball's Nine': Girls' teams flourished

Accordion music was a favorite

Neighbors visited, debated, staged chivarees.

Saturday nights and the 4th of July: The band played on the streets.

'Batter up': Baseball was every Sunday.

Storytelling was an art. Neighbors visited, played cards, sang, held debates. "The subjects were usually political," recalled a pioneer, "dividing the territory into states, or later, the question of writing prohibition into the state constitution."

Dances were popular and sometimes included box social lunches at auction to raise money for a local project. Said a Regent settler:

This was considered a lively community, often having dances in the various homes, taking all the kids along . . . some didn't sleep, but preferred to dance. There was always a fiddler in the group . . . some drove 20 miles with team and buggy to a dance.

Others rode horseback, 40 miles. Women wore divided skirts and rode astride, with their dancing clothes tied in a flour sack to the saddle. In winter, traveling home in dark and cold could be dangerous, so they danced 'til daylight.

Sunday afternoons featured baseball, church activities, or just visiting. Housewarmings, home weddings, chivarees were celebrated. In western Dakota, men brought together their toughest broncs to buck out. The original rodeo technique was: ear 'im down . . . throw on the saddle and cinch up tight . . . let the rider get a good seat (on the downed horse) . . . open the gate . . . and let 'er rip!

At Christmas the special nationality traditions blossomed more than at any other time. Norwegians celebrated the days of Christmas with socializing, and Juleboks went masquerading boisterously (Christmas fooling). When there were no evergreens, they adapted Christmas tree substitutes.

"Dad would get a big tumbleweed . . . Mother wrapped each branch . ."

"They worked down a fence post to form a trunk, drilled holes and inserted pegs for limbs . . . wrapped them in green crepe paper . . ."

"We whitewashed a boxelder tree for the school house . . . strung popcorn and cranberries and made paper chains . . . Gifts parents brought for their children were hung unwrapped on the tree."

Winter sports: Skating, skiing, sledding, sleighing were widely enjoyed.

161

There was no schoolhouse the first year, and as my shack was the better shape for that purpose, 14x8 feet, classes were held there in the daytime and I slept there at night. My bed was a spring fastened on the wall with hinges so it could be let down at night and pressed up against the wall in the daytime to make more room. My furniture had to be moved outside during school hours so there would be room for the homemade desks. The children sat two or three at each desk.

Divide County

School . . . as soon as possible

School terms were short at first, sometimes only six weeks. First school was a centrally located claim shack with makeshift "desks"; the teacher was often a volunteer neighbor. The stories recall sporadic but determined strivings for education.

MY BROTHER JOE and I horsebacked down to Cora's sod shack for the three "R's" that winter. We were her only pupils. All our education was during parts of a school term; we were never able to attend the entire term because we were needed at home to herd the sheep.

———————————

"Father taught the first district school. I can remember going the first day, father on skiis, pulling me along on my homemade sled. It was held in the new and cozy one-room house of Rasmus Wisness, still a bachelor, who later attended school. There were only a dozen children but they were joined by many of the young men and newcomers. For them father taught classes in English, American History, and other subjects they chose."

Just getting to school was sometimes a marvel of endurance and determination; children and teachers walked, rode horseback, drove a team for many miles. The teacher and older pupils did all the janitor work, carrying coal, stoking fires, and pumping water.

One new teacher had never heard of burning buffalo chips, and the school board was embarrassed to explain. She had a pile of damp lignite but it was hard to burn without kindling, so she requested kindling. None came. When she asked again, she was told shortly that it had already been delivered; but she could not find it. Finally one school board member sought out a relative of the teacher: "You tell your city cousin what we use for kindling out here. I can't." The cousin did, and the new teacher realized with amazement why all the dry pats of cow manure had been heaped so mysteriously beside her school.

Another teacher taught school in a deserted farm house where a family of skunks had made their home and left their odors. There was no well, so the children brought drinking water each day with their lunch pails. She and her own children lived in the school during the week, and had to be very saving of the water.

Fifteen or twenty pupils of all sizes in one room was not uncommon. Young teachers feared discipline problems with the big husky boys. Said one girl, "I was 17 when the school board asked me to teach school. I was scared stiff; the other teacher had quit because she had so much trouble with two 15-year-old boys. I put the pupils all to drawing when our work was over and they became so interested I never had any trouble with them. Fifty dollars a month and I thought there was never so much money in the world!"

Salaries were not easy for the school board to scrape together. One teacher said he, too, was paid $50 a month. "but they didn't have any money. I stayed at Ole Sneva's place six months before I got any salary, so Snevas didn't get any board or rent money either."

Children and teachers walked, rode or drove horses to school, often picking up others on the way. White frame schoolhouses soon replaced the claim shack. Right, inside a Griggs County school, 1914.

In crisis a teacher's first duty was safety of the children. It was understood that in a storm the children would stay at school.

Neighbor children rode double and bareback to school carrying their lard pail lunches.

Town schools might be two-story, with high school upstairs; janitor carried up coal daily.

This school with bell tower, near Maddock, also served as church for 13 years.

Along toward spring we got one of those spring snowstorms, and I looked to the west at recess time in the afternoon and noticed a big blue cloud in the west. I carried in loads of coal from the barn and piled it behind the stove. In about an hour it hit, and you couldn't see anything. The youngsters took it for granted they couldn't go home. I lit a few candles, that I had to start my fire. I also had some crackers and cheese in my desk. I read the little tots stories until they fell asleep, made a bed close to the stove, and laid them down as they fell asleep. The older ones didn't get a chance to sleep. When we ran out of candles, I opened the stove door a little bit just to get light. The blizzard raged all night and the snow was so deep we couldn't get the door open. At three in the morning we heard an awful stomping on the roof and a voice; "Is there anybody alive in here?" "Yes," I says. "We're all alive and it's nice and warm . . . what do you get out in this kind of weather for?" And he says, "We just had a new baby born at our place, and the wife wouldn't listen unless I got out to find out how the youngsters were at the school."

By noon, tumbleweeds began striking against the schoolhouse with a force that could knock down the sturdiest kids. Shortly after we heard the galloping hoofs of a horse. A rider paused at school to yell, "Prairie fire!" and galloped on. We ran out and could smell smoke; to the south gigantic billows of smoke rose . . . black, blue, red, and greenish white. The sun was obscured by 2 p.m. The teacher thought, "If it doesn't jump the river, the school will be safe." And it didn't jump, but the fire burned fast in tremendous wind along the Grand River's south bank. The older boys saddled their horses and went to help fight fire.

The churches

Religious groups, too, met first in homes; later in schools and local halls. Sunday schools and ladies aids formed for Bible study, and their leaders prevailed on traveling or not-too-distant ministers to hold services occasionally.

One summer a seminary student had Sunday services in Haley. Most of us would eat dinner at the hotel after services; all you could eat for $.35; others would bring their lunch and have picnic dinner. Then we would have a ball game and other sports. This young student was a good athlete, too, but most of those homesteaders were good and we had a ball team that was hard to beat.

Our Ladies Aid passed this resolution in 1910: The aim and purpose of this society shall be to aid this congregation in its work for the furtherance of the Lord's Kingdom both at home and abroad, and to gather funds for . . . furnishing and beautifying the church which it is hoped will be erected soon (it took 15 years) and to be diligent in the acts of mercy and in aiding missions, both local and foreign.

Ladies Aid: the men came, too.

Lone country church stood sentinel: They could be seen for miles. Top photo is of Golden Valley sod church near Hettinger. Below center, dedication of a new town church. The cemetery stood close by the country church; funeral in photo at right was of mother and three children who died of spinal meningitis.

there was deepfelt need for a church—and cemetery

THE CONGREGATIONAL MISSIONARIES served our area. Early pioneers met in homes for Sunday worship, once or twice a month. While my parents were Catholic, Mother always said to us, "No matter which church you attend we all pray to the same God. Go to church." Later Mother gave three acres near a good road for a Congregational church. A small building was moved there, remodeled and redecorated by community members. It served not only for a church but also for a center of other gatherings.

IN THE LIFE of all Scandinavian communities, their church has always been an integral part. They were all from Christian homes and from communities that had well established Lutheran congregations. The question of securing church services was one of the first problems up for discussion at meetings of the Viking settlement. When the seven-month-old child of Elken's died, a local committee selected a cemetery location from among several plots of land gratuitiously offered and the first funeral was conducted Nov. 29, 1887.

WE HAD JEWISH High Holy Day services at the homestead for all the scattered Jewish settlers . . . from South Dakota and Montana, too. We improvised a Synagogue in our home. This became a tradition and the Holiday was celebrated every year at our home. In the evening many of our non-Jewish neighbors would join us for delicious dinner.

The pastor of Tepee Butte Lutheran Church had 11 other churches under his charge. Each family was supposed to give $10 a year for his salary.

THE LADIES OF CEDAR CREEK had Lutefisk dinners in the homes of members to help finance a church. People came from far and wide. The lutefisk did not come ready for the pot, but dried and packed in wooden tubs and had to be soaked and resoaked in cold water for days to get the lye out. Another way they raised money was fancy work sales. Most women worked all year making fancy pillowcases, dresser scarves, aprons, pot holders, tableclothes and so forth. One of the men would be auctioneer. Price was usually high for those days . . . one set of pillowcases went at $9 a pair, an outstanding price.

SERVICES WERE HELD in a vacant ranch house about a mile from our home. It belonged to a sheepman. Church services were held about once a month, only in warm weather as the ranch house had no heat. One or two men of the parish would drive to Richardton with horse and buggy and bring a priest on Saturday. On Sunday people journeyed from far and near to attend mass. The ladies first gave the ranch house a thorough cleaning and decorated it with wild flowers and blossoming chokecherry branches for the bishop's visit. During services the sweet scent of chokecherry blossoms permeated the church.

Disaster and tragedy exacted their toll among the pioneers

Land and climate could be harsh, with pioneers vulnerable to the devestation of hail, flood, drouth, blizzard, biting cold, or prairie fire

THE FIRST FUNERAL held in our little church was for the two little Willis girls who drowned in July 1915.

WE HAD A CHINOOK in February after the heavy snow winter 1909-1910. Creeks and rivers ran wild and the bridge went out. Last one to cross was Dr. Poppe . . . he thought the warning lanterns were to light the travelers on . . . his team and buggy barely made the south side when the bridge collapsed. Then Mr. Coe operated a raft ferry. One man fell off and was drowned. Ole Viken attempted to cross with team and wagon and was swept downstream with the wagon box and was drowned. His body was found by the Anderson brothers in a sandbar near the Crowl ranch when they were looking for a place to ford the river with their steam breaking outfit.

THE DAY AFTER Winifred's sister came to homestead, hail shredded the tarpaper on her shack and broke windows. The ladies knelt and turned apple boxes over their heads for protection . . . with hailstones up to baseball size. A steady rain lasted for several days leaving everything wet including beds. They slept sitting under umbrellas.

THAT DAY OF THE BAD STORM in July, 1909, the wind, hail, and electrical storm took our house. We just got into the cellar, when off went the house. We had to run to the sod barn. The contents of the house was completely destroyed by fire and by breaking. All my wedding dishes were broken.

Blizzard

A GREAT TRAGEDY occurred on February 9, 1910. Our oldest son, 5 1/2 years old, was lost in a snowstorm. All our neighborhood searched for days but not until spring was he found . . . under a straw pile near the Centipede River.

ONE NICE WINTER DAY Nettie went to Hettinger to get a load of coal with a neighbor lady, Mrs. Koleman. They were caught in a blizzard on the way home. The storm was so bad and the drifts so deep the horses could no longer pull their load. The women unhitched and set out walking, holding the lines of the horses. Mrs. Koleman became exhausted and Nettie had to leave her covered with a shawl in an abandoned sod shanty and struggled on behind her horses who seemed to know the way home. Mr. Koleman made his way to the shack as soon as he could but found his wife dead.

WE ALWAYS EXPECTED a three-day blizzard to set in by November 22 each year. The two winters 1886-1887 and 1887-1888 were the most severe I have ever known. Many people died in the terrible blizzard of January 12, 1888. I saw ice cut from the Pipestem at Sykeston that month that measured 63 inches in diameter.

During blizzards, ropes or twine was strung between house, barn and outhouse to help everyone find his way back to the house and warmth. One of the worst blizzards was in March 1920, which raged for 3 days. Snow got higher than the buildings . . . tunnels were shoveled from house to barn.

Dad's brother Michael froze to death in March 1907 while walking to his homestead from working at the newspaper one Friday night. He lost his way in the blizzard and apparently became exhausted only a few feet from a vacant shack that held plenty of wood for the stove and food on the shelves. Dad formed a search party and hunted through the huge drifts to their horses shoulders . . . they had to get ahead of the horses and lead them through the deepest snow.

JOHN CAME FROM SWEDEN to Sheyenne in 1899 and took a homestead in Williams County. His mother and sisters took homesteads nearby. One winter John took his sisters Betty and Helda and a friend to Betty's homestead so she could stay there the night (putting in residence time). On the way back to John's homestead with sled and horses, they stopped to warm up at a neighbor's home. The team broke away and John told the girls to stay there till morning, but he would walk home so his mother would not worry when the horses came home without them. The girls insisted on going the couple of miles home with him although the neighbors told them it was too cold and too much snow to walk in. About halfway there a snowstorm came up and they turned east instead of north. They walked all night lost in the storm, passing right by John's shanty and by another homestead. Just west of these buildings Betty's feet gave out and she could not walk anymore. John put his fur coat on her and they left her to go for help. They walked on, lost in the storm, until the other two girls became too tired to go on. John dug a hole in the snow with his hands for a sort of windbreak for them while he looked for help. About a quarter of a mile away he saw a light and found an older couple's homestead. They had a light burning and a man visiting them who put on skiis and went to help John bring the girls to the house. They had gone to sleep and could hardly be roused so the men had to hold them up on the skiis and push them to the house. But they could not find Betty, until the next day after the storm subsided. Helda had frozen her fingers and was taken to the Minot hospital where all her fingers were amputated except for half her thumb and index finger on each hand. Betty's body was shipped to Sheyenne for burial.

Prairie fire—

ONE OF THE WORST PERILS was the terrible prairie fires which would rage for weeks in the fall after the grass was dry enough to burn. These fires usually originated far to the north and would burn for six weeks or more. Each day the smoke became more dense until at last the sun would be entirely obscured for days. Then at night the reflection of the fire on the clouds could be seen, gradually drawing nearer, and the reflection on the clouds growing brighter and larger each night. Finally after about ten days of this it would pass through, sweeping everything before it except in firebreaks. On a calm night it was a most beautiful sight to see the fires pass through and light the heavens as bright as day. Terrible fires passed through on Oct. 11, 1884. Millions of acres of burned prairie land and small plowed fields made one continuous field of black for miles and miles and left neither trees, shrubs nor any other green thing to rest the eye or break the monotony, giving it all the most dismal appearance of anything I have ever seen.

The two little girls, Anna and Mary, had gone to bring the cattle across the fireguard to safety. The cattle were frightened as the flames closed in on them and were running for shelter. In this terrible moment of danger each girl caught a cow's tail as the cows ran for home. Mary was pulled across the fire break to safety but little Anna's foot caught in a gopher hole and she fell as the flames caught her. Her mother ran to her, tore off her burning clothes and carried her across the fireguard. They were both badly burned and poor little Anna died that same night. The mother lived about two weeks when she, too, died after much suffering from her burns.

Nina Farley Wishek

We protected the ranch land, 10,000 acres of rich grassland for ourselves and our neighbors, by plowing and burning a fireguard. We plowed six furrows in three circles around the outside . . . each furrow 20 miles long . . . leaving about four rods between the circles. When the grass was dry enough to burn we would go at burning fireguards. We burned grass between the circles, burning alternate years between the outer or inner circles. The burning was alternated in this way so there would be a cleaner burn. We used two "torchmen." One torch would always stay far enough ahead of the other to allow the fire to burn back from the furrow in order to blacken a wider space before the main fire would come roaring across as the breeze fanned it along.

Children were sent to lie in the middle of a plowed field, their faces to the ground. Russian thistles would catch fire and bounce along . . . rolling balls of fire, bounding across the fireguards, igniting everything in their path. Afterwards, the landscape was black and it was hard to find feed for livestock because the fall grasses had all burned and many times the haystacks, too.

Chris went to fight side fire with team and wagon in the big prairie fire that started south of Belfield and went southeast in a 70-mile-per-hour wind. The wind shifted and he and the fellows with him were caught in the lead fire. They had to make a run for it and drove the team as fast as they could run, over a steep bank into the Cannonball River. The three other men jumped out of the wagon, but the flames were so close that their clothes caught fire. The fellows rolled down the bank, the horses slid down, but all were saved. Two men who lived in a stone house ran out, but caught fire and were burned. Many cattle which had badly burned feet had to be shot.

'Let it all go—they're safe!'

At noon, while Efford and I were at school, mother went outside and saw, to her amazement and horror, a raging prairie fire was almost upon our place. A high wall of leaping flames fed by tall grass from the network of dry creek beds to the west was fanned by a sixty-mile-an-hour wind. Mother grabbed little Ivan and they ran around the bend of the creek bank to the water's edge, thinking they could wade into the water if necessary. There they stood, watching the destruction of all our buildings. Burning haystacks were torn to pieces by the terrific wind and the flaming torches of loose hay swirled around the buildings and set everything ablaze at once. A neighbor came to tell us at school that our home had burned. We ran against the wind, crying and lamenting the loss of our home, our toys and possessions, naming them off as we thought of them. Papa saw the flames and immediately struck out for home with horse and buggy, almost frantic for fear. As he approached home, he stood up in the buggy, searching for sight of mother and Ivan in the burned wreckage of our homestead. Suddenly he saw them standing down by the water, black with soot and harrowed by the experience, but safe. He threw up his arms in thankfulness and cried out, "Let it all go; they're safe!"

The fire burned thirty miles beyond our place in thirty minutes. Our granery with its 1909 crop was burned, as was the house with all its furnishings, the calves in the barn, the chickens in the coop, the setting hens in their nests and the cat in the house. The cattle were all badly burned and they died later. The horses were found in a fence corner at the end of our farm, also badly burned. Shooting them was a heartbreaking task for father. Our sole possessions were the horse and buggy that Papa had with him. The dog was also saved, since he had followed mother and Ivan.

'Waiting for the mail'

Mail day

Each community was anxious to establish a post office for more convenient mail service. But post offices had to be petitioned and put through a trial run—in which everyone mailed as many letters as possible—before final approval from Washington. The postmaster's salary was figured by volume of cancelled stamps, and went lower if people started moving out.

Small country stores often had one official-looking corner inside with the glass post office cabinet of pigeonhole mail boxes, the gilt call window and drop letter slot.

One country storekeeper had his yard goods nearby with a counter, "just high enough for the customers to sit when the store was crowded and they were waiting for their mail. The habitual loafers, however, usually provided themselves with up-ended nail kegs, as they hated to be asked to move when we had to use the counter to measure off a yard of calico or jean."

Mail came three times a week, usually. Mail day brought settlers from miles around on foot, horseback, or with team and buggy or wagon to see what mail call might bring for them.

Mail was carried by relay from the railroad town down through the smaller towns and country post offices. Mail carriers were an important link with the outside world— sometimes, too, they took passengers.

When post offices were still scarce, a particular butte southwest of Rhame was called Post Office Butte because it had an iron box where mail could be left or picked up. Riders going to Dickinson or Belle Fourche would stop, sort through and take letters to be mailed, as well as pick up any mail for people in their locality.

Coming for the mail to Stowers post office and store.

One cold winter day our neighbor John went to town to pick up the mail for the community. It got dark on him coming home, the wind changed direction and he got lost. After a time he grew tired, sat down to rest and fell asleep. He awoke later to find he was surrounded by wolves. He reached into the mail sack and found some newspapers which he set afire and frightened the wolves away. He wandered on til daylight when a homesteader found him with his feet badly frozen. Some of the homesteaders griped, however, because their Decorah Postens had gone up in smoke.

Mrs. John Bergerson, carried mail from Stowers to Liberty, south of Mott, 1913-1915. Her small son rode with her in the buggy.

In 1910 Louis began work as rural mail carrier with a salary of $75 a month. He used to go by bicycle to Wolf Butte to pick up the mail, and also used horses, buggy, sled, and later, cars. It was a fine job when the weather was nice, but hard going in the winter. Sometimes he couldn't get home because of the blizzards but all the patrons would open their homes to him. Once his car burned up. Another time, his car was struck by a special train going through, but he was able to get his daughter and the mail bag out of the car in time. Another time as he came home after dark in his buggy, the horse refused to go on. He got out, walked ahead, and found that heavy rains had washed out the bridge in front of him.

Changing a tire, patching, pumping, became a familiar sight along the roadside as did tinkering with the engine, right.

Moving toward the great depression

Machinery increased on the farms and with it, cars on the roads. By 1920 57 percent of the state's farmers owned cars and soon North Dakota exceeded the national average in per capita car ownership. The auto was the answer to the long distances people had to travel. Good roads soon followed—though they were not always passable in all seasons. Drivers were often inexperienced and cars cantankerous. One pioneer recalls that he traded his rifle for "an old Model T that didn't have a top, windshield or lights. When we went to town after dark we hung a lantern in front. We couldn't get it started at first so pulled it to the top of a hill with a team of horses." Another said he and his brother bought a Model T touring car in 1918.

> Neither one of us had any idea how to run it so I drove like I would steer a header in the harvest field. When the Ford turned right I turned to the right too, and ran in a ditch. We had to push it up all the steep hills that we couldn't detour around. On our next trip to town we learned the carburetor had been set too rich—after that we had power for hills.

County-splitters swung into action with settlement, under various motives, petitioning and debating until the state was divided into 53 relatively small counties. With each new split a new county seat struggle developed as two or three towns fought for dominance. One newly-arrived immigrant watched such democracy at work in amazement, "Everybody was electioneering and arguing about it. And I felt it was a wild way of doing things, having just come from Norway where things were more settled and seemingly smoother running."

Each county had to finance a courthouse and full slate of county officials. During the '30's the state legislature tried to encourage consolidation of adjoining counties — because of the tax burden on property owners and the desperate financial state of the counties — but once split, there was no putting back together. No town would willingly give up its status as county seat.

Some good years came with bumper crops. But they were spaced by drouth, low prices, rust and hail. Serious drouth hit western Dakota in 1911, and again in 1912. The exodus from rural areas began, although there were still new waves of the hopeful coming west in a few good years. Many homesteaders left as soon as they could sell or mortgage their land. Everyone had been a speculator — convinced the land could only go up. Now it became clear the land was overpriced for the income it could produce. There were too many people trying to farm small acreages.

As rural areas declined in population, cities and towns grew. Between 1910 and 1920 North Dakota's small towns grew 29 percent, the cities 39 percent. Many people also left the state although total population did not decline until after 1930.

Those who stayed on the land increased their holdings if they could, by purchase or lease. There were many banks in the state, all willing to extend easy credit. Mechanization spread, and farmers invested heavily in machinery.

Agriculture became a powerful force in North Dakota politics with the collapse of the McKenzie machine and the rise of the Nonpartisan League. Under leadership of Arthur Townley, the League concentrated on farm problems, especially wheat marketing, preached anti-capitalism and fanned resentments against those in control of the elevators and businessmen in general. In 1916, through the Republican party, the Nonpartisan League elected Lynn Frazier governor and advocated a socialistic experiment of state ownership of marketing and purchase on wide scale. The League-sponsored Bank of North Dakota opened for business July 28, 1919 and the state Mill and Elevator was completed in 1923. But other attempts at state control of business met determined opposition.

By this time the Farmers Union was fully organized in the hands of Glenn Talbott and was successful in establishing cooperative marketing and cooperative buying and forced improvements on the wheat marketing system as a whole. Many of the state's immigrant farmers had come from countries strong in co-op marketing and socialistic practices. They united strongly behind both the Nonpartisan League and the Farmers Union in efforts to end unscrupulous outside control of their wheat market. Repeated investigations had exposed the unfair grading, price fixing, short weights, and excessive dockage of the line elevators, but little action was taken until the Nonpartisan League came into power.

The League included women's voting rights in their platform, and in 1917 North Dakota's women at last got the vote after meeting stubborn steady resistance since their first efforts in 1892.

In 1918 the Spanish influenza epidemic struck. Half of North Dakota's soldier deaths were from disease, mainly influenza. In November schools closed and all public

The '30's brought drouth, low markets, dust storms, grasshoppers . . . mortgage foreclosure

Hard times

gatherings were cancelled; nearly 3,000 North Dakotans died.

The crash came in 1919 and 1920 when the bottom dropped out of the market. Wheat, which was up to $3.30 a bushel in early 1920, dropped to $2.92 in July and $1.46 by the end of the year; the next year it was $1.01. There were brief rallies, but by 1930 wheat was 60 cents. Beef cattle brought 8 cents a pound in 1919; only half of that in 1921. Drouths again struck the plains in 1919 and a long severe winter killed many livestock.

Suddenly the banks began to fail. They had loaned out too much money and farmers without income couldn't pay up. Foreclosures and bank failure followed as the Federal Reserve Board called in their loans from the banks. Loss of confidence was contagious and caused more banks to collapse. During the '20's 62 percent of North Dakota's 898 banks failed, compared to 20 percent nationally. Montana and South Dakota had 70 percent closings, the highest rate in the nation. North Dakota depositors lost 50 million dollars.

People were leaving; for those who stayed there were high taxes and mortgages — and the hope of rain and better markets next year.

But instead, the '30's brought unprecedented drouth and relentlessly low markets. One-third of North Dakota farmers lost their land through foreclosure; 82 percent of the land in western and central North Dakota became tax delinquent.

The dreaded forced farm sale became commonplace as mortgages came due; banks and other creditors came to collect debts from farmers who had long since exhausted their last income sources. "If you could just carry me 'til fall," they would plead. "Maybe it will rain . . . and I'll get a crop." But the sale announced, out came the sheriff, the clerk, the auctioneer, the creditor, the buyers, and the angry neighbors. The farmer set his jaw, his wife wept, and their children ran to hide as their hard-won possessions went on the block: the milk cow, furniture, a favorite horse, their home, their land. No one had much money and the cherished items went cheap, and were thus further cheapened. The proceeds were seldom more than enough to pay off the debts.

And it did not rain. "The wind would blow three days from the northeast or the southeast . . . where we'd usually

get our rain," said one man. "And we'd think, it's just got to bring rain. But it didn't and next day it would turn around and come from the northwest with double force."

Grass didn't even turn green the spring of 1934 in western Dakota, with little snow the winter before. It was the driest year anyone had ever seen. State average that year was 9.47 inches; most of it fell in eastern North Dakota. But 1936 was worse. That year the state average moisture was 8.8. Even the eastern third of the state received only 3.17 inches of rain during the three months of growing season.

In 1936 less than six inches was measured in as scattered points at Ellendale, Bismarck, Ft. Yates, Linton, and Turtle Lake. Steele reported 4.86; Hettinger, 4.17. Creeks, lakes, and wells dried up. In Hettinger only .65 inch of rain fell during the three months of growing season.

Most markets hit bottom in 1932. Beef cattle were 2.7 cents a pound; milk cows $29 each; wool was 7 cents; horses were down to $27; wheat went as low as 25 cents a bushel. Even though crops were sometimes close to normal in the Red River Valley, there was little cash income because of low prices. And it was generally true that the farther west in North Dakota, the more severe the effects of the depression.

When the wind blew hard, clouds of dust billowed through the sky in dust storms caused by deep plowing of vast areas of the Great Plains . . . native grasses and cover had been destroyed and there were no crops or moisture to hold the soil. A Chicago paper reported a brown cloud of dust as high as 15,000 feet driven by 60-100 mile an hour winds enveloping the city on May 11, 1934. There were at least two deaths from this dust storm, said the paper. "A small boy in Hays, Kansas, was suffocated by the dust on his way home from school and a woman at Sykeston, North Dakota was pinned beneath a chicken coop blown over by the high winds." Next day the sun was blotted out over New York and Washington for five hours and it was said that the dust sifted in and covered President Roosevelt's desk . . . as it had sifted through rag-stuffed windows into the homes and spirits of thousands of Dakotans.

The fatal year 1936 shattered three records in many places throughout the state: driest, hottest, coldest. Of the July heat wave, the Minot newspaper said, "A hot wind from the parched areas of the south felt like the heat from a blast furnace . . . Wishek chalked up the highest official reading, 120 degrees." The bleak cold spell hit in mid-

Hard winds lifted billowing clouds of dust in a brown pall. Center photo shows drouth stricken western Dakota cattle awaiting the appraiser. Farmers met in school to hear government man explain one more New Deal program, the AAA, 1938.

February, 1936. On February 15 the mercury reached 60 degrees below in Parshall. Devils Lake's temperature had not risen above freezing for 96 days, from November 27 to March 1, 1936. For 37 consecutive days it had not reached zero in Devils Lake, except for one day; one entire week it averaged -28 degrees F.

"In all the years that people of this generation have lived, or for that matter in modern history," said the Farmers Union Herald, "there has never been a period like the present. Doubt and uncertainty are all about us."

There was no federal relief until 1933; the Red Cross had only a few dollars for the most needy. But even when relief became possible destitute families tried desperately to keep off welfare.

One day the game warden was called to Max to check a report that some farmers were capturing skunks and keeping them penned up until skunk season opened November 1, when it would be legal to kill them and sell pelts. The game warden found five skunks at one farm, fined the guilty farmer $8.45, and took the skunks. But when he arrived at the second farm, reported to have 30 skunks in a wire enclosure, the enclosure was empty, the skunks turned loose or escaped. Skunk pelts were worth $1 each; selling them required a $1 license. It must have seemed to some people that this man had surely earned his $4 after catching five skunks alive (to say nothing of 30), caring for them within smelling distance of his house, expecting to kill, skin them and stretch the hides.

In North Dakota the crisis produced a new leader with the election of the ambitious, controversial Bill Langer as governor in 1932. Langer was the champion of the common man, in sympathy with the aims of the militant Farm Holiday Association which was using various means of intimidation to halt forced farm sales. On April 17, 1933 Langer placed a moratorium on mortgage foreclosures and forced sale of livestock or personal property. Said Usher Burdick, president of North Dakota's Farm Holiday

Association, "The loan companies howled and wailed."

No doubt such support from the governor did prevent more acts of violence by the angry Farm Holiday men. There had already been 43,000 forced sales of farm land in the state since 1921. They called their first farm strike in September 1932, and shut down markets in Parshall. They stopped farm sales by threats and intimidation, by hanging the auctioneer in effigy, by turning out in armed force to send sale officials back to town. The creative idea of "penny sales", put into action, was the source of much grim humor among Holiday members and sympathetic neighbors. Holiday members infiltrated the sale crowd and permitted no bids but their own . . . a few pennies for the tractor . . . 29 cents for a team of horses. The creditor had to be satisfied with the receipts, and property was restored to the original owner after the smoke cleared.

"These people became violent out of desperation, because they were so frustrated," said an FERA administrator who was roughed up by Holiday members in Watford City when he took a father of five off relief rolls after finding the man had a milk cow, grain in the bin, and meat hanging in the shed. "They worked hard, but the harder they worked the worse things got."

Under Roosevelt the federal government launched a flood of relief measures after 1932, as promised. But many were ill conceived and poorly managed. A striking example was the livestock purchase program which was supposed to give meat to the needy, financial aid to the stockmen, and raise the price of beef. It made few friends in Dakota. Too little money was allotted to give a fair price: cows brought from $12 to $20, most calves brought about $4.

Cattle and sheep in good condition were shipped for relief food. Condemned livestock were shot and buried either on the farm or in a centralized location.

"We have not wastefully destroyed food in any form," insisted President Roosevelt. Yet a great deal of good food **was** destroyed.

Left, poisoning grasshoppers, 1939. Grasshoppers . . . swarms so vast they obscured the sun . . . descended to strip the country clean, crunching underfoot at every step. At right, dusting for mormon crickets near Whetstone Butte.

North Dakota's capitol burned in 3 hours, Dec. 29, 1930

A popular program: CCC camp near Medora

Hettinger's pit where condemned cattle were killed and buried in 1934

"No one wanted to sell to the government," explained a desperate rancher. "But we had no feed or grass and couldn't get a federal loan to buy hay unless we did. Market prices were even lower . . . sometimes cattle didn't pay the freight."

Officially the condemned animals were in extremely poor condition, but it turned out that a certain percentage of every herd had to be condemned in order for the government to buy any. Sometimes the entire purchase . . . especially of sheep . . . was condemned to avoid shipping costs.

In Adams County 14,189 cattle were purchased by the government between June 1 and Sept. 12, 1934. Of this number 234 were kept for local relief and 1,105 were condemned. Total payment was $196,000. Twelve hundred sheep were also purchased and of these over half, 708 were condemned. Sheep payment was $2,448 of which half went to producers and half to mortgage holders. Figures for other counties were similar.

"The whole program made you kind of sick," says a Reeder-area rancher. "They wouldn't let anyone take meat from the cattle they killed. Many times the women would be crying and wanting just a hindquarter, but they wouldn't let them have any. We had a roan calf we didn't want to sell at all. But the appraiser put a CONDEMNED tag on it. We couldn't talk him out of it. I remember how bad everyone in our family felt about that calf."

After the appraiser, a crew of four men came to the place to dig a hole; then a second crew which shot the condemned animals, pushed them in and covered them with dirt. In Hettinger there was also a big pit down by the railroad track where cattle were killed and buried.

With dry conditions, grasshoppers increased and ravaged crops. Each year there was a worse hopper problem despite extensive poisoning with a mixture of arsenic, bran, sawdust and molasses. Then came a new, dreaded species: migratory grasshoppers. They came in swarms so vast they obscured the sun, descending suddenly with a buzzing and a clattering, filling every inch of space with their hopping gray bodies that crackled underfoot wherever one walked, spitting their brown juices and laying waste to everything edible. Gardens, fields, clothes hanging on the line were all attacked by the horde of chawing, tearing, busy mouths. When they had stripped the country clean . . . and the wind was right . . . they would suddenly take flight again as if remembering unfinished adventures and disappear into the northwest, to lay waste to someone else's crops.

Mormon crickets were another new horror, migrating on foot in large bands from the southwest, eating everything in their path.

The hopeless conditions had far-reaching effects on the human spirit. People grew depressed or violent, some became mentally unbalanced. Families broke apart. A farmer who drowned himself in the Mouse River in 1937 left a note: "It is wrong to destroy one's self but debts, high taxes and the high cost of living and no crops for eight years . . . I bid you good-bye. I have no home and no money to start over."

A North Dakota family of five disappeared in March '34, and when two of their bodies were found hid under the floorboards of their house the hired man was charged and taken to jail. An enraged mob broke him out of jail and hanged him from the bridge of a country road.

North Dakota's political scene, too, was stormy and uncertain. Langer was removed as governor in 1934 after his conviction for soliciting political money from federal employees and conspiracy. Lt. Gov. Ole Olson, Republican, was sworn in to finish the two-year term. That fall Thomas Moodie, Democrat, was elected governor, but after taking office he, too, was declared ineligible and Lt. Gov. Walter Welford, NPL, took office. In seven months North Dakota had had four governors. His conviction reversed, William Langer was again elected in 1936, this time as an Independent. A desperate people were convinced that Langer would try to help them. Under his leadership and the Nonpartisan League, North Dakota gained the reputation of the most politically progressive state.

School districts were in desperate straits and many

many lost their homes, their land . . . but the grass came back

teachers had to accept warrants, or I.O.U.'s, instead of paychecks. Insurance commissioner Harold Hopton engineered a plan through the legislature to take money out of his hail insurance fund . . . one of the few places in the state with any money . . . to underwrite teachers' salaries. Teachers wrote Hopton gratefully, "It seems almost too good to be true that we are able to turn our warrants into cash . . . we have fought uphill . . . swapping warrants in order to keep going."

Federal New Deal programs provided millions of dollars worth of aid to North Dakotans. There was the CWA, the FERA, WPA, CCC, PWA, FSA, AAA, RA . . . alphabet soup, some called them. The CCC was a popular program in which more than 30,000 young men from the state worked and trained in conservation camps between 1933 and 1941 on soil erosion, recreational projects, flood control. Thousands also worked under the CWA and WPA on public works projects, 53,000 during late 1936 alone. The CCC boys earned $30 a month of which $25 was sent home to their families; Civil Works paid 50 cents an hour for unskilled, 60 cents for skilled with 30 hours work per week. WPA scale was similar, $40 a month for 100 hours.

For all the hardship and suffering of the depression, life continued . . . even smoothly in some quarters. Young people fell in love, married; babies were born, reared, and educated. People coped, with determination and amazing resiliancy. Dakotans could even laugh at sensational drouth stories published in eastern media picturing the state, and other plains states, as in far worse condition than they were, illustrated with photos of a bleached skull moved from one alkali slough to another.

Then the depression ended. Rain fell. Grasshopper and cricket eggs rotted in the soil. The grass came back. Markets boomed. Farmers bought new machinery to till their wider acreages. Stockmen built back their herds with better breeding lines. War loomed, but after war came a new era of prosperity and efficient production across the land.

A letter home

James W. Foley

Like to come and see you, Daddy, and perhaps I will some day;
Like to come back East to visit, but I wouldn't care to stay.
Glad you're doing well and happy; glad you like your country best,
But for me, I always hunger for the freedom of the West.
There's a wholesomeness about it that I couldn't quite explain;
Once you breathe this air you love it and you long for it again:
There's a tie you can't dissever in the splendor if its sky—
It's just home to you forever and I can't just tell you why.

It's so big and broad and boundless and its heaven is so blue
And the metal of its people always rings so clear and true;
All its billowed acres quiver like the shudder of the sea
And its waves roll, rich and golden, in upon the shore for me.
Why, your farm and all the others that we used to think so fine
Wouldn't—lump 'em all together—make a corner lot of mine;
And your old red clover pasture, with its gate of fence rails barred,
Why, it wouldn't make a grass plot in our district school house yard.

Not a foot has touched its prairies but is longing to return,
Not an eye has seen the sunset of its western heavens burn
But looks back in hungry yearning, with the memory grown dim,
And the zephyr of its prairies breathes the cadence of a hymn
That is sweet and full of promise as the "Beulah Land" we knew
When we used to sit together in the queer old-fashioned pew;
And at eventide the glory of the sun and sky and sod
Bids me bare my head in homage and in gratitude to God.

Yes I love you, Daddy, love you with a heart that's true as steel,
But there's something in Dakota makes you live and breathe and feel
Makes you bigger, broader, better; makes you know the worth of toil;
Makes you free as are her prairies and as noble as her soil;
Makes you kingly as a man is; makes you manly as a king;
And there's something in the grandeur of her seasons' sweep and swing
That casts off the fretting fetters of your East and marks you blest
With the vigor of the prairies—with the freedom of the West!

Foley, North Dakota's poet laureate, lived as a child at Ft. Lincoln,
punched cows near Medora around 1890.

and what of the future?

North and west pounded the hoofbeats. To a land of tall waving grass and rushing river; to a land of distance, blue sky, northern lights, and a halo around the moon.

Those who followed the call came into a country of western prairie and plain, and unpredictable climate.

Native plants adapted well; so did the animals. The jackrabbit's speed suited well his life in open spaces. The antelope's keen eyesight, speed, and white signal rump patch that flashed "danger" over long distance, developed in such country. Buffalo, with neither keen eyesight nor speed, grew to great size and multiplied into protective herds of ten-thousands to graze the rich grasslands.

Indians, too, adapted well and learned to live in harmony with the wealth of the land and breadth of climate. When Plains tribes came out of the woodlands they developed a new, nomadic life style. They discarded their birch bark canoes for a faster and more versatile means of travel: the horse.

When the pioneers came, they had to do the same. But the pioneers soon added the dimension of change. The task they claimed was enormous — to turn the plow and make of this grassland wilderness a bounteous garden. So well did they accomplish it that we need scarce adapt anymore, but can shape the environment to our own design.

It's not yet New York, nor California. And it has not one half-sized Disneyland. But this, too, we can accomplish if we like.

We can subdue the surging water of the mighty Missouri to sluggishness; we can change the course of this and lesser rivers and send their waters in vast ditches where we will; we can dig mile-wide trenches a hundred feet deep into the

We can shape the environment to our design

bowels of the earth to tear forth her treasures, and level it back and call it good; we can level butte and ridge for farmland and freeway; we can people our spacious lands with industrial workers, cover it over with buildings and cement and climate-controlled cities; we can obliterate nearly all the natural features of this land, if we like, and replace them with plastic Disneyland fantasies.

The rocky butte stands there on the horizon — still unchanged — watching over a valley of modern ranches with their bright cars and TV antennas in the same manner it watched over the Indian buffalo hunt, the wolf pack stalking antelope, the hardy French fur trapper. Here Dakotans have lived and died for whatever ideals, or lack of them, have for centuries entered full-stream into the drama of human existence.

And here we stand in some perplexity. Looking back on the way we have come in this headlong rush. Looking ahead in wonderment toward goals we have sought.

How shall we turn at this crossroad? To the left? Or the right? Or shall we depart from that custom of following only the surveyor's straight roads, turning only square corners, and find new trails that deal creatively with humanity in relation to this land?

North Dakota has not come quite so far down this broad straight road as have other, populous places, which bear more heavily the marks of "progress." Dakotans themselves are not entirely caught up in the plastic, the concrete, the TV, the chrome and frantic pace of a consumer-oriented society which has become willing slave to the zeal of industrialization. There is still, among them, a feeling for the land, for solid reality, for fresh air and sunshine, for neighborliness.

For Dakotans there is still the opportunity to get off the materialistic merry-go-round that clicks out the rhythm of the times: **buy**-waste-throw away-**buy**-waste-throw away-**buy.** There is the memory of how to live a more moderate kind of life, leaner and sparer, perhaps, but with its own deeply human satisfactions.

It's time to ask the hard questions. Time to look well at this mad dream of progress.

Dakotans are well equal to the task. No need to look to politicians for leadership; quite the opposite. The leaders are all about us, people of sensitivity, intelligence, and wide vision, people who regard justice, freedom, and the ethic of the land as reasonable considerations. These local leaders can forge out better grassroots planning and grassroots direction for this state's destiny. They need only insist that decision be based on fact — and that facts be examined in the light of human values.

Picture credits

Cover photo by Nancy Edmonds Hanson

Adams Co. Extension office — 170 b, d, e, f; 171 b

Alma Anderson — 115 a; 123 a; 130 a; 134 a, b; 143 c; 147 b; 153 d; 159 c; 160 f; 163 d

Beverley Badhorse — 56 b

Mrs. O. J. Bamble — 128 a; 144 a; 167 b, c

Chet and Margaret Barrett — 137 b; 152 a; 153 e; 154 c; 156 a; 158 b; 164 d; 168 b

Rolf Berg — 53 b; 70 a, e; 72 b

A. O. Brown — 119 a; 126 a; 128 b; 129 a; 136 a

Dakota Buttes Historical Museum — 123 b; 154 a, b; 160 b; 161 b

Dickinson Chamber of Commerce — 57 c

Dickinson Press — 60 a; 61 e

Dickinson State College — 10 d; 11 a; 18 c; 33 d; 53 g; 58 a; 59 a, b, c, e; 61 b, c; 62 a, c, d, e, h; 63 b; 73 a

Harley and Marge Erickson — 124 b; 138 a; 145 a; 148 b; 150 b; 151 c; 153 a, b; 156 b; 158 a; 160 g; 163 b; 164 b

Garrison brochure — 86 a

Hettinger High School — 10 f; 14 b, e; 49 a; 53 d; 57 b; 58 b, c, d, e, f, g, h, i; 62 b

Ed Holmquist — 18 b; 109 a; 125 a; 134 c; 147 c; 148 d; 150 d, e; 151 a; 155 a; 156 e; 160 c, h, i; 161 a, c; 162 c; 164 a; 168 a

Knife River Coal Mining Co. — 76 a, b

Dale Knittel — 11 b; 19 b; 36 d; 38 a; 49 b

Frank Korang — 140 a

Wilford Miller — 8 e

N. D. Dept. of Public Instruction — 85 a, b; 110 b, c; 112 a; 119 b; 121 b

N.D. Game & Fish — 2 a, b; 6 a, b; 7 a, b; 9 c; 10 b, c; 11 f; 14 c, d; 15 a, b; 34 a; 35 b; 36 a, c; 37 b, c; 38 c, d, e; 39 a, e; 40 a, b, c, d; 65; 67 d; 82 a; 172 a; 174 a; 175 b; 176 a

N.D. Historical Soc. — frontspiece; 41 b; 42 a, b; 81 b; 83 a, b; 84 a; 87 a; 88 a; 89 a, b; 90 b; 91 a, b; 92 a; 93 a, b; 94 a; 95 a, b; 96 a, b; 97 a, b, c; 99 a, b; 100 a; 104 a; 105 a, b; 106 c; 109 b; 110 a; 111 a, b, c; 112 b, c; 114 a, b; 115 b; 116 a; 133 b; 171 a

N.D. Inst. of Regional Studies — 113 a, c; 117 a; 124 a; 129 c; 141 a, b; 144 b; 146 b; 147 a; 154 d; 156 d; 160 a; 162 b

N.D.S.U. — 14 a; 51 a; 59 f

N.D. Travel Div. — 1 a; 10 a; 11 c; 24 a; 25 a, b, c, d; 26 a; 29 a, b; 31 a; 33 a, b, c, f; 35 c, e, f, g; 36 b; 37 a; 38 b; 39 c, d, g; 44 b; 45 b; 46 a, b; 48 c; 59 d; 61 d; 63 a; 66 b, c; 70 b; 72 a; 78 a; 80 a, b; 81 a; 116 b; 174 c

N.D. Weather Modification — 68 a, b

Morris and Gertrude Olson — 113 b; 127 b; 137 c; 138 b; 139 a, b; 146 a, c; 147 d; 148 a, c; 153 c; 155 b; 156 c, f; 159 a; 162 a, d; 167 a

Prairie Pioneers, Adams Co. — 145 b

Jan Prchal — 3

Soil Conservation (USDA and State Committee) — 10 a, g; 17 b, c; 21 a; 25 e; 28 a, b; 31 d; 35 d, h; 44 a; 45 a; 46 c; 47 a, b; 48 a, b, d; 63 c; 64 a, b; 69 a; 70 c; 71 a; 72 c; 78 b; 79 a; 84 b; 86 b; 111 d; 130 b; 135 a; 140 c; 173 a; 174 b

Dale and Kaye Schoeder — 141 b

D. J. Shults — 57 a; 67 c; 115 c; 129 b; 131 a; 138 c; 143 b; 145 c; 149 b; 160 d

Elmer and Mary Solseth — 152 a, b

S.D. Hist. Soc. — 106 b

Orval and Emily Stadheim — 70 f; 133 a; 164 c

Story of Flickertail State, Wemett — 108

Gus Swenson — 150 a; 151 b; 155 c; 171 c

Roger and Phyllis Thompson — 125 b; 157 a

USDA — 169 a; 170 a, c

United Tribes — 30 b; 54 a, b, c; 55 a, b, c, d, e; 56 a, c; 61 a; 66 f

Remaining photos from Berg family collection

———————————

Letters designate photos in clockwise order, beginning with upper left corner of page.

COLOR SEPARATIONS BY COURTESY OF THE FOLLOWING:

Bismarck Chamber of Commerce — 30 capitol; 31 zoo, civic center

Dickinson Chamber of Commerce — 8 Indian dancers; 22 prairie dog, canoe

N.D. HORIZONS — 1 Autumn scene, photo by D. J. Such; 12 Prairie Stage; 16 trees; 22 Medora; 23 pysanka; 26 Indian dancer

N.D. OUTDOORS — 8 meadowlark; 16 geese; 19 antelope

N.D. REC MAGAZINE — 16 berries; 23 rodeo

N.D. Travel Division — 1 buffalo; 4 all photos; 8 horses; 12 sailboat; 13 Metigoshe, combines, canoe; 16 hunters; 18 skiing; 22 hunters; 26 carnival, Scotch dancers; 27 boat, peace gardens; 30 girls, legislature; 31 sunset, camping, wild rose; back cover, badlands

WILDLIFE OF THE PRAIRIE, Wilford Miller — 9 crocus

TEXT CREDITS

I. Pg. 5 MILITARY LIFE IN DAKOTA: THE JOURNAL OF PHILIPPE REGIS DE TOBRIAND; Lucile M. Kane trans. & ed. 1951, with permission of Minn. Hist. Soc., St. Paul; pg. 50, p. 371

7 THE CRY OF THE WILD GOOSE, Terry Gilkyson, Am. Music, Calif.

10 MILITARY LIFE IN DAKOTA, Kane; p. 252

42 Ibid., p. 254

II. 64 TALES OF THE TRAIL, James W. Foley, 1905; p. 53

III. note 1 SOUL OF THE INDIAN, C. A. Eastman, 1911; p. 84

2 JOURNALS OF LEWIS AND CLARK, Feb. 11, 1805

3 Ibid., April 13, 1806

4 Ibid., April 22, 1805

5 Ibid., April 25, 1805

6 Ibid., May 5, 1805

7 Ibid, May 14, 1805

8 NORTH DAKOTA HISTORY, Vol. 33; p. 90; Boller Journals edited by Ray H. Mattison

9 PLENTY-COUPS, CHIEF OF THE CROWS, Frank Linderman, Copyright Wilda and Verne Linderman, p. 91

10 MILITARY LIFE IN DAKOTA; Kane; p. 277

11 NORTH DAKOTA HISTORY, Aug. 30, 1959; p. 210

12 MY LIFE ON THE PLAINS, George A. Custer

13 MILITARY LIFE IN DAKOTA: Kane; p. 328

14 BISMARCK TRIBUNE, May 27, June 17, 1874

15 CHICAGO INTER-OCEAN, July 30, 1874

16 Ibid., July 29, 1874

17 BOOTS AND SADDLES, Elizabeth Custer, Harper 1885

18 Ibid

19 MY FRIEND THE INDIAN, James McLaughlin, Hough Mifflin 1910

20 Ibid

21 HISTORY OF WELLS COUNTY AND ITS PIONEERS, Wal E. Spokesfield, 1929

22 As reprinted in the FARGO FORUM

23 PRAIRIE POEMS, Arnold Marzolf; Tumbleweed Press, Bismar with permission

24 Ibid.

Many pioneer stories were taken from the following excellent N.D. histories most of which were compiled through efforts of local committees:
OUR 50 YEARS, Regent
PRAIRIE PIONEERS, Adams County History, Taylor Publ., Bismarck
PRAIRIE TALES, Bowman County
PIONEER ASSOCIATION OF DEVILS LAKE, Henry Hale
STORIES AND HISTORIES OF DIVIDE COUNTY, 1964
HISTORY OF WELLS COUNTY AND ITS PIONEERS, Walter E. Spokesfield, 1929
VIKING SETTLEMENT DAYS, Hilda Wisness and Levard Quarve, 1936
ALONG THE TRAILS OF YESTERDAY, McIntosh County, Nina Farley Wishek, Ashley Tribune, 1941

In addition, the following not previously noted, contributed a great deal to the breadth of this book:
TOUCH THE EARTH, T. C. McLuhan, Pocket Books, 1972
OUR HETTINGER COUNTY HERITAGE, Enid Bern
CUSTER'S PRELUDE TO GLORY, Herbert Krause and Gary Olson, Brevet Press, Sioux Falls, 1974
STEAMBOATING ON THE UPPER MISSOURI, Wm. E. Lass, U. of Neb.
ADAMS CO. RECORD, 50th Anniversary Issue
OUT WHERE THE WEST BEGINS, Zena Trinka, Pioneer Co., St. Paul 1920
ONE TIME HARVEST, Mike Jacobs, N.D. Farmers Union 1975
WILDLIFE OF THE PRAIRIE, Wilford L. Miller, Record Printers, Grafton 1975
HISTORY OF NORTH DAKOTA, Elwyn B. Robinson, U. of Neb., 1966
THE STORY OF NORTH DAKOTA, Erling Rolfsrud, Lantern Books 1963
THE GREAT PLAINS, Walter Prescott Webb, Grosset & Dunlap 1931
NORTH DAKOTA BLUE BOOK, Bismarck Printing Co., 1942
NORTH DAKOTA, AMERICAN GUIDE SERIES, WPA; Knight Printing, Fargo 1938
THE PRACTICAL STOCK DOCTOR, edited by Dr. George Waterman, 1908
THE PEOPLE'S HOME LIBRARY, Dr. Ritter's Home Medical Book 1910
NORTH DAKOTA: THE NORTHERN PRAIRIE STATE, Bernt Wills, Edward Bros., Ann Arbor, 1963
OUR STATE: NORTH DAKOTA, Conrad Leifur, Am. Book Co. 1962
THE BONES OF PLENTY, Lois Hudson, Little, Brown and Co., 1962
THE YEARS OF DESPAIR, NORTH DAKOTA IN THE DEPRESSION, D. Jerome Tweton and Daniel F. Rylance, Oxcart 1973

A warm thank you to the many individuals who shared their photos, and who gave willingly of their memories, their time, their information. Some were state officials, some neighbors and friends, some were new acquaintances; all were most courteous, generous, and helpful.

Francie Berg lives in Hettinger, where her husband, Bert, is a veterinarian. A 10-year 4-H leader, adult education teacher, former county homemakers president, mother of four, Mrs. Berg was raised on a ranch just across the line in Montana. She has lived in North Dakota for nearly 20 years, has a Home Economics degree from Montana State University and a masters degree in Family Social Science and Anthropology from the University of Minnesota. She enjoys travel and has lived in Japanese and Swiss homes on two exchanges, 4-H Labo and IFYE.

INDEX